Miller

Workers and Wages
in an Urban Labor Market

THE GRADUATE SCHOOL OF BUSINESS
UNIVERSITY OF CHICAGO

FIRST SERIES (1916–38)
Materials for the Study of Business
Edited by Leon Carroll Marshall
and William Homer Spencer

SECOND SERIES (1938–56)
Business and Economics Publications
Edited by William Homer Spencer

THIRD SERIES (1959–)
Studies in Business and Society
Edited by W. Allen Wallis,
George P. Shultz, and Sidney Davidson

Workers and Wages
in an Urban Labor Market

Albert Rees and
George P. Shultz

with the assistance of
Mary T. Hamilton
David P. Taylor
Joseph C. Ullman

The University of Chicago Press
Chicago and London

International Standard Book Number: 0-226-70705-9
Library of Congress Catalog Card Number: 75-110114

The University of Chicago Press, Chicago 60637
The University of Chicago Press, Ltd., London
© 1970 by The University of Chicago

Contents

Tables

Foreword

It is a privilege to welcome this volume to the growing array of scholarly works sponsored by the Graduate School of Business of the University of Chicago.

The authors report here upon the findings of a comprehensive study, which they directed, of the characteristics and operations of a large urban labor market. They sought illumination on such topics as the explanation of wage differentials, the flow of information in the labor market, the spatial characteristics of the market, variations in the structural characteristics of markets for different occupations, and employer and union influence on wage movements; in the process, they made preliminary incursions into areas which other students of the field might profitably explore.

Mr. Rees and Mr. Shultz bring unusual credentials to their work. Albert Rees was a member of the Department of Economics of the University of Chicago from 1948 to 1966, and served for a time as chairman of the department; he is now professor of economics and public affairs and director of the Industrial Relations Section at Princeton University. George P. Shultz, professor of industrial relations at the Graduate School of Business (now on leave), was dean of the school from 1962 until early in 1969, when he became secretary of labor in the cabinet of President Richard M. Nixon.

Mary T. Hamilton is a research associate of the Graduate School of Business and the co-author with Albert Rees of two articles on labor economics. David P. Taylor is an associate professor at the Alfred P. Sloan School of Management, Massachusetts Institute of Technology, currently on leave to serve as executive assistant to the secretary of labor. Joseph C. Ullman is an associate professor at the Herman C. Krannert Graduate School of Industrial Administration, Purdue University, currently on leave as a fellow of the Brookings Institution.

This volume is the most recent expression of a significant publication program launched by the Graduate School of Business (then the School of Commerce and Industry) over half a century ago. The series *Materials for the Study of Business* was initiated in 1916 under the editorship of Dean Leon Carroll Marshall, and was continued by Dean William Homer Spencer. Fifty titles were published, and many became classics in their fields. In 1938 the series was renamed *Business and Economic Publications*, under the editorship of Dean Spencer, and thirteen titles were published. In the two decades before 1948, the school also published some seventy monographs under the general title *Studies in Business Administration*. The current *Studies in Business and Society* series was initiated under Dean W. Allen Wallis, who edited the first six volumes, and was continued under Dean Shultz, who edited the next nine.

The study which gave rise to this volume was made possible by a generous grant from the Ford Foundation. This work, sixteenth in the current series, is distinguished by the high qualifications of its authors and by their rigorous and disciplined approach to their subject. It is a pleasure and an honor to be identified with this outstanding work.

SIDNEY DAVIDSON
Dean
Graduate School of Business
The University of Chicago

Preface

THIS STUDY of the Chicago labor market was made possible by a grant of $80,000 from the Ford Foundation, made in the spring of 1962. We should like to thank the foundation for its very generous support, and in particular to thank the foundation executives who reviewed our proposal—Dr. Marshall A. Robinson, who in 1962 was director of the program in economic development and administration, and Dr. Victor R. Fuchs, then a program associate in that program.

The foundation furnished further support in the form of a faculty research fellowship to Albert Rees for the academic year 1965-66. Additional support needed for the completion of the study was provided by the Graduate School of Business of the University of Chicago and by the Industrial Relations Section, Princeton University. Needless to say, the findings and conclusions of the study are those of the authors and not of the Ford Foundation or the two universities.

The study has taken far longer to complete than any of us anticipated at the outset. The time involved in planning the project and collecting the data in the field were about what we had expected. However, much more time was consumed in data processing and analysis and in the preparation of the final report. Looking back, we can see how woefully naive we were at the beginning about data processing problems. But if we had realized how much we had to learn, we might have lacked the courage to continue.

Over the period of the study many people have contributed their help and advice. We should like to acknowledge our most important debts in this preface.

Three research associates, Mary T. Hamilton, David P. Taylor, and Joseph C. Ullman, have each made a major contribution to this study. Mr. Taylor and Mr. Ullman were involved in the early planning of the project and did the bulk of the data collection. In addition, David Taylor did the original analysis of the labor market for unskilled males, and Joseph Ullman did the original analysis of

xiii

the market for female clerical workers. Mrs. Hamilton has carried most of the burden of data processing and has participated actively in all of the statistical analysis. Without any one of these colleagues, this study could not have been done. All three have examined the final manuscript with great care and have made many suggestions for its improvement. An important contribution was made by Eaton Conant, who collected material on private employment agencies in the Chicago area and helped us with the use of test scores as a measure of worker ability. Kenneth Gordon was the third member of our data collection team and took special responsibility for the collection of material on fringe benefits.

In planning the project we were ably assisted by an industry advisory committee of eight industrial relations executives. Their names and a discussion of their work are given at the beginning of chapter 3.

We are also deeply grateful to colleagues on the faculties of the University of Chicago and Princeton University for advice at many points. Professor Harry V. Roberts at Chicago advised us on sample design. Professor H. Gregg Lewis at Chicago gave valuable help on frequent occasions in the early phases of the regression analysis. Professor Robert McKersie at Chicago and Provost William G. Bowen at Princeton read the final manuscript and made many helpful suggestions.

Among the others who have participated in our work are two very able computer programmers, Douglas Fisher and George Travers, and a research assistant, Ronald Oaxaca. Secretarial assistance was provided at the University of Chicago by Mrs. Carolyn Jordan Mosby, Mrs. Carolyn Johannsen, Mrs. Gladys Adams, Mrs. Delores Gardner, and Miss Jeanette Graham. The final manuscript was typed at Princeton by Mrs. Reba Titus and Mrs. Dorothy Silvester.

Portions of our results have been presented to seminars at the University of Chicago, Princeton University, Yale University, the University of Illinois, Massachusetts Institute of Technology, Ohio State University, Carnegie-Mellon University, the University of California at Berkeley, Rutgers University, and the London School of Economics. The participants in these seminars raised questions that led to the improvement of our work, and some of their comments are acknowledged in footnotes at appropriate points. Special mention should be made of the members of the Workshop in Labor Economics at the University of Chicago, who discussed our work helpfully on many occasions.

Those who have aided us so freely are not to be blamed for any errors or omissions in this work, for we may sometimes have misunderstood their advice or received it too late to incorporate it in our research program.

We have found the study of a large urban labor market a challenging and rewarding task. Many of the important problems raised by such a study remain unsolved, and we hope that this book may encourage others to pursue them.

Workers and Wages
in an Urban Labor Market

1

The Problems under Study

IN THE POSTWAR PERIOD, there has been a heavy commitment of resources to studies of the operation of local labor markets in the
United States. These studies have produced a wealth of information
about the demographic aspects of mobility and about the institutional forces operating in local markets, especially markets for blue-
collar workers. At the same time, they have a persistent theme that
is puzzling to many economists: an emphasis on the random, chaotic,
or purely institutional nature of wage structures and mobility
patterns.

This study was undertaken because of our concern over a number
of gaps and problems in this labor market literature, which are
discussed briefly in this chapter. These include the problems of
wage differentials, of information channels, of the spatial characteristics of large labor markets, and of the range of occupations and
industries that have been studied.

WAGE DIFFERENTIALS

A main focus of dissatisfaction with the present state of the literature on local labor markets is the size and nature of wage differentials within narrowly defined occupations. This is not merely our
own dissatisfaction; it has often been expressed by others. For
example, Professor Richard A. Lester begins a well-known article
with this sentence: "No satisfactory explanation has been developed
for the continued existence locally of genuine interfirm wage differentials."[1] He goes on to note that neoclassical wage theory presumed
that such differentials could not persist, but that empirical research
uniformly shows that they do.

The theory referred to is more accurately described as classical
than as neoclassical. Its best expression is still Adam Smith's chapter
"Of Wages and Profits in the Different Employments of Labour and
Stock" (chapter 10 of book 1), which begins with the famous passage:

1. Richard A. Lester, "A Range Theory of Wage Differentials," *Industrial and
Labor Relations Review* 5 (July 1952): 483.

The whole of the advantages and disadvantages of the different employments of labour and stock must, in the same neighborhood, be either perfectly equal or continually tending to equality. If in the same neighborhood, there was any employment evidently either more or less advantageous than the rest, so many people would crowd into it in the one case, and so many would desert it in the other, that its advantages would soon return to the level of other employments.[2]

Recent research has questioned both the tendency toward equality of net advantages and the existence of the mobility that is supposed to bring it about. The authors of interview studies with blue-collar workers have concluded that employed workers are reluctant to change jobs in search of higher wages and that they have very little information about alternative jobs. These findings have been interpreted as denying the presence of an important connection between mobility and wages. Professor Lloyd Reynolds has written:

Voluntary movement of labor—the only type of movement which is relevant here—seems to depend more largely on differences in availability of jobs than on differences in wage levels. Consequently, people engaged in setting wages often make little explicit reference to mobility as an influence on their decisions. The processes of wage determination and labor mobility seem to go on with only a peripheral relation to each other.[3]

Such conclusions about movement within local markets are somewhat surprising in view of the great importance of income differentials in inducing migration across long distances, as established both by casual observation and by empirical research.[4]

It should be noted that Adam Smith wrote of the tendency toward equality not of wages alone, but of the whole of the advantages and disadvantages of an employment. He recognized that certain nonmonetary advantages and disadvantages would be compensated for by persistent differences in wage levels. Some critics of classical theory have suggested that this formulation makes the theory tautological—some set of nonmonetary factors could be adduced to explain any set of wage differentials that might be observed.[5] This is

2. Adam Smith, *The Wealth of Nations*, Modern Library Edition (New York, 1937), p. 99.

3. Lloyd G. Reynolds, *The Structure of Labor Markets* (New York: Harper and Brothers, 1951), p. 3.

4. See, for example, Larry A. Sjaastad, "Income and Migration in the United States," unpublished doctoral dissertation, Univ. of Chicago, 1961.

5. One statement of this view reads in part as follows: "When one confronts the awkward fact that people do not always seek the better-paid job, even when they know it is there, the economist has always resorted to the argument that men do not maximize money but net satisfactions. . . . Once the assumption that man

indeed a valid criticism of writers who leave the set of nonmonetary factors unspecified or open-ended. It does not apply to Adam Smith, because he carefully specified the factors he thought important, and the direction in which he expected them to work. Not being blessed with labor statistics and an electronic computer, he was, of course, not very precise about their magnitude.

In the general context of comparisons of wages among occupations, Smith specified five factors accounting for persistent differentials. Four of these arise on the supply side of the market: wages are lower the steadier the employment and the more agreeable the work (a factor that includes cleanliness, the absence of strenuous physical effort, and the esteem in which the work is held in the community). Wages are higher the greater the cost of learning an occupation and the smaller the probability of success in it.

In modern studies of wage differentials within occupations, the factors on the supply side have been identified with the presence of fringe benefits and the physical conditions of the work place, such as good lighting, good ventilation, and such facilities as a cafeteria. The positive association of wages with fringe benefits and with pleasant working conditions has been cited as denying the current applicability of classical theory;[6] this view seems to us to interpret the theory too narrowly, since there are many possible applications to other nonpecuniary aspects of work.

Smith's remaining factor is very different from the other four, which arise entirely from workers' preferences. He argues that wages will be higher the greater the trust reposed in the worker. But this cannot mean that goldsmiths and jewelers dislike being trusted. Rather Smith seems to be arguing that the number of trustworthy people is small relative to the need for them, so that at wages no higher then those of ordinary jobs there would be excess demand. The bidding up of wages for such occupations reduces the number of workers demanded and induces additional workers to conduct themselves in such a way that they will be considered trustworthy. Clearly trustworthiness is but one example of a large set of characteristics related to the quality and productivity of labor and its value to the employer.

The role in wage determination of differences in quality among workers was developed by Alfred Marshall in the concept of "effi-

---

maximizes money is replaced by the assumption that he maximizes net satisfactions *which are not specified*, no predictions of his market behavior can be made." Kenneth F. Walker, "The Psychological Assumptions of Economics," *The Economic Record* 22 (June 1946): 72–73. Quoted in Wilbert E. Moore, *Industrialization and Labor* (Ithaca, N.Y.: Cornell University Press, 1951), p. 162.

6. See for example, Lester, p. 487; Reynolds, pp. 220–22.

ciency earnings." He argued that competition does not tend to equalize the hourly or weekly money wages of individuals in the same occupation, but rather tends to equalize their earnings per unit of work performed. Differences in weekly earnings are consistent with competitive labor markets if they correspond to differences in productivity.[7]

Recent studies of local labor markets have done relatively little with the relation between wages and worker quality. Lester reports little relationship except at the extremes, but his method of judging quality seems to be impressionistic.[8] Reynolds, also on the basis of nonquantitative evidence, concludes that wage differences are larger than quality differences, so that low-wage employers pay lower efficiency earnings.[9] One of the tasks of this study is therefore to try to develop objective measures or indexes of worker quality and see how they are related to wages. It should also be noted that widespread employer beliefs or prejudices about worker quality might have effects on wages similar to those of actual differences in productivity. If most employers believe, even without evidence, that nonwhites are less productive than whites, this can give rise to a wage difference between whites and nonwhites. It will therefore not always be possible to distinguish between characteristics that actually affect productivity and those that are merely believed by the employer to do so.

The factors mentioned so far, both on the supply side and on the demand side, are consistent with a competitive model of labor markets. There will be a unique wage in each occupation, determined by the forces of supply and demand, for workers of a given quality in employment of given attractiveness. There is, however, a second set of forces that is inconsistent with the competitive model. Smith called these forces "the policy of Europe" and included among them restrictions on the number of apprentices, terms of apprenticeship longer than were needed to learn the trade, and legal restrictions on the mobility of labor. The most comparable factor in the modern economy is the trade union. Recent research has found that wages are generally higher in unionized establishments than in otherwise similar nonunion establishments. This relationship can be obscured where nonunion establishments pay union wages or better in order to avert the unionization of their workers.[10]

7. Alfred Marshall, *Principles of Economics,* 8th ed. (London: Macmillan and Co., 1930), pp. 546–49.
8. Lester, pp. 487–88.
9. Reynolds, p. 219.
10. See H. Gregg Lewis, *Unionism and Relative Wages in the United States* (Chicago: Univ. of Chicago Press, 1963), and Leonard W. Weiss, "Concentration and Labor Earnings," *American Economic Review* 56 (March 1966): 96–117.

Many studies of wages have indicated that wages are higher in large firms or establishments than in small ones,[11] though there is no particular basis in theory for expecting such a relationship. It is not clear whether size should be interpreted as a proxy for some other variables, such as the rate of profit, the extent or threat of unionization, or the occupational skill mix, or whether it is a factor in the attractiveness of employments to workers, which would imply a preference for working in a small establishment.

Several recent studies suggest profitability or ability to pay as a major factor in wage differentials. A closely related hypothesis is that firms that are monopolists in the product market pay higher wages than those that are competitors. The first of these views arises in part from studies of local labor markets;[12] the second is based more on studies of interindustry wage differences at the national level.[13] Both views are inconsistent with the main body of neoclassical economic theory, which assumes cost minimization by both competitors and monopolists and argues that both profitable and unprofitable firms will pay no more for a factor of production than they have to. On the other side, it is argued that labor is unlike other inputs in ways that make it plausible for a monopolist to seek good will by paying high wages even while buying other factors at the lowest prices obtainable.

In some analyses, it is not profitability or product monopoly as such that raises wages, but the joint presence of profitability or product market monopoly and union pressure. Here again, there is no clear basis in theory for expecting unions to make larger gains when bargaining with monopolists than when bargaining with competitors.[14]

It is difficult in local labor market studies to obtain precise measures of ability to pay, since profits data relate to the firm as a

11. For some unusually strong relationships between average hourly earnings and establishment size within industries, see Albert Rees, *New Measures of Wage-Earner Compensation in Manufacturing* (New York: National Bureau of Economic Research, 1960), p. 12. For a very useful review of available evidence, see Richard A. Lester, "Size-of-Establishment Compensation Differentials," *Industrial Relations*, October 1967.

12. See, for example, Reynolds, pp. 162–66 and 189.

13. See Joseph W. Garbarino, "A Theory of Interindustry Wage Structure Variation," *Quarterly Journal of Economics* 64 (May 1950): 282–305, and Harold M. Levinson, *Postwar Movements of Prices and Wages in Manufacturing Industries*, Study Paper no. 21, Joint Economic Committee, 86th Congress, 2d Sess.; Washington, 1960.

14. For a development of this argument, see Albert Rees, *The Economics of Trade Unions* (Chicago: Univ. of Chicago Press, 1962), pp. 82–87; for a contrary view see Martin Segal, "The Relation between Union Wage Impact and Market Structure," *Quarterly Journal of Economics* 78 (February 1964): 96–114. For empirical evidence see Weiss.

whole and not to its local establishments. It would be possible to develop measures of market structure by grouping establishments by industry, and assigning industries to market structure categories. We have not done so in this study because of our limited resources and lack of expertise in industrial organization. To the extent that ability to pay and market structure are related to size of establishment, we may have measured them indirectly.

The studies that have stressed the importance of the noncompetitive factors in the determination of local wage structures have generally concluded that there is a considerable range of indeterminancy in the setting of wages, and that within broad limits a firm can choose its place in the wage structure without incurring any significant extra costs for any choice. Thus Lester writes,

> It seems likely that a wage position established by a firm anywhere within a community's wage range would be an equilibrium position even from a long-run viewpoint. Assuming underemployment or even relatively full employment such as the economy has enjoyed during the past decade, there appears to be little in the way of competitive pressures to force a firm to alter its relative wage position.[15]

Robert Raimon has argued that such indeterminancy is especially true of the wages of semiskilled workers, since semiskilled jobs are traditionally filled from within the firm through on-the-job training, and previous occupational experience may be unimportant or irrelevant. He supports his position by showing from published wage survey data that relative wage dispersion is greater for semiskilled than for skilled or unskilled blue-collar occupations.[16]

The literature touched upon here poses several challenges for new studies of local labor markets. Can such studies come closer than existing studies to explaining the substantial variance of wages within occupations? How much of the explanation is in terms of market forces and how much in terms of institutional and psychological factors? To the extent that the explanations run in terms of market forces of the classical type (that is, forces affecting the attractiveness of employments to workers and the productivity of workers in various employments), labor market studies could lead to the development of a new variant of traditional theory relevant to modern American conditions. The same study, however, cannot both develop such a variant of traditional theory and test its validity. The test must come by extending the model to evidence that was not used in formulating it in the first instance. The wider the range

15. Lester, "A Range Theory of Wage Differentials," p. 493.

16. Robert Raimon, "The Indeterminateness of Wages of Semiskilled Workers," *Industrial and Labor Relations Review* 6 (January 1953): 180–94.

of such evidence consistent with the model, the more useful the model.

MOBILITY PATTERNS AND INFORMATION CHANNELS

A salient aspect of the postwar studies of local labor markets has been the study of mobility patterns of workers within local markets and of the channels of information by which job seekers find jobs and employers find workers. This body of material presents fewer intellectual puzzles than the material on wage dispersion. Nevertheless, some hypotheses have been advanced about it that have not been fully tested.

Once source of such hypotheses is a recent article by George J. Stigler, who goes further than most writers in viewing search by both employer and worker as a process of rational choice among alternatives.[17] Among the specific hypotheses he advances is that wages and search costs are substitutes for each other from the point of view of the employer. In other words, employers who pay relatively low wages in an occupation will have to search for new workers more often than high wage employers because they will experience higher turnover, and they will have to use higher cost channels of recruitment than high wage employers because their vacancies will be more difficult to fill. Thus they will be more likely to use newspaper advertising and to pay the fees of private employment agencies than will high wage employers. We attempt in this study to test this hypothesis against data from the Chicago labor market. We also attempt to estimate the extent to which such differences in hiring costs offset the differences in wages, though only crude estimates can be made of this.

Much of the literature on mobility has been based upon studies in which movers were asked why they moved. The conclusions drawn have generally been that wage differentials are not an important reason for movement. This conclusion can be questioned to the extent that people cannot always disentangle their own motives, or tend to emphasize only one of an interrelated set of differences between the old and new employment.[18]

In this study, we tabulate certain information from the personnel records of job changers, to supplement the data generated in interviews. In particular, we look at the ratio of the final wage on the old job to the initial wage on the new, and at the length of the period

17. George J. Stigler, "Information in the Labor Market," *Journal of Political Economy* 70 (October 1962, Supplement): 94–105.

18. For an elaboration of this point, see Simon Rottenberg, "On Choice in Labor Markets," *Industrial and Labor Relations Review* 9 (January 1956): 183–99.

between jobs, and seek to relate these to such explanatory variables as the age of the job changer and whether the move was voluntary.

A number of previous studies have provided information on the hiring channels through which workers find jobs and employers find workers. In some cases the information was obtained by asking employers to list or rank the channels they use in hiring. Information obtained in this way tends to overstate the importance of channels that are used infrequently. This study will supplement the somewhat scarcer information on the number of workers who actually found their jobs through various hiring channels.

We have been impressed by the tendency in the literature to regard the widespread use of informal channels of employment—such as referrals by employees—as a sign of inefficiency in the labor market information system, and to regard the private formal channels, especially fee-charging employment agencies, as inherently inferior to the public employment service. The information developed in this study will provide a basis for a reconsideration of these conclusions.

THE SPATIAL CHARACTERISTICS OF LARGE LABOR MARKETS

There has been a substantial body of research on the economic aspects of migration between states and on the size and nature of regional wage differentials. Much less has been done on geographical movement of workers within local labor markets, and on spatial wage differentials in such markets.[19] Much of what has been done is largely a by-product interest in transportation and commutation on the part of students of urban geography, urban sociology, and transportation economics. One reason for the relative neglect of this topic in the labor market literature has been that so many of the leading labor market studies were made in small or middle-sized cities, and so few in large metropolitan areas. Because of its large labor force and area, metropolitan Chicago affords a good setting for studying geographical aspects of the labor market.

The problems relevant here can be approached by considering the costs of commuting. Many workers in large metropolitan areas

19. Some data on geographical movement between employers in a local labor market are given in Charles A. Myers and W. Rupert McLaurin, *The Movement of Factory Workers* (New York: John Wiley and Sons, 1943). Some data on geographical wage differentials within a large metropolitan area are given in Robert Evans, Jr., "Worker Quality and Wage Dispersion: An Analysis of a Clerical Labor Market in Boston," *Proceedings of the Fourteenth Annual Meeting, Industrial Relations Research Association* (Madison, Wisconsin, 1962), pp. 246–59. See also George Seltzer, "Pattern Bargaining and the United Steelworkers," *Journal of Political Economy* 59 (August 1951), especially pp. 328–29, and Martin Segal, *Wages in the Metropolis* (Cambridge, Mass.: Harvard Univ. Press, 1960), especially pp. 180–81.

spend a long time traveling to and from work, and have substantial direct expenses for carfare or the use of their own automobiles. Little is known about how the time spent in commuting is valued. Workers could consider it to be equivalent to time spent at work, and wish to be compensated for it at the same rate as for work, or conceivably at an even higher rate. At the other extreme, they might find it so enjoyable as to need no compensation for it.

There are two possible ways of compensating for the time and money costs of commuting. First, those employers who must recruit their work forces over the longest distances might have to pay a wage premium. Second, the costs of housing of given quality could be lowest in those places from which workers had to travel the farthest; that is, the compensation for the costs of travel could be reflected in lower residential land values rather than in higher wage rates. The second force would operate most powerfully if all employment was at the center of the metropolitan area and residences were dispersed around this core; the Washington D.C. metropolitan area approximates this model.[20] The opposite extreme is somewhat harder to imagine on a large scale; it would consist of an area in which all residences were clustered at the center and employment was dispersed around it. In the first of these cases, commutation costs would be largely reflected in residential land values and in the second they would be largely reflected in wages. The Chicago metropolitan area is not close to either pole; both residences and places of employment are widely dispersed. In such a setting, establishments too large to draw their whole work force from the immediate neighborhood might be expected to have to pay some wage premiums.

A somewhat less formal approach to the same problem is suggested by thinking about urban neighborhoods. Each neighborhood and each suburb of a metropolitan area has a special character created by the nature of the business establishments, population, and dwelling places located within it. There are areas of heavy and light industry, and commercial and business areas. There are areas of high and low income, of concentrations of Negro and foreign-born population, and of old and dilapidated or new and sound dwelling units. There are strong correlations among these characteristics, and they have many kinds of consequences for such varied things as the quality of education, the amount of crime, and the infant and maternal mortality rates. There must also be consequences for wages: industrial neighborhoods may have higher wages either because they are less pleasant places in which to work or because they

20. See William C. Pendleton, "The Valuation of Accessibility," unpublished Ph.D. dissertation, Univ. of Chicago, 1962.

may have to attract their work forces over long distances. Negro neighborhoods may offer lower wages to Negro workers because the supply is plentiful. Geographical wage contours could also be established by the uneven distribution of unionization within the metropolitan area.

In an effort to learn more about the spatial characteristics of a large labor market, we analyzed data on the location of each establishment in our sample, and the place of residence of each worker in the study.

COVERAGE OF OCCUPATIONS AND INDUSTRIES

With one significant exception, local labor market studies in the United States have covered a limited range of occupations and industries.[21] Most of these studies have concentrated on the mobility of blue-collar workers in manufacturing industries; three have dealt with female clerical workers.[22] Whereas the blue-collar studies give an impression of little rational organization of the market and a weak relation between wages and mobility or wages and worker quality, two of the three studies on female white-collar workers suggest a more efficient labor market and stronger relations between wages and mobility or quality. It is not clear whether these differences between major occupational groups are true interoccupational differences or whether they reflect the fact that the two sets of studies were undertaken in different places and at different times by investigators who approached the studies from somewhat different perspectives.

In an effort to resolve some of the problems of differences in labor market behavior among occupational and industrial groups, we have made the industrial and occupational coverage of this study as broad as we could within the limits of time and funds. In this we have been assisted by the large size and great diversity of the Chicago labor market area. A brief description of this area will be given in the next chapter.

Some previous studies of the labor market have been designed to explore its behavior in times of excess supply (for example, the clos-

21. The exception is the "six city" study of the Committee on Labor Market Research of the Social Science Research Council. This was a longitudinal study of mobility in the war decade, 1940–50. See Gladys L. Palmer, *Labor Mobility in Six Cities* (New York: Social Science Research Council, 1954).

22. George P. Shultz, "A Nonunion Market for White Collar Labor," in *Aspects of Labor Economics: A Conference of the Universities-National Bureau Committee for Economic Research* (Princeton, N. J.: Princeton Univ. Press, 1962), pp. 107–55; Eaton H. Conant, "Worker Efficiency and Wage Differentials in a Clerical Labor Market," *Industrial and Labor Relations Review* 16 (April 1963): 428–33, and Evans. The Shultz and Evans studies cover female clerical employees in Boston; the Conant study covers female clerical workers in Madison, Wisconsin.

ing of a large plant in a small market) or of excess demand (such as wartime). For our purposes, it was desirable to avoid both of these extremes, and we were fortunate that events permitted us to do so. Our data refer to mid-1963, when the Chicago labor market was reasonably well balanced. It had recovered well from the recession of 1960–61, but was not yet as tight as it was to become in 1966.

Interviews provided the bulk of the data for most previous labor market studies. Only a few researchers have collected substantial bodies of data from personnel records, and even fewer have attempted to reconcile interview data with records. We have placed primary reliance on the collection of data from personnel records, both because this sharply reduced the costs of collecting large bodies of data and because we feel that on many items the records may be more accurate.

Finally, most of the existing labor market studies were made in the 1940s and 1950s. Some of their findings may have changed with the passage of time and with the growth of new institutions and labor market policies on the part of governments, unions, and employers. Although no one reason for adding to the large stock of labor market studies seemed compelling, together they were sufficient to provide the impetus for the work reported here.

2
The Study Area
and Its Labor Force

THIS STUDY covers the Chicago–Northwestern Indiana Standard Consolidated Area as defined in the census of 1960, This area includes six Illinois counties (Cook, DuPage, Kane, Lake, McHenry, and Will) which comprise the Chicago Standard Metropolitan Statistical Area and two Indiana counties (Lake and Porter) which comprise the Gary–Hammond–East Chicago Standard Metropolitan Statistical Area. All references to the Chicago area or the Chicago labor market in this study are to the consolidated area, unless otherwise stated. Table 2.1 shows population and labor force by counties in 1960; Cook County had 76 percent of the total population of the

TABLE 2.1
Population and Labor Force, 1960, Consolidated Area by Counties

Place	Population		Civilian Labor Force[a]	
	Thousands	Percentage of Total	Thousands	Percentage of Total
Consolidated area	6,794	100.0	2,837	100.00
Illinois				
Chicago SMSA	6,221	91.6	2,625	92.5
Cook County	5,130	75.5	2,211	77.9
DuPage County	313	4.6	119	4.2
Kane County	208	3.1	86	3.0
Lake County	294	4.3	105	3.7
McHenry County	84	1.2	33	1.2
Will County	192	2.8	70	2.5
Indiana				
Gary–Hammond– East Chicago SMSA	574	8.4	212	7.5
Lake County	513	7.6	190	6.7
Porter County	60	0.9	22	0.8

SOURCE: U.S. Census of Population, 1960, volume 1, parts 15 and 16, tables 83 and 119. Detail may not add to total because of rounding.

[a]County figures include female members of the armed forces (approximately 700 for all counties combined).

14

area and 78 percent of the total labor force. The second largest county, Lake County, Indiana, had 8 percent of the population and 7 percent of the labor force.

COMMUTING PATTERNS

Table 2.2 shows the 1960 ratios of employed to resident workers in each of the counties and in the city of Chicago. Both Chicago and Lake County, Indiana, gained more commuting workers than they lost. For all other places, the ratio of employed to resident workers

TABLE 2.2

Ratio of Employed to Resident Workers and Commuting Patterns, 1960

Place	Ratio of Employed to Resident Workers	Percentage of Resident Workers Commuting to	
		Cook County	Chicago (City)
Consolidated area	.94		
Illinois			
Cook County	.98		
Chicago (city)	1.09		
DuPage County	.51	51.8	33.1
Kane County	.95	8.4	5.2
Lake County	.84	18.1	11.5
McHenry County	.78	16.4	11.0
Will County	.82	17.5	6.2
Indiana			
Lake County	1.04	6.8	4.7
Porter County	.62	5.4	4.7

SOURCE: Computed from U.S. Census of Population, 1960. Subject Reports, Journey to Work, table 1.

was below one, though in some cases it was not far below. The county with the heaviest concentration of "bedroom suburbs" is DuPage, with only about half as many employed as resident workers. Fifty-two percent of the workers who resided in DuPage commuted to Cook County; in no other case were commuters to Cook County more than a fifth of the resident workers.

Table 2.3 shows the commuting patterns of the area in more detail. In the census week of 1960, 353,000 persons worked in the city of Chicago who did not reside there, and 95,000 resided in the city and worked elsewhere in the consolidated area. The largest single intercounty flow in one direction consisted of 59,000 workers who lived in DuPage and worked in Cook. The next largest flow was made up of 21,000 who lived in Lake County, Illinois, and worked

TABLE 2.3

Workers Working in Consolidated Statistical Area by Place of Residence, Census Week, 1960 (in thousands)

Work in	Total	Reside in				
		Consolidated Area[a]	Cook County	Chicago (City)	DuPage County	Kane County
Consolidated area	2,535.1	2,493.4	1,915.8	1,345.5	107.3	76.6
Cook County	2,019.1	1,997.0	1,879.4	1,333.2	59.2	6.8
Chicago (city)	1,603.3[d]	1,587.1[d]	1,514.3[d]	1,250.2[d]	37.8	4.3
DuPage County	58.4	57.9	9.3	2.9	45.4	1.9
Kane County	77.8	73.5	2.7	0.4	1.9	66.9
Lake County, Ill.	99.7	96.0	5.1	1.8	0.2	0.3
McHenry County	24.8	23.0	0.4	0.1	0.1	0.5
Will County	54.4	51.2	1.6	0.4	0.4	0.2
Lake County, Ind.	187.8	182.9	17.2	6.5	0.1	b
Porter County, Ind.	31.1	12.0	0.1	0.1	b	b

Work in	Reside in					
	Lake County (Ill.)	McHenry County	Will County	Lake County (Ind.)	Porter County (Ind.)	Elsewhere[c]
Consolidated area	111.2	29.4	62.6	171.3	19.2	41.6
Cook County	21.5	5.2	11.5	12.3	1.1	22.0
Chicago (city)	13.7	3.5	4.1	8.5	1.0	16.2
DuPage County	0.2	0.1	0.9	b	b	0.5
Kane County	0.2	1.0	0.7	b	b	4.3
Lake County, Ill.	88.7	1.5	0.1	0.1	b	3.7
McHenry County	0.5	21.6	b	b	b	1.8
Will County	b	b	48.9	0.1	b	3.2
Lake County, Ind.	b	b	0.4	158.3	6.9	4.9
Porter County, Ind.	b	b	b	0.6	11.2	1.1

[a]Does not include Gary–Hammond–East Chicago SMSA if note (b) appears for both Indiana counties.
[b]Fewer than 50 workers.
[c]Includes places where note (b) appears.
[d]Totals given in source in error; recomputed from detail.

in Cook. Flows between Cook County and Lake County, Indiana, were heaviest away from Cook, with 17,000 workers commuting in that direction and 12,000 in the reverse direction.

It is our impression that the commuters from the Illinois counties of Lake and McHenry consisted largely of professional and managerial workers. For other workers, these areas are probably not fully part of the Chicago labor market, but constitute to some extent a separate market. Nevertheless, we chose the consolidated area to study, largely because this permitted the use of lists of firms for the two SMSAs as a sampling frame, and because it permits the comparison of our data with previously published data.

The Chicago area is tied together by an extensive system of expressways, and 56 percent of the workers in the area in 1960 got to work in private automobiles (see table 2.4). This makes it more plausible to think of the eight counties as one labor market area. There are also several commuter railroads running from outlying parts of the area into Chicago, and in 1960 5 percent of the workers in the area got to work by railroad. However, we realize that an area this large probably contains distinct geographical submarkets, and we looked for them in analyzing our data.

TABLE 2.4

Means of Transportation Used in Getting to Work, Census Week of 1960, Consolidated Area

Means	Number of Workers Working in Area (In Thousands)	Percentage of Total
Railroad	124.7	4.9
Subway or elevated	168.0	6.6
Bus or streetcar	463.2	18.3
Taxicab	7.9	0.3
Private automobile or car pool	1,428.2	56.3
Walked	233.8	9.2
Worked at home	62.1	2.4
Other	24.4	1.0
Not reported	22.8	0.9
All means	2,535.1	100.0

SOURCE: Computed from U.S. Census of Population, 1960. Subject Reports, Journey to Work, table 2. Detail may not add to total because of rounding.

RACE AND ORIGIN

Table 2.5 shows the population of the principal urban places in the area, by race. For the area as a whole, the 1960 population was 14.8 percent nonwhite and 14.4 percent Negro; the total Negro popu-

TABLE 2.5

Total and Negro Population of Urban Places 50,000 and over, 1960

Place and County		Population		Percent Negro
		Total	Negro	
Illinois				
Aurora	(Kane)	63,715	2,227	3.5
Berwyn	(Cook)	54,224	6	a
Chicago	(Cook)	3,550,404	812,637	22.9
Cicero	(Cook)	69,130	4	a
Evanston	(Cook)	79,283	9,126	11.5
Joliet	(Will)	66,780	4,638	6.9
Oak Park	(Cook)	61,093	57	0.1
Skokie	(Cook)	59,364	147	0.2
Waukegan	(Lake)	55,719	4,485	8.0
Indiana				
East Chicago	(Lake)	57,669	13,766	23.9
Gary	(Lake)	178,320	69,123	38.8
Hammond	(Lake)	111,698	2,434	2.2

SOURCE: U.S. Census of Population, 1960. vol. 1, parts 15 and 16, table 21.
aLess than 0.05.

lation was 977,332. As can be seen from table 2.5, the Negro population is very unevenly distributed within the area. Chicago, with 52 percent of the total population, has 83 percent of the Negro population. Negroes make up 39 percent of the population of Gary, but less than one-twentieth of 1 percent in Berwyn and Cicero. In suburbs where the Negro population is very small, it is disproportionately female, suggesting that it consists largely of domestic servants residing with their employers. Thus the village of Skokie in 1960 had 143 Negro females and only 4 Negro males.

Within the city of Chicago the distribution of Negroes by neighborhood is also very uneven. The main areas of Negro residence form an L-shaped pattern, with the shorter branch running west from the Loop (the central business district) and the longer branch running south from the Loop for a distance of about ten miles. This South Side branch contains two large neighborhoods (Grand Boulevard and Washington Park) whose total 1960 population was almost 124,000, of whom more than 99 percent were Negro. At the other extreme, there are several residential neighborhoods in the northwestern and southwestern corners of the city that had no Negro population in 1960. We will examine later the effect of the location of Negro population on the market for unskilled labor.

The occupational composition of the employed in the Chicago area is quite different for whites and for Negroes. Table 2.6 shows

18

total employment by sex and major occupation group and the percentage of Negroes in each group. Negroes are substantially underrepresented among professional, managerial, and sales workers of both sexes, among female clerical workers, and among male craftsmen. They are substantially overrepresented among operatives, service workers, and nonfarm laborers of both sexes. The areas in which Negroes are underrepresented are, of course, those that in general have the highest pay and prestige and require the most skill.

TABLE 2.6

Employment by Major Occupation Group and Sex with Percent Negro, Chicago Consolidated Area, 1960

Occupation	Employment		Percent Negro	
	Male	Female	Male	Female
All occupations	1,812,158	904,443	11.1	13.4
Professional and technical	197,971	102,072	2.9	8.0
Managers and proprietors	184,674	27,491	2.0	5.6
Clerical workers	164,226	338,758	11.1	6.1
Sales workers	128,997	65,460	2.6	4.6
Craftsmen and foremen	389,740	13,782	5.5	11.4
Operatives	365,611	148,323	14.7	18.0
Nonfarm laborers	115,921	5,542	27.1	33.7
Private household workers	1,712	33,949	46.1	46.2
Service workers, except private household	122,356	95,781	22.6	22.2
Farmers and farm managers	8,790	454	0.6	1.8
Farm laborers	5,029	874	3.0	4.5
Occupation not reported	127,131	71,957	27.7	28.2

SOURCE: U.S. Census of Population, 1960, vol. 1, parts 15 and 16, tables 121 and 122.

The Chicago area still has a substantial population of foreign-born whites: 628,000 in 1960, or 9.2 percent of the total population. The number of foreign-born whites has been declining since the census of 1930, when it was 1,100,000; their percentage of the total has been declining at least since 1910, when it was 33.7 percent. Of the foreign born of all races, 68.6 percent lived in the city of Chicago in 1960, as compared with 50.6 percent of the native born. In addition to 639,000 foreign born in 1960 (including foreign-born nonwhites), the area had 1,508,000 native born of foreign or mixed parentage; this group, together with the foreign born, is referred to in census statistics as the foreign stock. Poland was the most important country of origin of the foreign stock, with 17 percent of the total, followed by Germany with 14 and Italy with 10. Among the more recent arrivals in the area were 67,000 persons of Mexican origin. The Chicago SMSA also had 35,000 persons of Puerto Rican birth or parentage in 1960.

In large cities like Chicago, immigrants from the same country have typically clustered in particular neighborhoods, and some of these neighborhoods still preserved their identity in 1960. For example, in West Town, a neighborhood of 140,000 population west and slightly north of the Loop, just over half the population in 1960 was of foreign stock, and of this about half was Polish. In South Lawndale, a West Side neighborhood of 61,000 population, just under half the 1960 population was of foreign stock, with Poland and Czechoslovakia each contributing about a third of this half, or a sixth of the total.

The Chicago area has also been the destination of a considerable stream of migration originating within the continental United States. Of the native white population of 5,159,000 there were 1,196,000 born in a state other than the one in which they resided in 1960. Of the native nonwhite population of 996,000, almost half (496,000) were born in other states. The South contributed about a fourth of the white interstate migrants and 89 percent of the non-white interstate migrants; the east south central states alone account for three-fifths of these nonwhite migrants. Movement into the Chicago area from the east south central states has undoubtedly been assisted by the presence of two major railroads serving these states and having Chicago as their northern terminus: the Illinois Central and the Gulf, Mobile, and Ohio.

EDUCATIONAL ATTAINMENT

To some extent, the racial differences in occupational composition shown in table 2.6 reflect differences in educational attainment. Table 2.7 shows the educational attainment of persons in the Chicago area who were twenty-five years old and over in 1960. The proportions of nonwhites who had completed high school or attended college are substantially smaller than the corresponding proportions of whites. However, the differences in educational attainment by color in 1960 were smaller for the Chicago area than for all urban areas in the United States. The median number of years of school completed for nonwhite males in Chicago was 9.0 and for nonwhite females 9.6. For all urban areas in the United States, the corresponding figures are 8.5 and 8.9. For the adult population of all races, the Chicago area medians are below those for the urban United States.[1] The median number of years completed in the

1. For the Chicago area, the census does not give median years completed for whites separately, and this figure cannot be computed accurately from those given.

TABLE 2.7

Percentage Distributions of Educational Attainment of Persons 25 years of Age and Over, Consolidated Area, 1960

Years of School Completed		Whites		Nonwhites	
		Male	Female	Male	Female
None		1.8	2.2	2.6	1.9
Elementary:	1–3	4.2	3.7	12.4	8.9
	4–7	10.5	9.4	19.4	18.3
	8	18.9	20.5	16.4	16.7
High school:	1–3	20.3	20.9	22.5	24.1
	4	22.0	28.2	15.9	19.5
College:	1–3	10.7	9.0	7.0	7.3
	4	6.5	4.3	2.0	2.2
	5 or more	5.2	1.9	1.8	1.1

SOURCE: Computed from U.S. Census of Population, 1960, vol. 1, part 15, table 103.

Chicago area was 10.7 for both males and females; in all urban areas it was 11.0 for males and 11.2 for females.

EMPLOYMENT AND UNEMPLOYMENT

The proportion of Negroes in total employment in the Chicago area is somewhat lower than in the total population (11.9 percent as compared with 14.4 percent). In part, this is because a higher proportion of nonwhites are below working age. Nonwhites made up 14.8 percent of total population, but only 13.4 percent of the population fourteen years of age and over, and 13.3 percent of the civilian labor force. They were less heavily represented in the male civilian labor force (12.5 percent) than in the female labor force (15.0 percent). However, the main reason for the underrepresentation of nonwhites in employment is their much higher unemployment rate. The unemployment rates for whites in 1960 were 3.0 percent for males and 3.7 percent for females; for nonwhites the rates were 10.1 percent for males and 12.1 percent for females. Although nonwhites were only 13.3 percent of the labor force, they were 34.0 percent of the unemployed.

The level of unemployment in the Chicago area tends to be lower than the national average. Table 2.8 shows that in the Illinois portion of the area, unemployment was estimated to be below the national average in each of the years 1957–63. In the Indiana portion of the area, unemployment was above the national average in the recession years 1958 and 1961 and in the years immediately following them. However, by 1963, which is the reference year for this study,

21

unemployment in both SMSAs was well below the national level. The greater fluctuations in unemployment in the Indiana part of the area result from the heavy concentration of the basic steel industry in Gary, East Chicago, and Portage.

INDUSTRIAL COMPOSITION AND EARNINGS

The Chicago area has long been known as the home of a diversified manufacturing industry and a center for all forms of transportation. Table 2.9 shows employed workers living in the consolidated area by industry in 1960 and their 1959 annual earnings; table 2.10 shows employment in nonagricultural establishments in 1963 (the reference year for this study) in the Chicago SMSA, and average hourly earnings of production or nonsupervisory workers where available. Only the most important manufacturing industries are shown separately in table 2.9; table 2.10 shows all two-digit manufacturing industries. Data on employment and earnings in nonagricultural establishments are not published for the Gary–Hammond–East Chicago SMSA. The basis of industrial classification is not the same in the two tables; the largest difference occurs in the government sector. The statistics on nonagricultural employment show all government employees as a separate group. The census statistics for 1960 show only public administration separately; employees of public schools and hospitals, for example, are included under professional services.

There were 959,000 manufacturing employees residing in the Chicago area in 1960, of whom almost two-thirds were employed in durable goods manufacturing. The four durable goods industries shown separately in table 2.9 account for about three-fourths of employment in durable goods. The first three of these are heavy industries with little female employment; however, electrical equipment is a large employer of women.

TABLE 2.8
Unemployment as a Percentage of the Labor Force, 1957–63
(Persons fourteen years of age and over)

Year	National Average	Chicago SMSA	Gary–Hammond–East Chicago SMSA
1957	4.3	3.3	3.1
1958	6.8	6.2	8.2
1959	5.5	4.7	5.8
1960	5.6	4.2	5.5
1961	6.7	5.4	6.9
1962	5.6	4.3	6.2
1963	5.7	4.3	4.8

SOURCE: *Manpower Report of the President*, March 1965.

The textile, apparel, and shoe industries—which generally have low wages—are relatively unimportant in the Chicago area. This has a consequence that will be of considerable importance in our analysis of wages; earnings in nondurable goods in the area are not lower than in durable goods. The important nondurable goods industries

TABLE 2.9
Employed Workers by Industry and Sex, 1960, and Median Annual Earnings, 1959, Consolidated Area

Industry	Employment, 1960 (in thousands)		Median Annual Earnings, 1959	
	Male	Female	Male	Female
All industries	1,812.2	904.4	$5,602	$2,970
Agriculture, forestry, and fisheries	18.3	2.1	3,423	1,550
Mining	1.5	0.3	6,473	4,469
Construction	122.3	6.3	6,296	3,553
Manufacturing	711.7	247.0	5,742	3,313
Durable goods	481.7	139.2	5,644	3,422
Primary iron and steel	100.8	6.7	5,334	4,173
Fabricated metals	84.0	20.5	5,776	3,604
Machinery, except electric	93.9	18.7	5,865	3,550
Electrical machinery	86.6	54.7	5,734	3,373
Nondurable goods	227.2	106.3	6,001	3,166
Printing and publishing	61.0	25.8	6,397	3,280
Transportation, communication, and utilities	184.5	42.5	5,819	4,027
Wholesale and retail trade	292.3	191.0	5,215	2,272
Finance, insurance, and real estate	72.1	62.1	6,216	3,332
Business and repair services	51.6	23.6	5,501	3,034
Personal services	41.6	73.9	4,025	1,562
Entertainment and recreation	13.3	6.2	4,202	1,829
Professional services	116.8	158.1	6,036	3,174
Public administration	77.5	28.0	5,533	3,860
Industry not reported	108.8	63.4	4,512	2,618

SOURCE: U.S. Census of Population, 1960, vol. 1, part 15, tables 127 and 130.

such as printing and publishing, chemicals, and food products had average hourly earnings close to or above the all-manufacturing average. In the consolidated area male workers in nondurable goods had significantly higher annual earnings in 1959 than male workers in durable goods. Within each group, average hourly earnings vary widely among industries, although there was only a negligible difference between the mean hourly earnings of the groups themselves.

TABLE 2.10
Employment in Nonagricultural Establishments by Industry and
Average Hourly Earnings, Chicago SMSA, 1963

Industry	Total Employees (in thousands)	Average Hourly Earnings, Production or Nonsupervisory Workers
Nonagricultural employment	2,494.9	----
Mining	6.3	----
Contract construction	98.7	$4.23
Manufacturing	849.0	2.71
Durable goods	540.7	2.71
Ordnance and accessories	1.1	----
Lumber and wood products	6.9	2.11
Furniture and fixtures	23.5	2.47
Stone, clay, and glass	19.8	2.57
Primary metals	65.3	3.11
Fabricated metals	95.7	2.79
Machinery, except electrical	110.7	2.88
Electrical machinery	136.9	2.48
Transportation equipment	27.0	2.92
Instruments and related products	25.4	2.57
Nondurable goods	308.2	2.70
Food and kindred products	84.5	2.68
Textile mill products	4.1	2.01
Apparel and related products	28.8	1.83
Paper and allied products	28.9	2.42
Printing and publishing	82.7	3.27
Chemicals and allied products	40.6	2.72
Petroleum refining	6.3	3.02
Rubber and plastic products	22.4	2.49
Leather and leather products	9.5	2.31
Transportation and public utilities	193.1	----
Wholesale and retail trade	539.8	----
Department stores	58.1	1.87
Mail-order houses	29.1	1.86
Finance, insurance, and real estate	155.1	----
Service and miscellaneous	391.8	----
Government	261.1	----

SOURCE: BLS Bulletin no. 1370–1.

At the time of our study, two traditional Chicago industries were no longer of major importance. Employment in farm machinery and equipment in the Chicago SMSA was only 8,300 in 1963, although farm machinery companies had additional employment in such industries as basic steel and construction and material handling equipment. Employment in meat products in 1963 was only 15,400, less than a fifth of employment in food and kindred products. Railroad employment has also been of declining importance in the Chicago area. In 1963, railroad transportation had 54,000 employees in the Chicago SMSA, which is less than a third of the total in transportation and public utilities.

In trade, the Chicago area is distinguished as the headquarters of several large mail-order houses, which employed 29,000 workers in the Chicago SMSA in 1963. Among financial institutions, insurance carriers are the largest employers, accounting for 46,000 employees in the SMSA in 1963.

There were five private institutions of higher learning in the area with enrollments of 5,000 or over in 1959, as well as a number of smaller private institutions, public junior colleges, and branches of state universities. Employment in these institutions is included in the totals shown for professional services in table 2.9.

3

How the Data
Were Collected

The Selection of Occupations and the Pilot Study

Work on this study began during the summer of 1962, when we examined published data on the Chicago labor market, with emphasis on the distribution of workers by occupation and industry. This was a first step in deciding on the occupations to be selected for intensive study.

In the autumn of 1962 an advisory committee was formed of eight industrial relations executives who agreed to help us in the design of the study. The members of the committee were as follows (titles as of 1962):

Thomas G. Ayers, executive vice president, Commonwealth Edison Company

Frank W. Braden, general personnel manager, Illinois Bell Telephone Company

John Kajander, director of industrial relations, Warwick Electronics

Karl Klein, vice president, Pullman Trust and Savings Bank

Charles M. Mason, senior vice president, personnel, United Air Lines

Ralph J. Sturkey, vice president, personnel and public relations, A. B. Dick Company

Weir C. Swanson, personnel manager, Jewel Tea Company

George Yoxall, manager, personnel and training, Inland Steel Company

The principal problems discussed at the first meeting of the committee were the availability of data in company records and the selection of the study occupations. We wanted to choose occupations, both white-collar and blue-collar, covering a wide range of skills and including occupations that were largely or exclusively filled by members of one sex. We also wanted occupations in which there were substantial numbers of workers, and whose job content was readily identifiable and reasonably uniform across industries. For the most part, we sought occupations present in a wide variety of industries. Our first discussion led to the tentative selection of thirteen occupations.

Of these, five were white-colar and professional: typist, keypunch operator, accountant, draftsman, and tabulating machine operator. The remaining eight were blue-collar: material handler, janitor, janitress, fork lift trucker, punch press operator, truck driver, maintenance electrician, and tool and die maker.[1] As a result of the pilot study described below, the draftsman occupation was dropped from the final list because of excessive variation in job content.

TABLE 3.1

Employment in Selected Occupations by Sex and Race, 1960, and 1959 Earnings, Consolidated Area

Occupation	Employed Persons, 1960				Median Earnings of Experienced Civilian Labor Force 1959	
	Total		Negro			
	Male	Female	Male	Female	Male	Female
Accountants and auditors	23,477	5,082	206	172	$7,121	$4,555
Office machine operators	6,258	20,029	——	1,193	——	3,465
Typists	1,084	30,120	——	2,521	——	3,111
Electricians	16,589	75	362	——	6,854	——
Tool makers and die makers and setters	13,260	89	205	——	7,024	——
Truck drivers and deliverymen	70,182	575	6,230	——	5,841	——
Truck and tractor drivers	53,330	250	——	——	——	——
Charwomen, janitors, and porters	35,531	9,761	13,050	1,894	3,882	2,159
Charwomen and cleaners	2,201	3,915	——	——	——	——
Janitors and sextons	26,635	5,689	——	——	——	——

SOURCE: U.S. Census of Population, 1960, vol. 1, part 15, tables 121, 122, and 124. Where no figure is shown, separate data are not available.

1. The order in which these occupations are named will be followed throughout the study, because it is roughly the chronological order in which we analyzed
2. The number of observations deleted is shown in table 6.1 of chapter 6.

One of the study occupations, janitress, by definition is female; two more, keypunch operator and typist, were predominantly female, and we later deleted the few male observations and defined them as female.[2] Janitor was defined as a male occupation, and three more (maintenance electrician, tool and die maker, and truck driver) turned out to be exclusively male in our sample. Fork lift trucker and material handler were predominantly male, and were defined as exclusively male by deleting the few female observations. The remaining three occupations (accountant, tabulating machine operator, and punch press operator) contained enough observations of both sexes to be analyzed as mixed occupations.

For most of the study occupations, published data were available on the numbers of workers in the Chicago labor market in 1960 or

TABLE 3.2
Average Earnings in Selected Occupations, Chicago SMSA, April 1963

Occupation	Number of Workers Surveyed		Average Earnings	
	Male	Female	Male	Female
Office Occupations			*Weekly, Standard*	
Tabulating machine operators				
class A	1,117	——	$115.00	$ ——
class B	1,366	394	96.00	94.00
class C	517	421	86.00	83.50
Keypunch operators				
class A	——	2,672	——	84.50
class B	——	3,964	——	76.50
Typists				
class A	——	5,900	——	80.00
class B	108	10,442	73.50	69.00
Maintenance, custodial, and material movement occupations			*Hourly, Straight Time*	
Electricians, maintenance	3,365	——	$ 3.38	——
Tool and die makers	4,258	——	3.50	——
Truck drivers	14,822	——	3.04	——
Truckers, power (fork lift)	4,681	——	2.54	——
Janitors, porters, and cleaners	13,960	5,477	2.02	1.78
Laborers, material handling	22,463	——	2.38	——

SOURCE: Occupational Wage Survey, Chicago, Illinois, April 1963: BLS Bulletin no. 1345-65.

1963, and their earnings. Such data are shown in tables 3.1 and 3.2, and may be compared with the information given in later chapters on the size of our samples and earnings reported. No separate published data were available for punch press operators.

During the winter of 1963 we collected data on workers in the original thirteen occupations from a set of six establishments of four firms represented on the advisory board; this is referred to hereafter as the pilot study. The data collection included interviews with appropriate employer representatives in each establishment concerning hiring standards, sources of recruitment, wage policy, and related topics. Data were also collected from personnel files on 885 individuals, 357 in the five white-collar occupations and 528 in the eight blue-collar occupations. The pilot study confirmed the feasibility of our data collection scheme. In general, however, the data from the pilot study are not included in the work presented in this report because the establishments in the pilot study were not randomly selected. They represented firms whose industrial relations practices are more sophisticated than the average, and establishments that are in general much larger than the average establishment that entered the random sample.

THE SELECTION OF THE ESTABLISHMENT AND EMPLOYEE SAMPLES

The pilot study enabled us to estimate the number of establishments from which we could collect data within our time and money budgets. It was decided that these would permit collection from a random sample of seventy-five establishments. Since not all establishments surveyed contained each of our study occupations, the sample for each occupation is smaller than this total. It later became clear that our establishment sample was somewhat too small for our purposes; results might have been improved if we had studied fewer occupations in a somewhat larger number of establishments. However, this would have increased the costs of data collection.

In designing the establishment sample, we consulted Harry V. Roberts, professor of statistics in the University of Chicago's Graduate School of Business. He advised us that a sample of this size should be stratified in only one dimension. We then believed that the size of establishment was the largest single source of wage dispersion within occupations, and decided to stratify by size. As it developed, we did not find strong relations between wages and establishment size, and concluded we might better have stratified by industry. However, we were fortunate in that we nevertheless ended up with a good industry distribution, as shown in table 3.3.

Our industry universe includes manufacturing; transportation, communication, and public utilities; wholesale and retail trade;

TABLE 3.3

Number of Establishments in the Random Sample by Industry and Size

Industry	1,000 Employees and Over	250–999 Employees	50–249 Employees	All Sizes
Durable goods				
Primary metals	2	3	——	5
Fabricated metal products	1	2	2	5
Machinery	3	1	2	6
Electrical equipment	3	——	——	3
Instruments	1	2	——	3
All other durables	2	1	2	5
Total	12	9	6	27
Nondurable goods				
Food	——	2	2	4
Textiles and apparel	2	3	——	5
Printing	1	1	2	4
Chemicals	——	2	3	5
All other nondurables	——	1	2	3
Total	3	9	9	21
Transportation, communications, and public utilities	4	3	1	8
Wholesale and retail trade	2	3	2	7
Banking, insurance, and real estate	2	1	5	8
Other services	1	0	2	3
Total, all industries	24	25	25	74

finance, insurance, and real estate; and other service industries except private households. We excluded agriculture, forestry, fishing, and mining because they are not important employers in the Chicago area. Private households and government were excluded because of problems in data collection, arising in the first instance from the large number of employers and in the second from laws protecting the confidential nature of personnel records. Construction was excluded for a variety of reasons: it employs very few workers in our study occupations, has many very small firms and a high turnover of firms, and its on-site workers have no fixed work locations within the area.

To set the limits of the employment size classes within which to sample, we had to develop a list of establishments in our industry universe by size. The basic list was provided by the Illinois Division of Unemployment Compensation and showed Illinois establishments covered by unemployment insurance by size and location. This was supplemented with several lists of uncovered establishments. A list of establishments employing over five hundred persons in the Chicago SMSA was provided by the Chicago office of the U.S. Bureau of Labor Statistics (these were mostly railroads and nonprofit institutions); a list of hospitals showing numbers of employees was taken from publications of the American Hospital Association; and lists of Indiana employers of five hundred and over were obtained from the Calumet Area Personnel Association Yearbook and from the Gary office of the Indiana State Employment Service. It should be especially noted that both in setting up our size strata and in drawing firms from within them we omit all establishments in the Indiana part of the area with fewer than five hundred employees.

The size classes we chose were 1,000 employees and over, 250 to 999 employees, and 50 to 249 employees. We excluded establishments with fewer than 50 employees (which account for 28.1 percent of all employment in the area) because it would be hard to get access to them and because any one establishment in this size class was unlikely to have many, if any, workers in the study occupations. Table 3.4 shows our estimates of employment by establishments in each size class. The three included size classes have been chosen so that they represent roughly equal parts of estimated total employment.

TABLE 3.4

Estimated Employment by Establishment Size, Consolidated Area, March 1962

Number of Employees	Approximate Number of Establishments	Estimated Total Employment	
		Thousands	Percentage
1,000 and over	200	580	28.1
250–999	850	407	19.7
50–249	4,900	497	24.1
0–49	48,200	580	28.1
Total	54,150	2,064	100.0

NOTE: Data exclude employment by governments and private households, and Indiana establishments of under 500 employees. Illinois data for establishments under 500 employees are incomplete. A total of about 300,000 employees in establishments of under 500 employees are unaccounted for. For sources, see text.

TABLE 3.5
Establishments Drawn but Not Surveyed by Size Class

	Number of Employees			Total
	1,000 and over	250–999	50–249	
Surveyed	24	25	25	74
Refused	9	16	12	37
Omitted for other reasons[a]	1	8	20	29

[a]Includes (1) no workers in the study occupations, (2) establishment not within our industry coverage, and (3) establishment no longer in existence.

If the costs of collecting data were proportional to the number of individual observations, it would have been the best strategy to sample roughly equal numbers of *individuals* from each size class. In fact, however, a large part of the cost of data collection is the fixed cost of getting access to the establishment and visiting it. To economize on these fixed costs, we visited the same number of *establishments* in each class, consequently collecting data on more individuals the larger the size class. Establishments were drawn at random from each class until we had collected data from twenty-five in each.[3] Our procedure permitted us to draw more than one establishment of the same firm, and in a few cases we did.

In getting access to the establishments drawn we turned again to our advisory committee. Members of the committee called friends at firms with establishments in the two larger size classes and explained the study to them. As we finished gathering data at each firm, we asked its help in getting access to firms on the list with which we did not yet have contact. If this chain of contacts ran out, we turned to alumni of the Graduate School of Business who held management positions in the firms to be approached or who could help us gain access to them. When all else failed we approached firms with no introduction; this was the procedure used for all the establishments in the smallest size class.

In all, 137 establishments were drawn, of which 74 were surveyed. Table 3.5 shows the firms drawn but not surveyed, by size. Refusals to provide data were most numerous in the middle size class; the smallest size class produced the most omissions for other reasons. When an establishment had to be omitted for any reason we turned to the next establishment on the random list; we did not try to find a substitute in the same industry. This procedure led to some

3. One establishment in the size class "over one thousand" turned out to have no employees in the study occupations and was never replaced, so that this size class has only twenty-four establishments.

TABLE 3.6

Relation of Establishments in the Random Sample to Firms by Size

	Number of Employees			Total
	1,000 and over	250–999	50–249	
Single establishment firm	2	8	14	24
Multiestablishment firm:				
Headquarters establishment	15	8	2	25
Branch of firm with employment concentrated in Chicago area	4	4	2	10
Branch of firm with employment not concentrated in Chicago area	3	5	7	15

underrepresentation of miscellaneous services, the only industry category in which the number of firms drawn and omitted (nine) substantially exceeds the number surveyed. We experienced a higher rate of refusals among branch establishments of firms whose headquarters were not in Chicago, and such establishments may be somewhat underrepresented in the sample. Table 3.6 shows the way in which the establishments in the sample are related to the firms of which they are a part.

Additional information about the sample is given in table 3.7. The sample includes twenty-five establishments where no workers are represented by unions, including seven with one thousand employees or over. This is perhaps more than might be expected in view of the traditional strength of unions in the Chicago area. In another six establishments, including two with one thousand employees or over, only a few occupations are represented by unions.[4] In some of these the unionized occupations include one or more of our study occupations: maintenance electrician, tool and die maker, truck driver, or janitor.

Our definition of an establishment differs slightly from that used in government statistics; the change made it possible to gather additional data at very little extra cost. Several facilities of the same firm

4. Three of these six establishments are retail outlets, where the concept of "production and maintenance workers" used in table 3.7 is not really applicable.

TABLE 3.7

Distribution of Establishments in the Random Sample by Unionization and Size

Extent of Unionization	Number of Employees			Total
	1,000 and over	250–999	50–249	
No union	7	9	9	25
Union representing: Only selected occupations	2	1	3	6
All production and maintenance workers	10	13	13	36
Production, maintenance, and clerical workers	5	2	––	7

located in the Chicago area were considered one establishment if personnel records for all of them were kept at one facility that fell into our sample. In most such cases there was some centralization of personnel policy, such as uniform wage scales or central hiring. The separate facilities at different locations are considered subestablishments. In deciding whether to measure a variable for the establishment as a whole or for its subestablishments separately, we took into account the nature of the variable and the policies of the firm. For example, locational variables were measured for the subestablishments.

Employees in two of our occupations are employed in large numbers in specialized firms, few of which fell into our random sample—public accounting firms for accountants, and tool and die shops for tool and die makers. For each of these occupations, we obtained a list of specialized firms from trade sources and drew a small nonrandom supplementary sample, from which data were collected only for the occupation in which the firm specialized. Wherever data from the supplementary samples are reported, they are clearly distinguished from the random sample data.

Within each establishment we collected data for the last week of June 1963 on a maximum of forty workers in each study occupation represented there. Where there were more than forty workers in one occupation in the establishment, we sampled that occupation.

If the purpose of this study were to estimate mean earnings for the employees in an occupation in the Chicago area, it would be appropriate to weight these observations by the inverse of the sampling ratio; for example, if we took half the observations in a personnel file we should multiply each observation by two. Similarly, it would be appropriate to weight the observations from the smaller size classes of establishments, since we took equal numbers of establishments from each class rather than equal numbers of employees. However, it is not the purpose of this study to estimate mean wages; for this purpose the BLS data shown in table 3.2 are far better than any we could produce, because they come from a sample of almost thirty-five hundred establishments. Our main purpose is to investigate the interrelationships between wages and other variables at the level of the individual, and for this purpose weighting would be meaningless if not mischievous.

In addition to collecting data from personnel records for the workers in our sample, we interviewed subsamples of workers in five of the twelve study occupations (accountant, keypunch operator, tool and die maker, fork lift trucker, and janitor). The appendix lists in detail the items on which information was taken from personnel records. Not all firms would permit us to interview workers, especially blue-collar workers, so the interview subsamples are considerably smaller than the personnel record samples. In every establishment we visited, we interviewed appropriate management personnel about hiring practices, channels of recruitment, and wage policy.

We were especially interested in scores on tests designed to show intelligence or job-related aptitudes or skills. Where such information was available in company records we collected it, and in one case it proved to be useful in explaining wage dispersion. This was the scores on typing tests taken by typists at the time of hire, which were recorded by many employers.

In four occupations (accountant, keypunch operator, fork lift trucker, and janitor) we attempted ourselves to administer tests which, according to the United States Employment Service, are relevant to performance in these occupations. The number of firms permitting us to do this was so small that in most cases the data collected were not usable. In the case of accountants, however, we obtained data on a paper-and-pencil intelligence test from the General Aptitude Test Battery for ninety-two individuals in eighteen establishments.

Many Chicago employers give prospective employees a short paper and pencil intelligence test known as the Wonderlic Personnel Test,[5] and we recorded the scores where they were part of the personnel record. However, the samples again were very small, and little use was made of these data.

5. For further information in this test, see chapter 7, p. 90.

The Employers View the Labor Market

THE EMPLOYERS in our sample varied widely in the extent to which they were free to choose a wage and manning strategy and, for those with discretion on these matters, in the pattern of behavior adopted. These aspects of employer outlook and performance form an important part of the background for analysis of the data on individuals and occupations, and for an understanding of the results of that analysis. In addition, data from the employer interviews can be directly helpful in assessing the meaning of wage differentials, quality differences, information and employment networks, and the general operation of the labor market.

We will start with a discussion of the extent and nature of constraints on their behavior as seen by employers and as related to the channels of information and recruitment they use in the labor market; then we will explore various aspects of employer strategy, particularly with respect to unions, occupations, location, worker quality, and the problem of discrimination in the employment process. Our information is based primarily on interviews with personnel workers and tends to be qualitative in nature. This chapter will therefore be more impressionistic than the subsequent analyses of the mass of data accumulated on individual workers and occupations.

CONSTRAINTS ON EMPLOYER WAGE POLICY

The employer's outlook on and pattern of behavior in the labor market will depend in part on the extent and nature of the restraints placed on his ability to pursue an independent wage strategy. We have therefore classified the establishments in our sample into these three groups: those with no discretion in wage strategy (eight establishments); those with some control over wages (forty-three establishments); and those with wide latitude at the establishment level (twenty-three establishments). In the first group, wages were in effect fixed by a collective bargain whose scope extended beyond the establishment or by a policy set at the corporate headquarters of a multiestablishment firm. In the second group, rates for only

TABLE 4.1

Size of Establishment and Latitude in Wage Policy

Size of Establishment	Number of Establishments		
	No Control	Some Control	Wide Latitude
1,000 employees and over	2	14	7
250–999	4	13	9
50–249	2	16	7
Total	8	43	23

one or some occupations were determined elsewhere, or the more general constraints imposed still left local personnel with considerable room for maneuvering. None of the employing units in the third group had a unionized occupation. It is interesting to note that size of establishment did not exert any special influence on degree of latitude in wage policy (table 4.1).

In the no-control group, with rates of pay fixed by corporate policy or multiestablishment bargaining, local management had little need to collect wage information. However, in one case local management, just before union negotiations, supplied the home office with rates in three firms in the immediate area (table 4.2). Labor recruiting in this group took place predominantly through unsolicited applications and employee referrals, with relatively little and only specialized use of public or private employment agencies,

TABLE 4.2

Latitude in Wage Policy and Primary Sources of Wage Information

Sources of Information	Number of Establishments		
	No Control	Some Control	Wide Latitude
Own surveys	1	5	2
Other surveys, including BLS	0	22	14
Trade association	0	4	2
Informal sources[a]	0	19	14
Agencies	0	0	2
College placement bureaus	0	0	1
Applicants	0	0	4
Union	0	0	2

NOTE: The entries in this table do not add to the totals of table 4.1 because some establishments did not indicate sources of wage information, and others used more than one source.

[a]Includes calls to area and industry firms, information provided by current employees, information resulting from turnover, and responses to ads placed by individuals and other firms.

newspaper advertisements, and other formal channels (table 4.3). Indeed, in three cases there had been no new hires in recent years. This relaxed attitude toward the labor market is understandable in the light of the wage position of these firms: they tended to be in the fourth or fifth quintile of our sample in level of wages for most of the occupations in our survey. In one case, wage rates were well above the average in the area. As the personnel manager of this establishment remarked, "When a new firm comes into the area, they often call to see what we are paying, but they never call after that first time." By contrast, in another case where rates were below average in unorganized clerical occupations, the local manager was rebuffed in his effort to break through corporate policy, although he used a special wage survey covering fifty-two firms as the basis for his position. The local reaction is to circumvent the policy through the device of promotion whenever possible, and to request raises on an individual basis. "Permission to do this is given occasionally, but more often it is denied and the person then frequently quits."

More generally, the association of wage position in the labor market and degree of latitude in wage policy appears to be a strong one, as shown in table 4.4 and chart 4.1. This table and chart were developed by first classifying the mean wages in each occupation in each establishment by their quintile ranking among establishments where the occupation was present; then grouping these rankings into white-collar, skilled, and other blue-collar occupations separately

TABLE 4.3

Latitude in Wage Policy and Primary Sources of Recruits

Hiring Sources	Number of Firms with					
	No Control		Some Control		Wide Latitude	
	White-Collar	Blue-Collar	White-Collar	Blue-Collar	White Collar	Blue-Collar
Informal[a]	4	4	17	29	12	12
Schools	1	0	8	2	4	0
Agencies	1	1	18	1	13	2
Ads	2	1	16	13	8	6
State employment service	1	1	3	9	3	3
Union	0	0	0	7	0	0
Other[b]	0	0	6	6	4	4

[a]Includes unsolicited applications and referrals by current employees.

[b]Includes a miscellany of sources specialized to the firm or to an occupation such as recruiting from public accounting firms and organizations of particular nationality groups, by handbills, and by internal promotion.

TABLE 4.4
Distribution of Establishments by Wage Quintile in Each Occupation and Latitude in Wage Policy

Wage Quintile	White-Collar Occupations						Skilled Occupations						Other Blue-Collar Occupations						All Occupations					
	N		S		L		N		S		L		N		S		L		N		S		L	
	#	%	#	%	#	%	#	%	#	%	#	%	#	%	#	%	#	%	#	%	#	%	#	%
5	5	38	16	16	13	23	0	0	8	28	1	8	7	39	26	21	5	10	12	32	50	20	19	16
4	4	31	21	21	9	16	1	17	6	21	2	15	7	39	25	21	6	13	12	32	52	21	17	14
3	1	8	22	22	10	18	2	33	6	21	4	31	2	11	21	17	12	25	5	14	49	20	26	22
2	2	15	21	21	11	19	2	33	4	14	3	23	1	6	24	20	13	27	5	14	49	20	27	23
1	1	8	19	19	14	25	1	17	5	17	3	23	1	6	25	21	12	25	3	8	49	20	29	25

NOTE: N = Establishments with no control over wage policy.
S = Establishments with some control.
L = Establishments with wide latitude in wage policy.
# = Number of establishments with the mean wage in an occupation falling in the quintile. Not all establishments are represented in all occupations.
% = Percentage of establishments in the "control" category falling in the quintile.

40

CHART 4.1

Percentage Distributions of Frequencies of Quintile Rankings. Mean Wage per Hour at Work, All Occupations Combined.

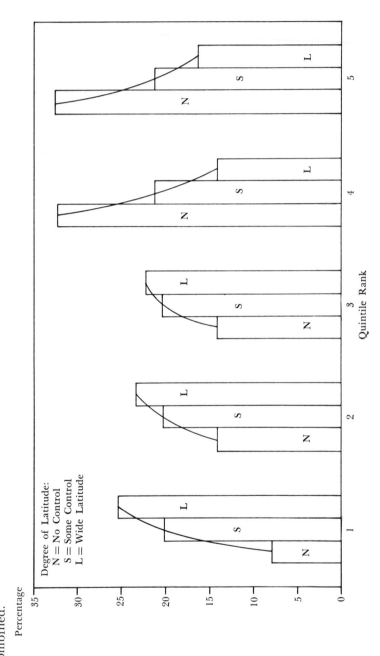

Percentage

Degree of Latitude:
N = No Control
S = Some Control
L = Wide Latitude

Quintile Rank

for each "degree of latitude" set of firms; and finally computing the percentage of establishments in each quintile for each set of firms. The results are striking, especially for the blue-collar occupations. Here 78 percent of the ranks for the "no control" group are in the fourth and fifth quintile, compared with 42 percent for the "some control" group, and only 23 percent for firms with wide latitude in wage policy. It may be noted that this gradation corresponds roughly to "degree of unionization," with the "wide latitude" group of firms being completely nonunion. The interview material suggests that the strong unionization of blue-collar workers in the "no control" firms was associated in some cases with wage compression affecting skilled workers who belonged to an industrial union.[1]

At the sixty-six establishments where the managements were free in varying degrees to develop wage policies of their own, we explored the nature of their decisions, including the factors that appeared to be most influential.

In the cases of a few small employers, the response was, in effect, that there was no particular policy but rather an ad hoc adaptation to particular circumstances:

> We pay what has to be paid to get people to work for us and what has to be paid to keep them.
>
> We don't have one. I can make any deal I'm able to arrange with an individual.
>
> There is no basic policy. If a good person comes along, they would get a good wage, but basically we hire inexperienced people at low wages, then train them ourselves. I guess you would say that we aim our wage policy slightly below average.

In a few cases, we heard about an explicit policy of high wages, expressed in one of them as follows:

> . . . to pay superior wages. We want to attract the best people by paying the best. We want to be at the top of the firms with whom we compare wages. This applies at the hourly and clerical levels as well as to management jobs.

On the other hand, several firms articulated a low wage policy and others apparently followed one, though perhaps not so consciously.

> We pay the least the traffic will bear.
>
> Let's face it. It's to get the most for the least as long as we can maintain the quality of our work force at the level we want.

1. These findings were supported by an additional set of calculations. The technique used above was applied where the wage range was divided into fifths instead of using number of establishments to determine quintiles. The resulting table showed the same general relationships between degree of latitude and wage level, except that five of the six observations for skilled workers in the "no control" group and half of the total observations were in the middle fifth of the range, which reinforces the conclusion about wage compression.

> That's what it should be in any decently run company . . . to maximize profits.
>
> We hire at the legal minimum wage—whatever it happens to be at the time.

And, striking a somewhat different note:

> . . . to get the help as cheaply as you can, given your efficiency requirements, and not to let the employee subsidize you. We don't want people working here for less than they can get elsewhere.
>
> A monopoly can't pay the highest wages because of their obligation to the public to keep prices low.

As these quotations suggest, a dominant response was to identify policy in terms of some standard, for the most part rates of pay in the area where the establishments are located or in the firms with whom they compete in the product market. Table 4.5 shows the distribution of these considerations, which is about the same for the "some control" as for the "wide latitude" group of employers. Samples of statements on the area and industry influences are:

> In general we aim our wage level somewhere in the middle of rates in the area. However, I don't know how important that idea is because we vary rates somewhat according to the importance of the job and the quality of the person.
>
> It's foolish to say we are going to pay superior wages in this industry. We aim at the fifty percent mark in the area and plan to change our policy manual to say just that.

These area and industry influences were, in effect, sharpened in a significant number of cases by more explicit attention to the union rate or the rate disclosed by a survey in one or more skilled or white-collar occupations. These union and occupational factors will be

TABLE 4.5
Primary Considerations in Wage Policy and Degree of Latitude

Considerations	Number of Establishments with Some Control[a]	Number of Establishments with Wide Latitude[a]
Merit	0	1
Local area rates	19	8
Industry rates	17	8
Union rates	6	3
Occupational rates	3	5

[a]Totals add to more than the number of establishments, since more than one response was tabulated in a few cases. We have tabulated only responses that received emphasis in the interviews with employer representatives.

explored more fully in the next section; we note here their general role in the formulation of a firm's wage policy.

As is certainly to be expected, the effort to collect information about the labor market is much greater where firms are free to a significant degree to establish their own wage and manning strategy. The information net was cast most widely by the firms with the most latitude and the greatest freedom from direct union influence (table 4.2).

Table 4.3 on sources of recruits shows the same wide variety that has been found in other studies of labor markets. In addition, it shows the greater use of relatively formal sources, such as agencies, ads, and schools, for white-collar workers. Employers volunteered many comments about the channels they used to get workers and these comments tended to emphasize the quality—or perhaps lack-of-quality—dimension in their reactions. Agencies came in for mixed reviews:

> Their referrals are better because they don't want to refer a poor applicant since that would reflect on their own reputation.

and

> Agencies have the market cornered. Everybody goes to the agencies.

but

> A large percentage [of counselors] know nothing about personnel and just want the fee. They have dollar signs for eyeballs. But some good gals know the applicants and companies and do a good job.

On the other hand, comments about the state employment service were almost all on the negative side:

> They don't handle the type of help we like. Their referrals are people who don't want to work, they just want their compensation checks. It costs too much to screen out their referrals to find a good one.

> Instead of trying to meet our qualifications, they just send out people who have trouble finding jobs and they aren't the best people. A guy who comes here on his own has some incentive.

In some cases, the comments struck a racial note:

> They are all Negroes and we are trying to keep a racial balance in the shop. Also, it seems to us that these Negro referrals are of the very worst type.

A few firms did report satisfaction with the use of the state employment service.

Our interview notes are full of comments on the information-gathering and recruiting activities of firms, with pros and cons expressed about all sources of information and recruits. This and other aspects of the networks of information in labor markets will be discussed more fully in chapter 13, but we may note here two refrains that characterize the comments of employers. The first is their consciousness of the relative quality of applicants produced through various channels and their tendency to judge those channels by that standard. The second is their attitude toward the relative costliness of different sources, usually expressed in terms of the amount of screening necessary to get a satisfactory employee from a given group of referrals.

DIMENSIONS OF EMPLOYER STRATEGIES

Five further dimensions of employer strategies deserve special attention since they have special relevance to our objectives in this study and since each is of interest and importance in its own right. All have been touched upon already to some degree so that we will be picking up pieces of the earlier discussion as we go along. We will first take up union influences as they appear to the employers and as they affect employer behavior. Then we will look at the extent to which differential approaches are made to individual occupations, consider the impact of location on employer manning strategies, review the question of worker quality in relation to pay and employment patterns, and finally discuss the question of discrimination in the employment process.

THE INFLUENCE OF UNIONS

We have already noted that twenty-five of the seventy-four establishments on which we have data are nonunion; the remaining forty-nine are unionized to some degree. In six cases unions cover only selected occupations, in thirty-six cases they cover all production and maintenance workers, and in seven cases they cover clerical workers as well (table 3.7). We have also noted that the classification of firms according to latitude in wage policy corresponds roughly to degree of unionization, and that relative wage levels are lowest in the group of twenty-three firms with the widest latitude and with a complete absence of unionization.

The influence of unions in the organized plants goes beyond the direct processes of collective bargaining, with its varying impact on wage rates. In some occupations, particularly truck driver and tool and die maker, and to a lesser extent maintenance electrician, the union rate is widely taken as a "given" by many firms, accounting for the clustering of rates in these occupations. As one personnel man put it, "The IBT (Teamsters) just mails in the contract and I sign it."

Further, though clerical employees are unionized in only a small proportion of the establishments, union settlements for other employees often enter into the consideration of changes in rates of pay and especially fringe benefits of the clerical workers. This was referred to explicitly in eighteen of the establishments studied; in eight it was asserted that there was no direct or automatic effect, but in ten a definite policy of passing on changes in fringe benefits was indicated. The motivation appears in large part to be to prevent unionization:

> Our white-collar people wouldn't be human if they didn't want the union to get a hell of a big increase every year. We've changed that for the exempt people and we'd like to do the same with the nonexempt but we can't because we'd lay ourselves wide open. . . . You know what I mean without my mentioning it.
>
> We pass on the negotiated wage and fringe benefits to the nonexempt workers to prevent organization. In other words, they get the same here as in other company plants which are organized.[2]

In five cases where the union had organized skilled and production workers in the same unit, the negotiation of increases on a cents per hour basis produced a flattening effect on the wage structure. In one of these cases, some headway had been made, with union cooperation, in widening differentials in favor of skilled workers; but in the others the flattening apparently produced a problem in terms of recruitment. These seemed clearly to be cases where a craft form of organization or even nonunion status would probably have led to higher wages for skilled workers. In yet another case, where clerical workers were organized, the entry rate was considered to be too low, but it could not be raised at this unit of a large multiplant firm.

At least half the nonunion employers were conscious enough of union activity to bring it explicitly into our interviews. In many of these cases, recent attempts at organization had failed or further attempts were expected. Here is a sampling of statements:

> We use our own surveys to be sure we're on the high side and we keep careful track of union contracts in other company plants. So far we haven't had serious threats of unionization.
>
> The union is always in the wings and we keep informed about our employees' needs and about going wages.

2. The references to "exempt" and "nonexempt" people in the quotations pertain to exemptions from the hours provisions of the Fair Labor Standards Act, which apply to executive, administrative, and professional employees.

The methods used to keep informed about employee needs included plant grievance committees of various sorts. In one case, the probability that truck drivers would be organized seemed so high that trucking is now contracted out. In another case, to forestall threatened unionization of skilled model makers, the employer shifted them from an hourly wage to a monthly salary basis of pay.

In our subsequent regression analysis of data on individual workers, we have not been able to see much effect of unionization (see chapter 12). In view of the importance of unions in the thinking of employers, this is a little puzzling. However, the effects of unions may be masked by industry and locational variables and by the influence of the threat of organization on wages in nonunion establishments. In any case, unions are clearly an important factor in employers' thinking about changes in wages and fringe benefits.

OCCUPATIONAL DISTINCTIONS

One of the questions to be explored in this study is how wage policies and manning strategies differ in different occupations, and the concomitant distinctions between the labor markets for these job categories. We therefore collected information about professional, white-collar, and skilled occupations as well as about the less skilled blue-collar jobs covered in the bulk of earlier studies of labor markets. We turn now to the employer view of these occupational groups.

It may be noted, first of all, that the employers did tend to distinguish among these occupational groups as they developed their wage and manning strategies. This general impression gained from the interview material is buttressed by the results of a simple correlation analysis, relating the mean wages by establishments for those pairs of occupations in each of which the establishments employed two or more persons. Thus we searched for pairs or clusters of occupations in which a firm that paid high wages in one was likely to do so in the others. Wages of accountants were not significantly correlated with those in any other occupation, nor were wages of maintenance electricians, tool and die makers, or truck drivers. Relationships significant at the 1 percent level were found between the wages of tab machine and keypunch operators, keypunch operators and typists, punch press operators and material handlers, and among the wages of fork lift truckers, material handlers, janitors and janitresses (table 4.6). Although we do discover some clusters of occupations in which wages are significantly related, we do not find many firms that are consistently high wage or low wage firms across the whole spectrum of occupations. It appears that a firm's position in the wage hierarchy of a labor market is not a simple

TABLE 4.6

Simple Correlations between Establishment Means by Occupation of Wages per Hour at Work (Excludes Establishments with Fewer Than Two Observations in an Occupation)

Occupations	Correlation Coefficient	Number of Establishments with Sufficient Observations in Each Occupation of the Pair
Accountant	No significant correlations	——
Tool and die maker	No significant correlations	——
Maintenance electrician	No significant correlations	——
Truck driver	No significant correlations	——
Tab machine operator and		
Keypunch operator	0.637	23
Janitress	0.779	14
Keypunch operator and		
Typist	0.753	30
Fork lift trucker	0.844	15
Janitor	0.639	22
Punch press operator and		
Material handler	0.763	11
Fork lift trucker and		
Material handler	0.821	22
Janitor	0.771	22
Janitress	0.720	12
Material handler and Janitor	0.763	24
Typist and Janitor	0.550	30

NOTE: All correlations significant at the 1 percent level, and only those, are listed here. Five additional correlations were significant at the 5 percent level: accountant and tab machine operator, maintenance electrician and punch press operator, material handler and janitress, janitor and janitress, and typist and janitress. One additional correlation was significant, but with a negative sign: key punch operator and janitress.

thing to summarize, contrary to impressions given in some of the previous literature that has examined narrower ranges of occupations.

For accountants the main determinant of salary policy and manning strategy appears to be the size of the parent organization. Large firms recruit at colleges, transfer among establishments, and do substantial training within the firm. Smaller companies hire to specific openings, often requiring persons with experience, and use agencies or public accounting firms rather than colleges. Salaries are usually set at the national level in larger companies, with local management having little authority in this area. When firms are ranked according to the salary paid accountants and then judged in terms of quality standards applied to recruits, there appears to be a rough positive relation between these two variables: only high salary firms require a college degree and only some low salary firms set no general standards.

The factors affecting wage and manning strategy for our other white-collar occupations appear to be more diverse. Location may have several effects: the character of the neighborhood may make it difficult or easy to attract clerical workers, and locations not easily reached by public transportation restrict some firms to workers who live nearby or who have access to an automobile. Size of establishment also affects recruiting methods.

Many of the larger firms particularly reported that changes in clerical wages—as distinct from those of accountants, where no special union effect was noted—were closely tied to changes in wages for unionized blue-collar workers, either in or outside the company. On the other hand a number of companies, especially smaller ones, asserted that changes in wages for their clerical workers were in no way related to union settlements or pressures. Where the establishment was part of a firm with headquarters elsewhere, salary administration was often outside the control of local management, sometimes leading to local complaints about recruiting problems and to the suggestion that more attention be paid to conditions in the local labor market. Finally, there did not seem to be any obvious correlation between wage level and educational standards for recruits; however, high wage firms more often list experience as a requirement in hiring.

The dominant theme in employer comments on the tool and die and maintenance electrician occupations was the importance of the unions involved, principally the International Association of Machinists and the International Brotherhood of Electrical Workers. Most unionized firms took part in or were guided by occupation-wide bargaining involving the Tool and Die Institute, and many nonunion firms followed this lead "in order to recruit tool makers." On the other hand, some nonunion companies who trained their own skilled workers took no special note of union pressures. As mentioned previously, the flattening of wage structures through bargaining by industrial unions for workers in these occupations kept the relative wages of skilled workers low in some firms. Our interview material on wage level and information on worker quality was too sparse for these occupations to enable us to draw any conclusions about a possible relationship.

The jobs included in our other blue-collar categories are, of course, highly diverse and the considerations used in wage strategy have already been described and tabulated. Two additional points may be emphasized here. First, firms employing truck drivers were almost unanimous in pointing out that "everyone has to observe the union scale." In a number of cases, employers also indicated that workers in closely related jobs (such as material handler) benefited from the presence, actual or potential, of teamsters locals. Second, there does appear to be some relationship between general hiring standards for blue-collar work and the wage level, especially where the individual is hired with the expectation that he may move up the occupational structure in the establishment. Despite the tendency of personnel workers to say in general conversation that they did not believe in rigid educational standards for these jobs, the hiring policies followed did relate in a rough way to educational attainment: the range was from "high-school graduates only" in the higher wage firms to "no special standards," "literacy only" or "we hire everyone who walks in" in the low wage firms.

In general, then, the management perception is of genuine distinctions among the clusters of occupations in this study, with a need to consider varying characteristics of their respective labor markets in developing an approach to wage and manning problems.

LOCATION

The physical location of an establishment was apparently related to the manning strategies of about half the firms in our sample. This relationship appeared in two ways: in twenty-five establishments it led to hiring standards involving the distance between home and work, travel time, and the type of transportation available to the potential employee; in another seventeen establishments, location had certain manning implications that were reflected in special actions or attitudes of the firm rather than in requirements expected of employees. Examples of such special adjustment by the firm are given below. Turning first to the question of hiring standards, we find considerable variety in the rules set forth, the reasons for them, and the degree of insistence on them. In six cases, concern is limited to women, sometimes as a reflection of experience and sometimes because of fear of crime in the neighborhood, particularly where night shifts are required. For example,

> Distance is the big cause of tardiness and turnover among female office workers. We want them to be able to walk to work.

In another case, a distance rule (must live within thirty minutes' travel) was limited to maintenance electricians, who were on call in the event of an emergency.

The degree of insistence on distance and transportation requirements also varied, with eight establishments expressing preferences and with seventeen using these factors as rigid hiring standards. In some cases rules were quite specific. For example:

> No more than one hour one way and no more than two transfers when using public transportation.

> Recruit only in certain areas where public transportation to the plant is good.

> Car transportation necessary since no public transportation is available.

Other establishments made efforts to compensate for location. Thus, one provided bus and taxi service, and another furnished ample parking space for its employees. Five employers restricted recruits to the immediate area, three simply lived with the recruiting difficulties caused by their locations, and seven viewed their locations as desirable and a positive part of manning strategy.

These rules and attitudes on the part of employers can be described as reflecting their views of employee preferences, which had consequences for the employers in terms of cost. For example, it was considered foolish to hire people with difficult commuting problems since the probability of their quitting is high, and a quit wastes the costs of induction and training. If the employers are right about worker preferences, such factors as the distance from work to home, the regional location of the establishment, or the ratio of people working to people living in the immediate area should show up in our subsequent analysis of wage differentials among individuals.

WORKER QUALITY

We have already noticed a wide variety of ways in which the quality of the worker is evidently taken into account in employer thinking about aspects of wage and manning strategy. These include ad hoc decisions in small firms on wage rates for especially able individuals, the association of high or low wage policies with expected quality, the evaluation of different sources of recruits according to the quality of worker they produce, and the rough associations of some hiring standards and wage levels for accountants, clerical workers, and semiskilled blue-collar workers.

We may now look a little further into hiring standards of individual establishments. These appear to be most explicit and demanding in the large units that also pay relatively high wages. For example, in the case of a large utility that hires almost exclusively at the lower end of the job range, an elaborate set of tests is administered and hiring is restricted (with variations by gross level of occupation) to those with a high-school or college education, but experience is not necessary or even desired, since this firm carries on extensive training programs. A large manufacturing firm had made an effort (successful in its view) to upgrade the quality of new hires by new tests of "adaptability," and by renewed attention to the requirement of experience or high-school graduation, extensive reference checks, physical examinations, and by interview evaluations that put the interviewer on the spot.

These are examples of relatively sophisticated programs administered by sizable personnel departments. In many other cases, education was used as a general screening device but the most general effort took the form of reference checks. In yet others, mostly in small firms, a long probationary period was explicitly regarded as a substitute for extensive hiring standards, and a conscious effort was made to look the new employee over carefully before he or she became a regular member of the work force.

Our employer interviews also contain considerable evidence of flexibility in hiring standards. In one case this is in response to a changing neighborhood:

> My total impression is that it is harder and harder to meet our hiring standards. I'm thinking of the clerical occupations particularly. This is partly due to the change in the composition of the neighborhood.

In others, flexibility is a recognition of fluctuations in the tightness of the labor market:

> Our hiring standards are very flexible. They depend on the job to be filled and on the state of the labor market. It doesn't make sense to talk about hiring standards except at a particular time and for a particular job.

> The ad varies from "must be high-school graduate" to "average piece work earnings, $3.19 per hour."

Still another adaptation is to change the reject points on the various tests administered.

We do not wish to present here a picture of employers working uniformly and carefully to test for quality across the board in all their new hires. Certainly many employers, especially those at the lower end of the wage distribution, seem simply to hire whoever comes along, and even those with testing programs have little evidence to present of validation of the test in their own shops. At the same time, our feeling from the employer interviews adds up to this: the employers in our sample by and large are convinced that workers do differ substantially in the potential quality of their performance, and the employers make an effort—conscious and explicitly implemented in some cases, rough and ready in others—to discover quality in the hiring process.

RACIAL DISCRIMINATION IN EMPLOYMENT

In one highly important respect we found systematic deviation from any "quality of worker" standard on the part of many employers. This problem of discriminatory policies toward Negroes was the subject of special study by David P. Taylor, who analyzed the relevant data collected in the present study and some gathered separately. Here we will report on employer views and actions in this area, quoting directly from Taylor's published work.[3]

> A small group [of employers] thoroughly endorsed both the letter and the spirit of the Illinois Fair Employment Practices Act, while a few reported unequivocal violation. A much larger number were neither in clear-cut compliance nor outright violation of the statute. One striking aspect of employer responses to inquiries about racial hiring policies was their ability to explain their activity in economic terms, through either the labor market or the product market, no matter what these policies were.
>
> The labor market factors included:
>
> (1) *Morale of current employees.* One employer noted that a large proportion of his current employees were Polish and other Eastern Europeans. "Now, if we were to start hiring Negroes in here, these people would raise the roof, and we'd end up with a terrific morale problem. I really believe that integrating this plant would cost us money. I know it would."
>
> In contrast, other firms found little resentment among current employees when Negroes were introduced into the plant. Some companies took the precaution of forewarning supervisors and foremen, but others did not on the ground that it should be considered a routine matter. One personnel man said he received a

3. David P. Taylor, "Discrimination and Occupational Wage Differences in the Market for Unskilled Labor," *Industrial and Labor Relations Review*, April 1968. For the material quoted here, see pp. 378–79. See also "The Market for Unskilled Negro Males in Chicago," unpublished Ph.D. Dissertation, Graduate School of Business, Univ. of Chicago, June 1966. Our analysis of the effect of race on wage differentials among individuals is to be found principally in chapter 8.

call from a foreman when he sent their first Negro worker to the production line. The foreman asked the personnel man if he realized that the worker was a Negro. He replied that he did and that a new company policy was being implemented. The personnel man reported that he had virtually no problem as a result of the change in policy.

(2) *Relationship between the firm and the community.* An employer whose firm was located in a white residential neighborhood said, "We have always tried to be a good neighbor, and we rely on this neighborhood to provide a supply of labor. So we will hold off on changing our policy on this as long as we can. It really isn't much of a problem as we have very few [Negro] applicants and, of course, all of them live quite a distance from here."

In a different setting, an employer did not hesitate to import Negro workers to a fairly remote suburban town. The personnel officer contacted the state employment office in another city and asked for applicants, knowing that some would be Negro. He was confident that the townspeople would cause very little trouble, since the plant was the largest employer in the area.

(3) *Perceived quality of Negro workers.* Some employers insist that Negro workers are of lower quality than the whites in their current work force. They cite aggregate education, work experience data, and crime statistics to support this claim. In contrast, one employer said, "Since we started hiring Negroes, we've found that we can get better quality people at the same wage rate. Their attendance record is better, and they have lower turnover."

(4) *Negroes never apply at the firm's employment office.* A shortage of Negro applicants can be either a legitimate or a hypocritical reason for failing to hire Negroes. Thus, one employer said he preferred personal referrals to want ads, because want ads generated so many Negro applicants. Another employer switched his advertising from the *Chicago Tribune* to *Cicero Life*, because he was getting too many Negroes from his ads in the *Tribune*. In 1960, the city of Cicero had four Negro residents in a total population of nearly 70,000. Of course, some firms never get Negro applicants because of long-standing reputations for discrimination.

Product market factors also affect hiring policy:

(1) *Relations with the government.* If a firm, because of the nature of its product or service, has frequent and intimate dealings with the government, particularly the federal government, it is probably difficult for it to maintain a discriminatory hiring policy. This is especially true if the company is in a regulated industry or as a contractor is frequently visited by government representatives. On the other hand, it is not clear that just any business relationship with the government was sufficient to affect hiring policies. A firm which sold a substantial amount of its regular production to the government was not overly concerned. "We have to make quarterly reports to the government, but we have a Chinese engineer, and some Mexicans here at the main plant, and some Negro janitors at our sales offices throughout the country.

We lump them all together on the report, and it doesn't look too bad. I suppose if the government people come around to inspect the plant and find no Negroes, we'll be in hot water. But until then I guess we'll just go along as we have been." This interview obviously took place before the passage of Title VII of the Civil Rights Act.

(2) *Consumer product vulnerability.* Similarly, if a firm's product or service is utilized or consumed directly by the public, it is susceptible to Negro consumer boycotts.

By no means all of the employment problems of Negroes are the result of current discrimination in the employment process, of course. Indeed, the material presented earlier suggests the pervasive orientation in the personnel community toward screening out those whose education has been limited, whose exposure to work-related discipline has been meager, and whose opportunities to live close to their work are restricted. We may remind the reader that our interviews with employer representatives took place and our data were collected in 1963, before the major efforts of the last few years to help the disadvantaged worker find a place in the world of work rather than the world of idleness. Our interviews provide a look back to this earlier time. The objective then was to screen out these workers, and the whole apparatus of personnel recruitment was oriented in this direction. The shift to a new look, bringing new considerations into play, is a great one and will succeed only with strong and persistent leadership from the top.

CONCLUDING COMMENTS

The views of employers on employment processes, as reported in this chapter, may provide insights into policies and patterns of behavior on the employer side of the labor market. The information obtained through employer interviews also suggests many avenues of possibly fruitful analysis of the main body of data collected in this study—information on wages paid to individual workers and on a variety of their characteristics.

It will obviously be important to examine a wide range of individual characteristics that may be associated systematically with worker quality. Location of the work place may be important in view of the emphasis on area rates and of the variations in patterns of residence. Unionization of the establishment appears to be a significant factor to a great many employers, as do industry wage levels, since many compare their wage and manning costs with those of competitors. Size of establishment is apparently a factor in some aspects of recruitment. Since it is evident that racial discrimination exists in this labor market, we will want to find out what we can about its influence on wage differentials.

5
An Overview of Data
on Individual Workers

THIS CHAPTER has two principal objectives. The first is to define somewhat more precisely the twelve occupations selected for study. The second is to present some descriptive statistics—largely percentage distributions—on certain characteristics of the samples of individuals in each occupation. These will permit us to observe some of the salient differences between the occupations under study and to see the range of variation of some of the individual variables that will be used later in the regression analysis of wage dispersion.

DEFINITIONS OF THE STUDY OCCUPATIONS

All of the study occupations have been defined to exclude trainees and apprentices at one extreme and foremen or supervisors at the other, at least to the extent that such status could be determined from job titles or other information in the personnel records. Other factors in the selection of the individuals in the samples are peculiar to the twelve occupations, and will be discussed for each occupation in turn. More detailed definitions of these occupations may be found in the *Dictionary of Occupational Titles* and the occupational wage surveys of the Bureau of Labor Statistics.[1]

TYPIST

This occupation was called clerk-typist in some of our firms. A typist types letters, reports, tables, invoices, and other similar material from rough copy or from a dictating machine. The typing may be on stencils or on forms. A clerk-typist may in addition do filing or, in a small office, answer telephone calls, sort mail, or perform other miscellaneous clerical duties. The occupation does not include stenographers or secretaries whose duties include taking dictation in shorthand, arranging appointments, receiving visitors, and making travel arrangements. Male typists were omitted from our sample.

1. *Dictionary of Occupational Titles*, vol. 1, *Occupational Titles*, 3d Edition (Washington: Government Printing Office, 1965) and U.S. Bureau of Labor Statistics, *Wages and Related Benefits*, part 1: 82 Labor Markets, 1962–63, Bulletin no. 1345–83, Appendix B.

KEYPUNCH OPERATOR

A keypunch operator operates an alphabetic and numeric keypunch machine to transcribe data onto punch cards for use in a tabulating machine or an electronic computer. More experienced keypunch operators may locate data to be punched in source documents rather than working from coded data. This is one of the easiest occupations in the study to identify, since other duties are seldom performed by keypunch operators, and there are no closely similar occupations.

ACCOUNTANT

An accountant designs, modifies, and oversees the operation of a system or part of a system of financial or cost records. His work requires a higher level of skill and the exercise of more judgment than that of a bookkeeper, who makes routine entries in books of account. We included in our sample accountants who have supervisory responsibility over bookkeepers, but not those whose duties consisted substantially of supervising other accountants. We also excluded corporate financial officers such as controllers or treasurers. The job titles of our accountants included "cost accountant" and "internal auditor" in some firms. In the supplementary sample of public accounting firms described in chapter 7, the accountants in our sample were junior accountants engaged in auditing the books of client firms. We excluded the senior accountants who supervised the work of teams of auditors.

TABULATING MACHINE OPERATOR

A tabulating machine operator sets up or wires and operates tabulating or electrical accounting machines, including machines that tabulate, sort, and reproduce punched cards. He may prepare reports based on data he has tabulated. He is to be distinguished from the operator of an electronic computer, a newer occupation that is not included in our study.

MATERIAL HANDLER

A material handler loads and unloads trucks or railroad cars and moves materials, boxes, and other containers in and around a plant, warehouse, store, yard, or loading dock, using hand trucks and other unpowered equipment. He may unpack boxes or cartons and store or shelve their contents. He is to be distinguished from a fork lift trucker, who moves materials with power equipment. Female material handlers were omitted from our sample.

JANITOR AND JANITRESS

These two occupations involve similar duties, although the janitor may perform heavier tasks requiring more strength. Janitors are sometimes called "porters" and janitresses "charwomen." Janitors sweep, mop, and polish floors, vacuum carpets, dust furniture, empty wastebaskets, clean washrooms, and perform other similar duties in factories, offices, and stores. Since our sample of firms did not include any that operated apartment buildings, flat janitors—who have a somewhat wider range of duties than industrial janitors—were not included.

FORK LIFT TRUCKER

A fork lift trucker operates an electric or gasoline powered fork lift truck or other industrial truck to move goods or materials, frequently loaded on pallets, in and around a warehouse, factory, or yard.

PUNCH PRESS OPERATOR

A punch press operator sets up and operates a machine that forms or shapes metal or plastic parts by punching them out of a sheet or strip of stock. The work pace is usually under the control of the operator. Punch presses differ greatly in size and in the heaviness of stock used.

TRUCK DRIVER

In our study, we gave the occupation "truck driver" a more restricted definition than that in general usage. We excluded driver-salesmen, such as milk-wagon drivers who make all or a part of their income from commissions on products sold. We also excluded over-the-road truck drivers because they are generally paid on a mileage basis, and it is difficult to ascertain their hourly wages. Because there are substantial differences in pay and duties between drivers of light and heavy trucks, we excluded drivers of light trucks (under three tons capacity) from our sample.

MAINTENANCE ELECTRICIAN

A maintenance electrician repairs, maintains, and installs motors, generators, transformers, lights, wiring, and other electricial equipment in an existing building. His work involves a wide variety of duties and requires a well-rounded training. He is to be distinguished from a construction electrician, who installs the original electrical wiring and lighting in a new building at the time it is constructed, or during substantial renovation done by an outside contractor.

TOOL AND DIE MAKER

A tool and die maker makes and repairs metalworking dies, cutting tools, gauges, jigs, and fixtures used in metalworking industries. His work requires him to exercise substantial amounts of judgment, to plan his own tasks, to read blueprints and plans, to make calculations, to work to close tolerances, and to use a variety of machine and hand tools. His work requires a well-rounded training, often acquired through formal apprenticeship.

CHARACTERISTICS OF WORKERS IN THE SAMPLE

This section will present some data on the distributions of workers in the random samples for each study occupation by earnings per hour at work, age, seniority, schooling, race, and distance traveled from home to work. These distributions are based on the number of observations used in the regression analysis of chapters 7 through 10, after the deletion of some observations for which data were not complete. The number of such deletions in each occupation by reason is given in chapter 6.

EARNINGS PER HOUR AT WORK

Earnings per hour at work is the usual measure of wages in this study, and will often be called "wages" to save space. It is basically earnings per payroll hour for the regularly scheduled work week, adjusted for the length of paid vacation and number of paid holidays to which the worker is entitled. If two workers have the same wage per payroll hour, but one is entitled to more paid vacation, this one will have the higher earnings per hour at work. A more complete description of this measure will be given in chapter 6.

The percentage distributions of workers by earnings per hour at work are shown in table 5.1. It is apparent that the occupations differ radically in the level of earnings, the dispersion of earnings, and the shapes of the distributions. The distributions for the two lowest wage occupations, typist and janitress, and the highest wage occupation, tool and die maker, do not overlap. The highest paid typist received less than $2.95 an hour, and the lowest-paid tool and die maker received $2.95 or more.[2] The highest paid janitress earned less than $2.75 an hour. This occupation includes the lowest paid worker in the whole sample; she earned less than $1.15 an hour.

By far the most disperse distribution is that for accountants. The lowest paid accountant earned less than $1.90 an hour, and the high-

2. Statements in the text are based on a distribution of earnings per hour at work by five-cent intervals. Therefore a statement such as that made above for typists should be interpreted as reading that the highest paid typist had hourly earnings in the range $2.90 to $2.94.

est paid earned $6.25 or more.[3] No twenty-five cent class interval in table 5.1 includes as much as 15 percent of the accountants. The earnings of maintenance electricians also cover a wide range; the lowest paid earned less than $2.00 an hour and the highest paid earned $5.10 or more. However, there is more tendency in this occupation for observations to be clustered in the middle of the distribution, with 34 percent falling in the range of $3.75 to $3.99.

The distribution with the least dispersion is clearly that for truck drivers, with 64 percent of the observations in one twenty-five cent class interval. This probably reflects the fact that a large portion of our drivers were represented by two local unions of teamsters that made uniform collective bargaining agreements with large employers' associations.

Most of the distributions show to a greater or lesser extent the long upper tail characteristic of income and earnings distributions. It is particularly marked in the case of punch press operators, where the use of incentive pay may explain the observations that lie far above the mean. The distribution for janitors is unusual because the lower tail is by far the longer of the two.

AGE

Table 5.2 shows the distribution of workers in our sample by age. Three of the white-collar occupations have the lowest mean age: thirty-one. In the two female clerical occupations the mean age is low because of the presence of many very young workers—10 to 14 percent are under twenty and more than half are under thirty. Tab operator is similar in that more than half the workers are under thirty; however, few are under twenty. The low mean age of tab operators results in large part from the small percentage of workers over forty—smallest in all the occupations. The youngest worker in the entire sample is a sixteen-year-old tab operator.

The highest mean age is forty-eight, for janitresses, followed closely by janitors at forty-seven and tool and die makers at forty-six. All but two of the occupations have some workers over sixty-five. The oldest person in the entire sample is an eighty-one-year-old accountant, followed by a seventy-six-year-old janitor.

The age distribution for typists shows a dip in the thirty to thirty-nine group. This is a period in which married women tend to withdraw from the labor force to take care of preschool children; some then reenter when their youngest child is in school. Inspection of

---

3. The range is not a reliable statistic in comparing samples of different size, since, other things equal, it increases with the size of the sample. However, table 5.1 suggests no correlation between sample size and range, indicating that the differences in ranges are attributes of the populations being sampled.

the distribution by single years of age shows that the dip actually begins in the middle and late twenties, and that the numbers are increasing by the late thirties. The distribution for keypunch operators by single years of age shows a similar dip that is hidden in the decade totals. The largest number of typists at any single year of age is seventy-three at age twenty.

TABLE 5.1
Percentage Distribution of Sample by Earnings per Hour at Work

Earnings per Hour at Work	Typist	Keypunch Operator	Accountant	Tab Operator
Less than $1.50	0.7	0.3	———	———
$1.50–$1.74	17.1	4.8	———	0.9
1.75– 1.99	36.6	19.3	0.4	5.6
2.00– 2.24	27.3	36.8	0.4	10.6
2.25– 2.49	11.0	23.0	2.2	16.7
2.50– 2.74	6.5	12.4	2.2	15.7
2.75– 2.99	0.9	2.1	5.3	25.5
3.00– 3.24	———	———	12.3	11.6
3.25– 3.49	———	———	10.5	5.6
3.50– 3.74	———	———	11.0	5.1
3.75– 3.99	———	———	9.2	1.9
4.00– 4.24	———	———	10.5	0.5
4.25– 4.49	———	———	14.9	0.5
4.50– 4.74	———	———	7.9	———
4.75– 4.99	———	———	6.1	———
5.00– 5.49	———	———	2.6	———
5.50 and over	———	———	4.4	———
Number in sample	557	378	228	216
Mean earnings[a]	$2.01	$2.20	$3.93	$2.73

Earnings per Hour at Work	Material Handler	Janitor	Janitress	Fork Lift Trucker
Less than $1.50	1.6	1.1	2.9	———
$1.50–$1.74	3.3	2.7	12.7	0.6
1.75– 1.99	13.5	12.9	34.1	2.2
2.00– 2.24	14.4	12.3	24.9	10.1
2.25– 2.49	15.8	19.7	16.8	21.9
2.50– 2.74	30.9	44.2	8.7	27.2
2.75– 2.99	18.4	7.0	———	15.7
3.00– 3.24	1.5	0.2	———	15.4
3.25– 3.49	0.5	———	———	2.0
3.50– 3.74	0.2	———	———	3.9
3.75– 3.99	———	———	———	0.8
Number in sample	550	473	173	356
Mean earnings[a]	$2.41	$2.39	$2.02	$2.68

TABLE 5.1 (Continued)

Earnings per Hour at Work	Punch Press Operator	Truck Driver	Maintenance Electrician	Tool and Die Maker
Less than $1.50	----	----	----	----
$1.50–$1.74	----	----	----	----
1.75– 1.99	3.3	----	0.4	----
2.00– 2.24	18.2	----	----	----
2.25– 2.49	27.7	----	0.7	----
2.50– 2.74	18.5	1.8	1.8	----
2.75– 2.99	21.8	8.4	6.5	0.4
3.00– 3.24	4.0	63.9	10.2	2.2
3.25– 3.49	3.0	22.3	8.0	5.8
3.50– 3.74	0.3	3.0	26.2	11.9
3.75– 3.99	2.3	0.6	34.2	33.1
4.00– 4.24	0.3	----	5.5	21.9
4.25– 4.49	0.3	----	4.4	20.5
4.50– 4.74	0.3	----	1.1	4.3
4.75– 4.99	----	----	0.4	----
5.00– 5.49	----	----	0.4	----
Number in sample	303	166	275	278
Mean earnings[a]	$2.59	$3.18	$3.36	$3.99

[a]Computed from ungrouped data

SENIORITY

The distribution of the sample by year of hire is shown in table 5.3. Seniority is calculated by subtracting the year of hire from 1963. The year of hire is the beginning of continuous service with the employer in any occupation, not necessarily in the occupation in which the worker is now classified.

The lowest mean seniority is in the two female clerical occupations, both under four years. More than 40 percent of the typists and keypunch operators were hired in or after 1961. The occupation with the next largest percentage of short-service workers is material handlers, with 38 percent hired in 1961 or later. Tab operators, although they have about the same mean age as typists and keypunch operators, have on average more seniority: 6.3 years.

The skilled blue-collar occupations have the highest mean seniority: fourteen years for tool and die makers and thirteen for maintenance electricians. Almost a third of the tool and die makers have twenty years seniority or more. Some workers with as much as twenty years seniority were found in the sample for each of the twelve occupations. The two senior workers in the entire sample were a punch press operator and a maintenance electrician hired in 1917: six more workers were hired before 1920.

TABLE 5.2
Percentage Distribution of Sample by Age

Age	Typist	Keypunch Operator	Accountant	Tab Operator
Under 20	13.8	9.8	———	1.4
20–29	44.0	42.6	19.7	56.0
30–39	12.4	21.4	34.2	19.4
40–49	17.8	19.3	21.5	13.0
50–59	10.6	6.3	17.5	8.3
60–65	1.3	0.3	5.7	0.9
Over 65	0.2	0.3	1.3	0.9
Mean age[a]	31.3	31.4	40.5	31.2

Age	Material Handler	Janitor	Janitress	Fork Lift Trucker
Under 20	3.1	0.6	———	1.4
20–29	38.7	14.8	4.6	33.7
30–39	25.1	10.6	16.2	32.6
40–49	19.5	23.9	27.7	18.5
50–59	10.2	33.8	37.0	11.0
60–65	2.9	12.9	13.3	2.8
Over 65	0.5	3.4	1.2	———
Mean age[a]	34.6	47.1	48.4	35.6

Age	Punch Press Operator	Truck Driver	Maintenance Electrician	Tool and Die Maker
Under 20	0.3	———	———	———
20–29	16.8	11.4	14.5	5.8
30–39	24.8	34.3	27.3	17.6
40–49	36.0	29.5	30.9	42.1
50–59	17.8	20.5	20.4	23.4
60–65	4.0	4.2	6.2	10.4
Over 65	0.3	———	0.7	0.7
Mean age[a]	41.2	41.7	42.3	45.9

[a]Computed from single years of age.

SCHOOLING

The distribution of the sample by year of school completed is shown in table 5.4. The categories shown are those in which the data were originally recorded (except that years beyond four of college were recorded separately), so that no distribution by single years of schooling is available. The means are computed by assigning midpoints to class intervals of more than one year. No account is taken

TABLE 5.3
Percentage Distribution of Sample by Year of Hire

Year of Hire	Typist	Keypunch Operator	Accountant	Tab Operator
1962–63	45.2	44.2	22.8	24.1
1959–61	29.1	33.1	22.4	33.3
1954–58	13.8	13.0	19.2	22.2
1949–53	6.6	6.6	10.1	8.3
1944–48	2.2	1.6	5.7	5.5
1934–43	2.5	1.3	10.5	3.7
Before 1934	0.5	0.3	9.2	2.8
Mean seniority (years)[a]	3.9	3.5	10.3	6.3

Year of Hire	Material Handler	Janitor	Janitress	Fork Lift Trucker
1962–63	37.8	21.8	10.4	12.1
1959–61	24.0	23.7	19.1	22.5
1954–58	18.7	20.3	29.4	23.9
1949–53	10.2	19.2	20.8	23.9
1944–48	5.1	8.7	15.6	11.8
1934–43	2.5	5.3	4.0	4.5
Before 1934	1.6	1.1	0.6	1.4
Mean seniority (years)[a]	5.3	7.8	8.8	8.6

Year of Hire	Punch Press Operator	Truck Driver	Maintenance Electrician	Tool and Die Maker
1962–63	16.2	13.3	6.5	11.9
1959–61	25.1	23.5	21.4	10.8
1954–58	20.5	20.5	11.6	18.3
1949–53	15.1	12.7	14.2	8.6
1944–48	11.9	17.5	21.5	18.7
1934–43	9.9	11.4	21.1	27.7
Before 1934	1.3	1.2	3.6	4.0
Mean seniority (years)[a]	8.8	9.6	12.8	13.8

[a]Computed from single years.

in table 5.4 of attendance at private trade schools or of training received in the armed forces or in full-time apprenticeship programs. Such training is analyzed where relevant by means of separate variables.

TABLE 5.4
Percentage Distribution of Sample by Years of School Completed

Years of School Completed	Typist	Keypunch Operator	Accountant	Tab Operator
None to elementary 4	———	———	———	———
Elementary 5–8	0.9	1.3	0.4	2.3
High school 1–3	11.1	18.5	5.3	11.1
High school 4	69.8	69.6	16.2	55.1
College 1–3	14.5	9.3	37.3	27.3
College 4 or more	1.3	0.3	39.9	0.9
Unknown	2.3	1.1	0.8	3.2
Mean years completed[a]	12.2	11.9	14.4	12.4

Years of School Completed	Material Handler	Janitor	Janitress	Fork Lift Trucker
None to elementary 4	4.0	8.2	7.5	2.8
Elementary 5–8	21.5	47.1	48.6	26.1
High school 1–3	35.5	25.1	26.0	37.6
High school 4	32.4	12.1	8.7	24.7
College 1–3	4.2	3.2	2.9	5.9
College 4 or more	———	0.2	———	———
Unknown	2.5	4.0	6.4	2.8
Mean years completed[a]	10.3	8.6	8.5	10.1

Years of School Completed	Punch Press Operator	Truck Driver	Maintenance Electrician	Tool and Die Maker
None to elementary 4	4.6	0.6	0.7	0.4
Elementary 5–8	36.3	20.5	10.5	9.4
High school 1–3	36.0	38.0	29.5	28.4
High school 4	17.5	28.3	45.1	48.6
College 1–3	3.3	3.0	12.7	9.4
College 4 or more	———	———	1.1	0.7
Unknown	2.3	9.6	0.4	3.2
Mean years completed[a]	9.4	10.5	11.4	11.4

[a]Computed from grouped data after assignment of values to unknowns (see table 6.1).

As might be expected, accountants have the most formal education. The mean number of years of school completed is fourteen, and almost 40 percent of the sample are known to have completed college. Thirteen of the accountants had some graduate work, and five of these had M.A. degrees.

Almost 70 percent of the typists and keypunch operators had graduated from high school but had gone no further. This was true of 55 percent of the tab operators, with a larger percentage in this occupation attending college.

TABLE 5.5
Percentage Distribution of Sample by Race

Occupation	White[a]	Negro	Latin[b]	Other Nonwhite	Unknown
Typist	93.5	2.7	0.7	——	3.0
Keypunch operator	93.9	4.2	——	1.3	0.5
Accountant	98.7	0.4	——	0.9	——
Tab operator	96.3	1.4	1.4	0.5	0.5
Material handler	68.0	23.6	3.6	0.5	4.2
Janitor	60.7	32.1	5.7	0.2	1.3
Janitress	68.2	30.6	1.2	——	——
Fork lift trucker	61.0	35.1	2.2	——	1.7
Punch press operator	74.3	15.2	5.6	——	5.0
Truck driver	95.2	1.8	1.2	——	1.8
Maintenance electrician	91.3	1.1	——	0.4	7.3
Tool and die maker	99.3	0.7	——	——	——

[a]Other than Latins; see note *b* below.
[b]Whites with Spanish surnames, largely of Puerto Rican or Mexican origin or parentage.

The blue-collar workers with the most schooling are the skilled craftsmen. More than half the maintenance electricians and tool and die makers had completed high school or gone beyond, although the mean number of years of education in these occupations is below twelve. Those with the least schooling are janitors and janitresses; more than half of them had eight years or less of elementary school.

RACE

The composition of the sample by race is shown in table 5.5. In the rest of the study, we combine Negroes and other nonwhites and will speak of color rather than race. As table 5.5 makes clear, there are too few other nonwhites to justify treating them separately.

The term "white" in this section refers to whites other than those with Spanish surnames; the latter are listed under the heading "Latin," and are largely of Puerto Rican or Mexican origin or parentage.

The racial composition of the samples varies sharply from one occupation to another. In three occupations—janitor, janitress, and

TABLE 5.6
Percentage Distribution of Sample by Distance Traveled to Work (Blocks)[a]

Distance Traveled (Blocks)	Typist	Keypunch Operator	Accountant	Tab Operator
Under 20	29.8	27.0	11.0	21.3
20–39	23.5	24.6	13.6	19.4
40–79	25.0	28.3	36.4	28.2
80–119	11.5	9.3	18.0	13.4
120–159	3.4	3.2	8.3	5.1
160–200	1.4	1.9	4.4	2.3
Over 200	1.3	3.2	5.7	4.2
Unknown	4.1	2.6	2.6	6.0

Distance Traveled (Blocks)	Material Handler	Janitor	Janitress	Fork Lift Trucker
Under 20	22.4	20.7	25.4	17.7
20–39	21.8	21.8	19.7	19.4
40–79	34.2	27.9	31.2	29.8
80–119	10.4	18.8	12.7	18.5
120–159	5.1	3.6	3.5	3.4
160–200	1.8	3.0	0.6	5.6
Over 200	0.7	2.5	1.2	3.1
Unknown	3.6	1.7	5.8	2.5

Distance Traveled (Blocks)	Punch Press Operator	Truck Driver	Maintenance Electrician	Tool and Die Maker
Under 20	20.1	10.8	16.0	18.3
20–39	29.0	22.3	20.7	24.8
40–79	31.4	31.9	26.5	31.7
80–119	10.6	13.3	14.5	11.5
120–159	3.6	6.6	8.7	6.5
160–200	1.3	4.2	5.1	1.8
Over 200	1.7	4.8	2.2	3.5
Unknown	2.3	6.0	6.2	1.8

[a]Eight blocks to the mile; sum of the north-south and east-west distances.

fork lift trucker—more than 30 percent are Negroes. At the other extreme, in four occupations less than 2 percent are Negroes, and in none of the white-collar occupations is the percentage of Negroes as much as 5. There is some tendency for the percentage of Negroes to decline with skill and schooling, but the pattern is by no means regular. Truck drivers and fork lift truckers have very similar patterns of schooling, but very different percentages of Negroes. Unwritten policies of the two teamster union locals in the Chicago area probably reinforced employer preferences in the case of truck drivers. The very small representation of minority groups in the skilled manual occupations could also reflect union and employee attitudes as well as those of employers.

Latin-Americans are most important in the samples for janitors and punch press operators; they make up almost 6 percent of the total in each of these occupations.

DISTANCE TO WORK

Whenever the personnel files gave the necessary information, we recorded the employee's address. From this, we calculated the distance to work in city blocks (eight blocks to the mile) as the sum of the north-south and the east-west distances. This measure was used instead of airline distance because the street pattern of the Chicago area is for the most part a rectangular grid, with few diagonal transportation routes. However, the possibility of diagonal routes is greater the longer the trip, and so our data may tend to overstate the length of the longest trips relative to others.

The distribution of distances traveled is shown in table 5.6. There is a clear tendency for workers in the all-female occupations to travel shorter distances than those in other occupations. In all three of these occupations, more than one-fourth of the employees travel less than 20 blocks to work, and this is not true in any other occupation. Accountants travel farthest; 18 percent of them live 120 blocks or more from their work places. The corresponding percentage is 16 for the next two most-traveled occupations, maintenance electricians and truck drivers.

The two champion individual travelers in the sample live more than 400 blocks (50 miles) from their place of work, which cannot be less than 35 miles airline distance; one is an accountant, the other a fork lift trucker.

6
Methods Used in
the Regression Analysis

BEFORE PRESENTING the results of our analysis of wage dispersion, it seems useful to give some general information about our analytical methods.[1] The regressions presented in chapters 7 through 10 are designed to explain the sources of wage dispersion within each occupation, as of the last week of June 1963. Chapters 11 and 12 consider how some of the more important explanatory variables behave across the whole set of occupations. They also consider some relationships in which wage differences are, at least in part, a causal force that affects some other variable. However, in the chapters immediately following this one, independent variables are discussed only where they contribute to the explanation of wage dispersion in a particular occupation. Discussing occupations in turn and then explanatory variables in turn inevitably leads to some duplication, but we could see no better way to present our results.

THE DEPENDENT VARIABLE

In almost all of the regressions shown, the dependent variable is earnings in dollars per hour at work. This variable has been constructed from data on stated earnings (weekly, monthly, or hourly), on hours of work, and on the number of days of paid holiday and vacation to which the employee was entitled. If Jones and Smith received the same stated wage, but Smith was entitled to a longer paid vacation, we recorded Smith as having a higher wage per hour at work. Employees on the payroll for less than one year were given credit for the vacation earned after one year of service. At times, for comparison purposes, we will present results from a few regressions in which the dependent variable is stated earnings without adjustment for vacations and holidays.

1. This chapter assumes that the reader is familiar with the basic concepts of regression analysis. Any readers who are not may wish to consult the article "Linear Hypotheses: Regression," *International Encyclopedia of the Social Sciences* (New York: Macmillan and Free Press, 1968), 9: 310–23, or a textbook in statistics or econometrics. The footnotes in this chapter are also intended to help readers with little familiarity with regression analysis, and can safely be skipped by others.

The effect of the adjustment for vacations and holidays is to raise the general level of the dependent variable. For example, among keypunch operators, the mean stated wage was $2.07, and the mean wage per hour at work was $2.20. In this case, the relative dispersion of the two variables is almost identical (the coefficients of variation are 0.133 and 0.137, respectively).[2]

In some of our establishments, work weeks of more than forty hours, with premium wages for the additional hours, were normal practice. In such cases, we have computed wages per hour at work, including overtime premiums, for the number of hours normally worked in those establishments. However, we have not included premiums for *occasional* overtime, even when it occurred in the week of 23 June 1963.

In a few blue-collar occupations, especially punch press operator, some of the workers in our sample received piece rates or incentive rates. In such cases, we did not use the wage for the last week of June 1963, since it might have been atypical. Instead, we attempted to identify a typical month in 1963 and used mean hourly earnings for that month as the unadjusted dependent variable. If no month seemed typical, we divided annual earnings by total hours worked.

We wanted originally to include in our dependent variable the value of pensions, insurance, and welfare plans, so as to get a measure of total compensation per hour at work. We collected a good deal of material about such fringe benefits from the establishments in our sample, but it proved to be impossible to reduce it to a dollars per hour equivalent so that it could be added to the wage variable. At the end of this chapter, we present briefly some results on the presence or absence of various kinds of fringe benefits in establishments by level of money wages.

THE INDEPENDENT VARIABLES

Our independent variables fall into two distinct groups. The first consists of observations on the individual worker, such as his age, race, education, or the distance from his home to his place of work; we shall refer to these as "individual variables." The second consists of observations on the establishment in which the worker is employed, such as its size, industry, or location. Most of the individual observations, such as age or distance traveled to work, relate to the same date as the dependent variable. A few, such as marital status, were recorded only on the worker's application for employment and refer to the date at which he was hired.

---

2. The coefficient of variation is the standard deviation divided by the mean. The standard deviation is a measure of absolute dispersion: the square root of the sum of the squared deviations from the mean of the individual observations.

Because we collected our own data, we had a great deal of freedom in defining independent variables and choosing their form. We have used mixtures of linear variables, continuous nonlinear variables (logarithmic or quadratic), and dummy variables (sometimes called binary variables).[3] The choice of form is determined largely on pragmatic grounds—that is by the goodness of fit. For continuous variables, we generally get the best results with the linear form when the underlying distribution of the variables is approximately normal. The logarithmic form generally produces better results when the underlying distribution is J shaped. The quadratic form has been used for age, because it approximates the shape of the age-income profiles shown in a number of previous studies.

Our ability to use sets of dummy variables was somewhat constrained by the size of our samples; to include many dummies would have used up degrees of freedom and resulted in cells containing small numbers of observations. In many cases, we could overcome this difficulty by defining a set of dummies, using it in a regression, and then collapsing it by combining adjoining classes where the coefficients of the dummy variables were not significantly different from one another. As we gained experience with this process, we found we could often get better results with dummies than with continuous variables whose form had to be specified in advance.

The base or reference group (the omitted group) for the dummy variables is often intuitively obvious. For example, a dummy for females has males as a base group and a dummy for nonwhites has whites. If there is possible doubt, the identity of the base group is explained in the text.

Deletions and Missing Observations

After data for an individual had been obtained, it was sometimes necessary to drop him from the sample. In some cases, closer examination of the data indicated that he was not in the study occupation because he was a supervisor or an apprentice. In other cases, he had not been hired until after June 1963. In yet others, there had been a violation of the rule that no more than forty observations would be accepted in one occupation in one establishment, and this required further sampling of the completed data sheets. The cases mentioned were not considered true deletions from the sample; the observations should not have been collected in the first instance.

3. A dummy variable takes only the values zero and one. For example, a dummy variable for nonwhites would take the value of one if the worker is nonwhite, and zero if he is white. The coefficient of the dummy variable can be interpreted as a shift in the position of the regression plane (of its intercept with the axis on which the dependent variable is measured) without any shift in its slope.

A second set of observations were properly collected, but in the end could not be used. These deletions, by occupation, are shown in the top portion of table 6.1. The deletions of male typists and keypunch operators and of female material handlers and fork lift truckers are included, since the decision to make these occupations all female and all male was not reached until the distribution by sex had been examined. The remaining deletions were required by

TABLE 6.1

Numbers of Cases (Individuals) in Which Observations Were Deleted or Were Assigned Values

Treatment and Reason	Typist	Keypunch Operator	Accountant	Tab Operator
Deleted				
Sex	2	4	——	——
Unknown wage	2	6	——	3
Unknown year of birth	4	——	1	——
Unknown year of hire	——	1	——	——
Total deletions	8	11	1	3
Assigned values				
Education				
Establishment mean	11	1	——	5
Sample mean	2	3	2	2
Distance				
Establishment mean	20	7	5	7
Sample mean	3	3	1	6
Total assigned values	36	14	8	20
Size of final sample	557	378	228	216

Treatment and Reason	Material Handler	Janitor	Janitress	Fork Lift Trucker
Deleted				
Sex	15	——	——	3
Unknown wage	11	1	1	——
Unknown year of birth	5	——	——	2
Unknown year of hire	——	——	——	——
Total deletions	31	1	1	5

TABLE 6.1 (Continued)

Treatment and Reason	Material Handler	Janitor	Janitress	Fork Lift Trucker
Assigned values				
Education				
Establishment mean	10	14	6	8
Sample mean	4	5	5	2
Distance				
Establishment mean	17	5	7	9
Sample mean	3	3	3	——
Weight				
Establishment mean	18	10	——	——
Sample mean	8	15	——	——
Total assigned values	60	52	21	19
Size of final sample	550	473	173	356

Treatment and Reason	Punch Press Operator	Truck Driver	Maintenance Electrician	Tool[a] & Die Maker
Deleted				
Sex	——	——	——	——
Unknown wage	——	3	4	——
Unknown year of birth	1	——	——	2
Unknown year of hire	——	——	——	——
Total deletions	1	3	4	2
Assigned values				
Education				
Establishment mean	7	——	——	8
Sample mean	——	16	1	1
Distance				
Establishment mean	7	8	13	5
Sample mean	——	2	4	——
Total assigned values	14	26	18	14
Size of final sample	303	166	275	278

[a]In the sample including tool and die shops (final size 354) an additional 22 cases were assigned the establishment mean education and an additional 3 cases were assigned establishment mean distance.

absence of data for the dependent variable (wages) or for one of two crucial independent variables, date of hire and age.

In a number of cases, data were missing on one or two independent variables of somewhat less importance. We were reluctant to omit these cases from the regressions because of the relatively small sample sizes, especially for subsamples having certain properties in which we were particularly interested. We therefore included the observations and made assumptions about the missing variable. If the missing independent variable was inherently dichotomous, such as previous experience in an occupation, we assumed its absence if it was not known to be present. Where the missing variable was continuous, such as years of schooling, we assigned to a worker for whom it was unknown the mean value for the occupation in his establishment, if this establishment had five or more people in the occupation. Otherwise we assigned the mean value for the occupation in the sample as a whole. The bottom part of table 6.1 shows the number of cases in which such values were assigned. One firm in our sample employed janitors at several different locations, and the records did not specify where, so we could not measure distance to work. Since the number of individuals was large (thirty-five) and we already had a number of other assigned values for distance, we were reluctant to assign the sample mean to them, and instead deleted the firm from the sample for this occupation.

FORM OF THE REGRESSIONS

Our regressions attempt to explain wage differences between employed individuals. At this level of disaggregation, it is hard to view wages usefully as being determined by the interaction of a supply function and a demand function. Each person is presumably working at or above his supply price; those who cannot get their supply price are not working and therefore are not in our sample. Personal characteristics of the worker, such as his schooling, are in a sense a dimension of the quantities of services he supplies; in another view they are determinants of his productivity and hence of the demand for his services.

We have skirted these difficulties by using single-equation models in which all forces thought to influence wages enter the same regression, whether they operate from the supply or the demand side. This, of course, means that we do not have a system in which wages and employment can be viewed as simultaneously determined. We must therefore be careful about the direction of the causal relationships among our variables, which has to be determined by a priori reasoning. When we are explaining wage dispersion we want to exclude variables for which the causal relation runs from wage dispersion to the dispersion of the other variable.

Formally, we use ordinary least-squares regressions of the general form

$$w = a + b_1 I_1 \ldots + b_n I_n + c_1 E_1 \ldots + c_m E_m + u,$$

where the w's are the wages of the individual workers in the sample; a is a constant; b_1 through b_n are the estimated coefficients of the individual variables, I_1 through I_n; c_1 through c_m are the estimated coefficients of the establishment variables E_1 through E_m, and the u's are disturbances. The independent variables enter additively, with no interaction terms.

We can often observe interaction when the addition of one independent variable causes a large change in the coefficient of another, and in such cases we often, but not always, also observe a high simple correlation between the independent variables. We must then decide which variable to leave out on the basis of our a priori beliefs about the nature of the relationship involved. For example, in a particular occupation we might have a group of workers in one industry who were relatively highly paid and predominantly single, so that there was strong interaction between a marital status variable and an industry dummy, both having positive signs. There is no particular reason to expect single men as such to be highly paid, whereas there might be aspects of the job content in this industry that would require particular skill; on such grounds we would probably omit the marital status variable from the regression.

As this discussion suggests, we have been unable to reduce our criteria for the inclusion of independent variables to mechanical rules. However, we do systematically exclude any independent variable whose inclusion does not lower the standard error of the regression corrected for degrees of freedom. When our purpose is to explain wage dispersion, we also exclude variables that do not have the expected sign. For example, we expect on the basis of other studies a positive relation between wages and years of schooling. Suppose that in a particular regression we find a negative sign for years of schooling. We must then ask whether schooling really has a negative effect on wages in this occupation, or whether it happens to be associated by chance in this case with some unidentified factors depressing earnings. Since the second of these alternatives seems more probable, we would regard it as unfair to include the schooling variable and allow it to "contribute" to the "explanation" of wage dispersion by raising the coefficient of determination. In a sense, the negative effect of schooling increases the amount of explaining that must be done by the other variables. We would, however, report the unexpected result in our discussion of the effect of schooling across all occupations.

All of the individual variables have an expected sign in the sense of the last paragraph, but this is not true of all of the establishment variables. In particular, it is not true of industry or region. These variables stand for constellations of conditions such as job content, or the balance of local demand and supply, whose outcome cannot be predicted from theory or even very well from earlier empirical study. Their inclusion thus represents simple fact-finding as opposed to hypothesis testing.

In each of our twelve occupations, we will show first one or more regressions in which only the individual variables appear and then one or more regressions in which both individual and establishment variables appear. In part, this is because it is of interest in its own right to see how much wage dispersion is explained by each set of variables. However, it is also important to see whether the coefficients of the individual variables change substantially when the establishment variables are added. Our confidence in the results is often strengthened when they do not, though sometimes a change suggests a hypothesis about the forces producing wage dispersion.

When we first began to analyze our data, we tried including dummies representing the different establishments in regressions in which the other independent variables were individual variables. We then ran a second-stage regression across establishments in which the coefficients of the establishment dummies from the first-stage regression were the dependent variable, and our usual establishment variables were the independent variables. This two-stage procedure was far more expensive because of the large number of variables in the first-stage regression, and it did not produce noticeably better results.

In almost every case, the regressions presented here are the result of a large number of trials using different combinations and forms of independent variables. This raises the suspicion that the results we choose to show are fortuitously good—that the prolonged search for a tight fit will eventually be successful, even when the investigator has no theory to guide it.

The force of this reservation is somewhat blunted by the other criteria discussed above that guided our selection of final models. We have repeatedly discarded models whose R^2 was higher than that of the model we retained because some other feature of the discarded model disturbed us.[4] Moreover, we ordinarily got quite close

4. The R^2 statistic, or coefficient of determination, is a measure of the extent to which the independent variables explain the variance in the dependent variable. It can assume values from zero, when the independent variables have no explanatory power, to one, when they explain all of the variance.

to our final R^2 in the first few trials; the differences in R^2 made by subsequent modifications usually lie in a narrow range.

Complete disclosure of our methods would require us to show all of our trials somewhere in this volume. However, the most patient reader would be exhausted by such a presentation, and little would be shown except the very large number of seemingly plausible hypotheses that can be devised that are not supported by our data.

STATISTICAL SIGNIFICANCE

For each of our independent variables we present the t value (the ratio of the coefficient to its standard error) in parentheses below the coefficient. For normally distributed variables, tables of the significance of t are available. For samples of roughly the sizes used here, a t value of 2.00 would be significant at about the .05 level.[5]

However, our individual variables are not normally distributed because we have sampled establishments and not individuals. To the extent that hiring standards and other employer practices produce some degree of homogeneity within establishments, our variables show more clustering of values than would corresponding variables from a random sample of individuals selected from the occupational population at large. Moreover, where we combine individual and establishment variables in one regression, the number of possible values for the establishment variables cannot exceed the number of establishments, whereas the number of degrees of freedom used in computing t is the number of individuals.

We have been unable to discover or devise any precise way of measuring statistical significance for regressions from a sample having these properties. For that reason, we have tried to avoid making statements about statistical significance. We have tended to regard t values of two or better as indicating significance, but leave the reader to judge for himself how much meaning to attach to t values in the neighborhood of two.

It should be pointed out that for normally distributed variables, the level of significance would not be highly sensitive to whether we took n to be the number of establishments or the number of individuals. The t value corresponding to the .05 level of significance is 2.042 for thirty observations and 1.960 for an infinite number, and

---

5. The t statistic measures the confidence with which one can assert from the estimated coefficient that the independent variable whose coefficient is being estimated does have an effect on the dependent variable. A significance level of .05 means that one would expect a coefficient this large (in absolute size) to occur by chance only one time in twenty in repeated samplings of the same population using the same methods if in fact the variable in question had no effect. See the article "Significance, Tests of," *International Encyclopedia of the Social Sciences,* 14: 238–49.

the number of establishments in our regressions is almost always larger than thirty.

A NOTE ON LIFE INSURANCE AND RETIREMENT BENEFITS

We noted in this chapter that the hourly earnings equivalent of holiday and vacation pay was added to the stated wage to produce our basic concept of wages per hours at work. The question naturally arises whether the inclusion of life insurance and retirement benefits, the two major elements of private fringe benefit costs, would alter the pattern we observe in wage differentials. Since we were unable to reduce the information we collected on fringe benefits to a dollars per hour basis, we cannot answer this question with precision. Several points may be mentioned, however, to support our belief that whatever the alteration in our observed pattern, it would be relatively small. These points are based on the material in table 6.2, where establishments are classified according to fringe benefit categories and then the number of people in each category for each occupation is shown along with the mean wage paid to these people.

First, it may be noted that the vast majority of individuals (86 percent on an overall basis) fall into the category "both life insurance and retirement benefits." Although benefit levels themselves vary considerably, this concentration in one category suggests that inclusion of these fringes would not change appreciably the distribution of wage differentials.

Second, on the assumption that the categories shown move from left to right across the table in terms of relative costliness, the fact that the mean wage tends to rise in most occupations as you move from left to right suggests a distribution of these fringes that is more or less in line with the distribution of other parts of the wage package. To be sure there are a few exceptions to this pattern of rising mean wages, but they result primarily from means calculated on the basis of a very small number of individuals. The only occupation where this is not true is truck drivers, where the mean is lower for workers entitled to both life insurance and retirement benefits than it is for workers entitled to retirement benefits only.

Finally, national estimates suggest that the cost of life insurance and retirement benefits approximates that of holiday and vacation pay.[6] If this is roughly correct for the firms in our sample, then the dollars per hour equivalent of these benefits amounts to roughly 6 percent of the mean wage we are using. This fraction is small

---

6. See, for example, U.S. Bureau of Labor Statistics, *Employer Expenditures for Selected Supplementary Compensation Practices for Production and Related Workers*, Manufacturing Industries, 1962, Bulletin no. 1428, April 1965.

TABLE 6.2
Mean Wages of Individuals—By Occupation and Fringe Benefit Class

Occupation	Fringe Benefit Class							
	Neither Life Insurance nor Retirement Benefits		Life Insurance Only		Retirement Benefits Only		Both Life Insurance and Retirement Benefits	
	wage	number	wage	number	wage	number	wage	number
Typist	$1.899	10	$1.886	20	$2.011	23	$2.020	504
Keypunch operator	1.944	11	1.728	2	1.974	5	2.219	360
Accountant	3.902	11	4.086	5	3.670	7	3.932	205
Tab machine operator	2.253	5	3.152	4	2.365	5	2.741	202
Material handler	———	—	1.948	79	2.354	92	2.516	379
Janitor	———	—	1.866	30	2.422	45	2.426	398
Janitress	1.842	3	1.863	2	1.887	14	2.036	154
Fork lift trucker	———	—	2.139	30	2.693	25	2.734	301
Punch press operator	———	—	2.417	17	———	—	2.601	286
Truck driver	———	—	3.179	5	3.251	53	3.165	108
Maintenance electrician	———	—	3.810	10	3.857	8	3.626	257
Tool and die maker	———	—	4.017	18	———	—	3.984	260

NOTE: Mean wages indicate earnings per hour at work

enough so that, when it is combined with the force of the preceding two points, we feel confident in assuming the distribution of wages based on our concept of the mean wage is very close to the true distribution.

The general pattern of table 6.2 supports the findings of other research that indicates that fringe benefits are positively related to money wages. They therefore do not help to explain the variance in money wages as they would if they were negatively related, in which case high money wages could be viewed as an offset to substandard fringe benefits (see chapter 1, p. 5).

7
The White-Collar Occupations

THIS IS the first of four chapters that present the analysis of the dispersion of wages in individual occupations. The occupations considered in this chapter are the two female clerical occupations (typist and keypunch operator), accountant, and tabulating machine operator. The last two occupations include both males and females.

TYPISTS AND KEYPUNCH OPERATORS

The two female clerical occupations, typist and keypunch operator,[1] will be discussed together because the same general model was used to explain wage dispersion in both. Table 7.1 gives the results of the best regressions for the two occupations, first using individual variables only and then adding establishment variables. The models have somewhat greater explanatory power for keypunch operators than for typists, although fewer variables are used for keypunch operators. Most of the explained variance is accounted for by the individual variables. Only two establishment variables are helpful, and in the case of keypunch operators they contribute only modestly to raising the coefficient of determination.

AGE AND SENIORITY

Age and seniority are closely related variables; when both are expressed in linear form, the simple correlation between them is .56 for typists and .54 for keypunch operators. We are able to discriminate between them by using different curvilinear forms, quadratic for age and logarithmic for seniority.

The quadratic age function shows the effect of age on wages per hour at work when the other variables in the regression, including seniority, are held constant. After the peak of the age function, the

1. The original analysis of the female clerical occupations was done by Joseph C. Ullman. His work is concerned primarily with the relation between wages and the costs of search for new employees, rather than with the explanation of wage differentials. The variables that measure costs of search are excluded from this chapter on the ground that differences in wages and in search costs are determined simultaneously in the firm's manning strategy, and that the causal relation therefore does not run unambiguously from search costs to wages. Search costs will be introduced in chapter 13.

TABLE 7.1

Regressions for Typists and Keypunch Operators
(Coefficients in Dollars per Hour at Work; t Values in Parentheses)

Variable and Unit	Individual Variables Only		Including Establishment Variables	
	Typist	Keypunch Operator	Typist	Keypunch Operator
Age (years)	0.020	0.016	0.021	0.014
Age squared	−0.00026	−0.00021	−0.00024	−0.00016
Seniority (years)[a]	0.164	0.230	0.149	0.210
	(11.52)	(14.00)	(11.81)	(13.46)
Experience (D)	0.062	0.177	0.051	0.175
	(2.88)	(7.37)	(2.66)	(7.77)
Attended college (D)	0.038	——————	——————	——————
	(1.41)			
Nonwhite (D)	−0.096	——————	−0.094	——————
	(1.56)		(1.71)	——————
Distance to work	0.018	0.035	——————	——————
(blocks)[a]	(1.89)	(3.09)		
Nonresidential	——————	——————	0.117	0.116
neighborhood (D)			(6.52)	(4.72)
Nondurable	——————	——————	−0.097	——————
manufacturing (D)			(3.80)	
Trade, finance,	——————	——————	−0.195	−0.096
or service (D)			(10.03)	(3.98)
R^2	.333	.492	.474	.555
Constant term	1.418	1.465	1.486	1.568
Number of				
establishments	55	38	——————	——————
Number of				
individuals	557	378	——————	——————
Dependent variable:				
mean	2.013	2.205	——————	——————
standard deviation	0.281	0.302	——————	——————

NOTE: (D) Dummy variable
[a]Natural logarithm

earnings of individuals who stay with the same employer will on the average rise if the positive effect of seniority outweighs the negative effect of age.[2] It is the presence in the sample of some older workers with low seniority that permits us to estimate the two relationships separately.

2. For example, at age fifty the estimated value to a typist of being one year older is a negative 0.4 cents an hour, calculated from the regression that includes establishment variables. If she has ten years of seniority, the estimated value of one more year of seniority is 1.3 cents an hour, so that the estimated net gain in wages from staying with the same employer for another year (apart from gen-

The t values for age and age squared separately are not meaningful and are not shown in table 7.1. Instead, table 7.2 shows t values computed at certain preassigned ages,[3] together with the mean age, the age of peak earnings, and the value of another year of age at age twenty-five.

Typists and keypunch operators have almost the same mean age, and the same age of peak earnings as estimated using only individual variables. However, the peak age is raised more for keypunch operators than for typists when establishment variables are added to the regression. This shift in the peak occurs because the regression using only individual variables shows in full the effect of any tendency for the youngest and oldest workers to be concentrated in the lower wage establishments. The inclusion of the establishment variables partially controls for this, and lowers the coefficients of both age and age squared.

The negative coefficient of age squared is larger for typists than for keypunch operators, perhaps because there is more opportunity for typists to be promoted to higher-paid occupations, particularly stenographer or secretary. Those who remain typists at the higher ages may be on average less able than the younger typists.[4] This reasoning, of course, can also be used to explain the earlier age of peak earnings for typists in the regressions using establishment variables.

It should be noted that the effect of age on earnings in the clerical occupations is not large. At age twenty-five, one more year of age is worth only half a cent an hour for keypunch operators and six-tenths of a cent for typists.

Seniority is measured as the natural logarithm of the number of years plus one from the date of hire by the present employer (in any occupation) to 1963. The extra year has been added to avoid the impossible operation of taking the logarithm of zero. Since the

---

eral increases in the firm's wage level) is 0.9 cents per hour. The same calculation for keypunch operators shows a similar estimated net gain (0.8 cents an hour). These estimates are subject to substantial error since the t value of the age-earnings functions from regressions including establishment variables are below two at age fifty.

3. These are computed by the formula

$$t = \frac{b_1 + 2b_2 A}{\sqrt{\operatorname{var} b_1 + (2A)^2 \operatorname{var} b_2 + 4a \operatorname{cov} b_1 b_2}}$$

where b_1 is the coefficient of age, b_2 is the coefficient of age squared, and A is the age at which the t value is computed. Since the numerator of the ratio is the slope of the age-earnings function, the t value will be zero where the function is at its peak.

4. One of the firms in our sample stated this position in a very strong form. It hired typists between the ages of eighteen and twenty-five only, on the ground that "if a girl is still a typist at twenty-six, she is of poor quality."

contribution of coefficients of variables expressed in natural log units is not immediately obvious, we have calculated some values in arithmetic units, which are shown in table 7.3.

TABLE 7.2
Statistics Relating to the Age-Earnings Functions for White-Collar Occupations

	Typist	Keypunch Operator	Accountant		Tab Operator	
			Random Sample	Combined Sample	All	Male
Mean age	31.3	31.4	40.5	36.9	31.2	30.7
	Results of Regressions Using Individual Variables Only					
Age of peak earnings	38.0	38.0	49.7	51.0	38.6	36.0
t value at age						
25	3.33	2.43	4.44	2.80	5.45	3.05
35	1.53	1.03	4.25	2.74	2.34	0.45
50	−2.64	−1.76	−0.10	0.19	−5.59	−5.29
Value of one year older at age 25 (dollars per hour at work)	$0.006	$0.005	$0.052	$0.029	$0.029	$0.020
	Results of Regressions Including Establishment Variables					
Age of peak earnings	42.0	45.5	50.1	49.2	38.0	35.5
t value at age						
25	4.60	3.00	4.19	4.80	5.28	2.85
35	3.74	2.79	4.04	4.54	1.98	0.22
50	−1.86	−0.51	0.04	−0.30	−5.90	−5.40
Value of one year older at 25	$0.008	$0.006	$0.048	$0.047	$0.028	$0.018

In all of the regressions of table 7.1 the *t* value for seniority is the highest of any variable included. One reason for this strong relationship between earnings and seniority is our adjustment of the dependent variable for the length of vacations. Most firms explicitly relate length of vacations to length of service.

The value of seniority is shown by these calculations to be substantial. On the average, a keypunch operator with ten years of seniority makes an estimated fifty-five cents an hour more than one with none, and a typist with ten years of seniority makes an esti-

83

mated thirty-nine cents an hour more than one with none. The value of seniority declines slightly when establishment variables are added to the regression, suggesting a tendency for higher wage establishments to have lower turnover (higher average seniority).

TABLE 7.3
Statistics Relating to the Seniority Functions for White-Collar Occupations (Dollars per Hour at Work)

	Typist	Keypunch Operator	Accountant		Tab Operator	
			Random Sample	Combined Sample	All	Male
Mean seniority (years)	3.9	3.5	10.3	8.2	6.3	6.0
Results of Regressions Using Individual Variables Only						
Value of						
one year	$0.114	$0.159	$0.180	$0.152	$0.237	$0.253
five years	0.293	0.412	0.464	0.394	0.613	0.654
ten years	0.393	0.552	0.621	0.527	0.821	0.875
One more year at five	0.025	0.035	0.040	0.034	0.053	0.056
One more year at ten	0.014	0.020	0.023	0.019	0.030	0.032
Results of Regressions Including Establishment Variables						
Value of						
one year	$0.103	$0.146	$0.174	$0.180	$0.261	$0.273
five years	0.267	0.377	0.450	0.464	0.675	0.706
ten years	0.357	0.504	0.602	0.621	0.904	0.945
One more year at five	0.023	0.032	0.039	0.040	0.058	0.061
One more year at ten	0.013	0.018	0.022	0.023	0.033	0.034

Two interpretations of the seniority variable are possible. One is that it reflects the value of experience in the firm (specific training). The other is that it is an institutional variable reflecting pay increments based on length of service that are required by collective bargaining agreements or offered by employers to maintain morale. In these occupations, few employees are covered by collective bargaining. Moreover, the logarithmic form fits these data much better than the linear form. The logarithmic form produces increments in earnings with seniority that are much more rapid in the early years, which seems consistent with the view that the seniority variable reflects some kind of learning curve.[5]

EXPERIENCE AND SCHOOLING

The experience variable is a dummy that takes the value of one if the worker has had experience in her present occupation on a previous job, and zero otherwise. Experience gained on the present job will, of course, be reflected in the seniority variable.

The experience dummy has a coefficient of more than five cents in both typist regressions and of more than seventeen cents in both keypunch regressions. The coefficients change very little when establishment variables are added. The higher value of experience for keypunch operators may indicate that keypunching is less frequently learned in high school than typing. It may also reflect the greater variety of duties of the clerk-typist; the nontyping components of this job vary greatly from one establishment to another and experience in them is not readily transferable.

Formal schooling never contributed to the fit of the regressions for keypunch operators. For typists, a dummy variable for attending college for one or more years lowers the standard error of the regression that includes only individual variables, but its coefficient is less than four cents an hour and the t value is well below two. This variable does not lower the standard error of the regression containing establishment variables. This suggests that attending college is of more value in gaining entrance to a high wage establishment than in improving a girl's earnings position within an establishment. Other forms of the schooling variable, such as the number of years of schooling and a dummy for high-school graduation, did not perform as well as the dummy for college attendance.

The relatively weak performance of a schooling variable in these occupations may be explained by the small dispersion in years of school completed. The mean number of years of school completed for typists was 12.2 with a standard deviation of 1.1 years. Only 12

---

5. For further discussion of these possible interpretations of seniority, see chapter 11. See also Robert Evans, Jr., "Worker Quality and Wage Dispersion: An Analysis of a Clerical Labor Market in Boston," *Proceedings of the Fourteenth Annual Meeting of Industrial Relations Research Association* (Madison, Wisconsin: 1962), pp. 246–59. Evans examined sources of wage dispersion in a sample of 230 stenographers, and concluded that length of service was the only clearly significant factor. He questions whether continued increments in pay with long service can represent increased quality. However, Evans used rank correlation to measure the association between wages and length of service, and therefore does not present any evidence on the form of the relationship. Since he relates his variables to wages one at a time, rather than in a multiple regression, his measure of seniority also picks up the effects of age.

percent had not completed high school, and only 16 percent had attended college. For keypunch operators, the mean number of years completed was 11.9 with a standard deviation of 1.0. Twenty percent of keypunch operators had not completed high school.

COLOR

In our typist sample, less than 3 percent of the workers were nonwhite. Nevertheless, a dummy variable for nonwhites lowers the standard error of both regressions. The percentage of nonwhites in our keypunch sample was slightly larger, but the use of a color variable was not successful.

The coefficients of the color variable for typists are a negative ten cents an hour when only individual variables enter the regression and a negative nine cents an hour when establishment variables are added. These coefficients indicate the amount of the difference in earnings between white and nonwhite typists after the other variables entering the regression have been held constant, and are therefore a "purer" measure of discrimination than the gross pay differentials between whites and nonwhites.

DISTANCE AND LOCATION

The distance variable in table 7.1 is the natural logarithm of the number of city blocks (eight blocks to the mile) between the worker's residence and place of work. Since there are few diagonal transportation routes in the Chicago area, this distance is measured by adding the east-west distance to the north-south distance. We expected the distance variable to have a positive sign on the theory that workers have to be induced by higher pay to commute longer distances.

The distance variable was tried in both linear and logarithmic form, and generally performed better in the latter. This is consistent with the view that the costs of commutation are a nonlinear function of distance. Bus or elevated fares within the city of Chicago are related to distance only through a small additional charge for a transfer. Our interview data suggest a nonlinear relation between the time taken to travel to work and distance, which no doubt involves the use of faster modes of transportation for the longer distances.

The distance variable has a higher coefficient and t value for keypunch operators than for typists; there is no obvious explanation for this.

In the regressions including establishment variables, distance is replaced by a dummy variable indicating whether the establishment was located in a nonresidential neighborhood, where a nonresidential neighborhood is defined as one in which employment exceeds resident labor force. Outside the city of Chicago, the "neighborhood" is the individual city or suburb. In Chicago, it is one of the neighborhoods defined by the Chicago Community Inventory. The typical size of such an area is about three square miles.

The data for measuring the ratio of employment to resident labor force in neighborhoods came from an atlas that presented this ratio in five classes, one of which was open-ended.[6] We could not reconstruct the underlying ratios for lack of data on employment by neighborhoods. When we tried using the five ranges as a set of dummies, we found that the only significant break came between the ratios above and below one.[7]

The dummy variable for nonresidential neighborhoods has a high t value in both occupations, and almost identical coefficients (11.6 and 11.7 cents an hour). The variable is positively correlated with distance, indicating that women employed in residential areas do not travel as far to work as those employed in nonresidential areas. The good performance of the dummy for nonresidential neighborhoods helps us to rule out an alternative explanation of the distance variable. It might be argued that causation runs from wages to distance; that high-paid employees choose to live farther from work. On this line of reasoning, our distance variable would measure a kind of income elasticity of demand for living in more distant but more desirable areas. However, this reasoning should apply to income differences within as well as between establishments and would lead one to expect the individual variable to perform better than the establishment variable.

The fact that the dummy for nonresidential neighborhoods performs so much better than the distance variable suggests that more than just distance is involved. Female clerical workers may dislike industrial neighborhoods as such, for such reasons as dirtiness or threats to personal safety. This should not apply to the central business district (the Loop), which may be an especially attractive place to work because of the presence of stores, theaters, and restaurants, and because there is good transportation to the Loop from all parts of the metropolitan area. However, examination of the residuals for Loop establishments from the regressions including establish-

6. *An Atlas of Chicago's People, Jobs, and Homes* (Chicago: Community Renewal Program, 1963), p. 6.
7. We are indebted to Professors Karl Brunner and Jon Cunnyngham of Ohio State University for suggesting the use of dummies for location. In our early work, we coded the locations from one to five to form a continuous variable, a procedure that is both arbitrary and gives coefficients with lower t values.

ment variables shows that the regressions fit these establishments quite well, indicating that they do not pay lower wage than establishments in other nonresidential neighborhoods.[8]

INDUSTRY AND UNIONISM

In both regressions including establishment variables, a dummy for establishments in trade or services has a negative coefficient and a high t value. In the two female clerical occupations, the largest establishments in trade, finance, and services are home offices of insurance companies. The coefficient is substantially larger for typists than for keypunch operators. It is possible that this industry dummy reflects some differences in job content, or a dislike for working in offices that are in or adjacent to factory buildings. Some part of the difference may also reflect the much higher degree of unionization (of production and maintenance workers) in establishments not in the trade, finance, and service sector.

For typists, but not for keypunch operators, a dummy variable for nondurable manufacturing contributes to the regression including establishment variables, with a negative coefficient smaller than that for trade and service. The reference base for the industry dummies for typists is durable manufacturing and utilities; for keypunch operators, it is all manufacturing and utilities.

We are unable to include unionism as a variable in these regressions because it is strongly correlated (negatively) with "trade or service" and positively with "nonresidential neighborhood." The latter correlation prevents the use of a unionism variable even if trade and service establishments are omitted from the regression.

TEST SCORES

We collected scores on various tests for both typists and keypunch operators. The best results were obtained for typists, with data showing the number of words typed per minute. The regressions for the subsample of typists for whom these test scores were available are shown in table 7.4.

The test score subsample includes 34 percent of the typists in the main sample. These do not form a random subsample, since only nineteen establishments had test score data. The regressions for the

8. The Evans study of Boston stenographers cited in note 5 above advances the "Jordan Marsh" hypothesis that the farther the establishment is from Boston's largest department store, the higher will be its clerical wage. Evans concludes that his data provide some support for this hypothesis. Our data, as reported in the text, do not support the corresponding hypothesis (the Marshall Field hypothesis) for the Chicago area. Evans's data are again in the form of the simple association between wages and location, and are not from a multiple regression in which other factors are controlled. He notes that controlling for industry and seniority greatly weakens the association.

test score subsample are therefore shown first without the test score variable, to show how the subsample differs from the random sample.

The overall explanatory power of the regressions for the test score subsample is about the same as that of the regressions for the main sample, but the results for individual variables differ. In the subsample, years of education does slightly better than the dummy for college attendance, and the education variable has a higher t

TABLE 7.4

Regressions for Test Score Subsample, Typists

Variable and Unit	Individual Variables Only		Including Establishment Variables	
	Without Tests	With Tests	Without Tests	With Tests
Age	0.015	0.010	0.027	0.025
Age squared	−0.00022	−0.00017	−0.00037	−0.00034
Seniority	0.191	0.200	0.154	0.159
	(7.17)	(7.53)	(7.48)	(7.63)
Experience (D)	0.054	0.042	-----	-----
	(1.41)	(1.11)		
Schooling (years)	0.034	0.038	-----	-----
	(1.92)	(2.17)		
Distance to	0.042	0.036	-----	-----
work (blocks)[a]	(2.63)	(2.23)		
Test score				
(words per	-----	0.0039	-----	0.0019
minute)		(2.35)		(1.41)
Nonresidential				
neighborhood	-----	-----	0.233	0.221
(D)			(8.38)	(7.65)
Nondurable	-----	-----	−0.074	−0.069
goods (D)			(1.48)	(1.39)
Trade, finance,	-----	-----	−0.196	−0.200
or service (D)			(6.83)	(6.95)
R^2	.305	.325	.557	.562
Constant term	1.060	0.932	1.413	1.374
Number of				
establishments	19	-----	-----	-----
Number of				
individuals	194	-----	-----	-----
Dependent variable:				
mean	2.012	-----	-----	-----
standard				
deviation	0.277	-----	-----	-----

NOTE: (D) Dummy variable
[a]Natural logarithm

value. It may be that the establishments that give typing tests and record the scores are also those that pay the most attention in hiring to years of schooling. The experience variable no longer contributes to the fit of the regression when establishment variables are added. The coefficient for nonresidential neighborhoods is about twice as large, and has a high t value.

The result of main interest is that for the test score variable. The test scores were taken from the personnel records and measure words typed correctly per minute at the time of hire. The mean test score is a surprisingly low forty-three words per minute. Although, on the average, the wages refer to a date almost three years later than the test scores, the score still has a coefficient of four-tenths of a cent per hour per word typed when the regression includes individual variables only. Over a range of scores from thirty to sixty words (well within the range in our sample), this would be a difference of twelve cents per hour. Although this is substantial, it is of course much less than the differences in productivity at time of hire.

When establishment variables are added, the coefficient for test score drops to two-tenths of a cent per word and the t value falls substantially. The contribution of the test score to the fit of the regression is very slight. This result seems to arise from interaction between the test score variable and the dummy for nonresidential neighborhoods, which have a substantial positive simple correlation.

For a different subsample of sixty-seven typists, the personnel records gave us scores on the Wonderlic Personnel Test, a short "intelligence" test.[9] We have encountered mixed opinions on the value of this test among personnel men and industrial psychologists. In our regressions this test score always had a positive coefficient but never had a t value as high as 1.5, which may be due to the small size of the sample.

For keypunch operators, several establishments had records of an occupational aptitude test or permitted us to administer one. However, the sample of test scores was small and the results were not significant.

ACCOUNTANTS

Accountants, the only professional occupation included in the study, have both the highest mean wage and the largest relative

9. The Wonderlic Personnel Test is a twelve-minute test of fifty items covering verbal abilities, numerical abilities, and reasoning abilities. It is available in nine forms said to be equivalent. Users typically set a minimum score for a given occupation, screening out applicants who fail to meet the minimum. For typists, the typical minimum score is twenty correct answers in twelve minutes. See E. F. Wonderlic, *A Cooperative Research Study of Minimum Occupational Scores for the Wonderlic Personnel Test* (Northfield, Illinois: E. F. Wonderlic and Associates, 1966).

dispersion. Our random sample included no public accounting firms. Since such firms employ large numbers of accountants, we collected additional data on this occupation from two large public accounting firms. Where indicated below, these firms have been added to the random sample to produce what is called the combined sample.[10]

The accountants in the public accounting firms differ from those in the random sample in a number of respects, some of which will be elaborated later. All of the former are male; they are on average younger and have less seniority; and a much higher proportion are college graduates and have not had a previous job as an accountant.[11] They also receive, on the average, slightly higher wages. Since being male, age, seniority, college graduation, and previous occupational experience are all positively associated with earnings in the random sample, the addition of high-wage public accounting firms employing many young, inexperienced, short-service, male college graduates substantially lowers the proportion of wage variance explained by individual variables alone. (Compare the R^2 in the first and third columns of table 7.5.) When the establishment variables are added for the combined sample, including a dummy variable for the public accounting firms, the individual variables regain the power they had in the random sample, and the R^2 for the two samples is almost identical.

AGE AND SENIORITY

Age is a more powerful variable for accountants than for the female clerical occupations, and seniority is somewhat less powerful. The age of peak earnings for accountants is quite high—close to fifty in all regressions (see table 7.2). The value of being one year older at age twenty-five, as estimated from the random sample, is five cents an hour—ten times as much as for typists. The lower coefficients for age and age squared in the first regression for the combined sample reflect the lower average age in public accounting firms, combined with their higher pay for given values of the individual variables.

The absolute value of seniority is greater for the random sample of accountants than for the female clerical occupations (see table 7.3), but it is less relative to mean earnings. The value of one more year of seniority at five years is 1.2 percent of mean earnings for typists, 1.6 percent for keypunch operators, and 1.0 percent for

10. The public accounting firms were not randomly selected; both are among the largest in the area. We are indebted to Professor Sidney Davidson for assisting us in the selection and in getting access to the data.

11. Our sample from public accounting firms consists entirely of men called junior accountants in these firms. The senior accountants are in charge of auditing teams and have substantial supervisory responsibilities, and we have excluded supervisors from our sample throughout the study.

TABLE 7.5

Regression Results for Accountants

Variable	Random Sample		Combined Sample	
	Individual Variables Only	Including Establishment Variables	Individual Variables Only	Including Establishment Variables
Age	0.108	0.099	0.057	0.098
Age squared	−0.0011	−0.0010	−0.00056	−0.0010
Seniority[a]	0.259 (4.21)	0.251 (3.98)	0.220 (3.88)	0.259 (4.76)
Experience (D)	0.301 (3.06)	0.332 (3.44)	0.139 (1.64)	0.364 (4.40)
College graduate (D)	0.282 (3.03)	0.254 (2.77)	0.434 (5.04)	0.265 (3.24)
CPA (D)	1.176 (5.38)	1.073 (4.95)	0.906 (6.27)	0.724 (5.43)
Female (D)	−0.440 (2.49)	−0.432 (2.50)	−0.629 (3.71)	−0.441 (2.81)
North and West region (D)	-----	−0.188 (2.00)	-----	−0.216 (2.57)
Nondurable goods (D)	-----	0.198 (1.53)	-----	0.203 (1.73)
Trade, finance, and service (except public accounting firms) (D)	-----	−0.169 (1.68)	-----	−0.159 (1.74)
Public accounting firms (D)	-----	-----	-----	0.682 (5.47)
R^2	.404	.444	.310	.440
Constant term	0.720	1.002	2.032	1.020
Number of establishments	44	-----	46	-----
Number of individuals	228	-----	297	-----
Dependent variable: mean	3.926	-----	3.964	-----
standard deviation	0.799	-----	0.726	-----

NOTE: (D) Dummy variable
[a]Natural logarithm

accountants in the random sample. The t values of the seniority variable are substantially smaller for accountants than for the other white-collar occupations, and mean seniority is substantially higher. The relatively low t value of the seniority variable may indicate that the regressions for accountants do not separate out the effects of age and seniority as well as the regressions for the other white-collar occupations. This in turn could occur because of the high age of peak earnings, which restricts the range in which the age and seniority functions have opposite signs. The age variable could be picking up some of the positive effect of seniority on earnings.

EXPERIENCE AND TRAINING

The value of previous experience in the occupation was considerably greater for accountants than for the female clerical occupations. In the random sample, a dummy variable taking the value of one for individuals having known previous experience as accountants had a coefficient of over thirty cents an hour in both regressions. We arrived at this form of the experience variable after long and costly work with measures of the total length of known experience as accountants, which we thought would be more relevant in a professional occupation. As it turned out, these did not work quite as well as the dummy variable.

For the combined sample, the experience dummy has a much lower coefficient and t value before the establishment variables are added. This is because the public accounting firms hire many accountants at graduation from colleges or universities. (There is a substantial negative correlation between the experience dummy and the dummy for the public accounting firms in the combined sample.) Once the establishment characteristics are added, the experience variable has a somewhat larger coefficient and t value than in the random sample.

The best form of variable for length of formal schooling turned out to be a dummy having the value of one for college graduates. This has a coefficient between twenty-five and twenty-eight cents an hour in three of the four regressions. In the fourth, the regression using individual variables alone for the combined sample, the coefficient is much higher (forty-three cents), reflecting the necessity of college graduation for gaining entry to the public accounting firms. In the random sample, 40 percent of the accountants are college graduates; in the combined sample, 54 percent are. All but one of the sixty-nine observations in the public accounting firms are for college graduates.

The third variable reflecting experience and training is a dummy taking the value of one for Certified Public Accountants (CPAs). In the random sample there were nine CPAs, or 4 percent of the total; in the combined sample there were twenty-one, or 7 percent. The coefficient and t values of this variable were all very high. The estimated value of the CPA is somewhat greater in the random sample than in the combined sample. It is also greater when only individual variables enter the regression, indicating that part of the value of the CPA is in gaining entry to higher wage firms rather than in wage advantage relative to one's fellow employees.

At two thousand hours of work per year, the value of a CPA in the random sample was over $2,300 a year and in the combined sample about $1,800 a year. This suggests a high rate of return on the additional training a college graduate with numerical aptitude would need to get the CPA. However, because our sample of CPAs is so small, we have not attempted to use these data to calculate the rate of return.

SEX

There were fourteen female accountants in our random sample and none in the public accounting firms. They made up 6 percent of the random sample and 5 percent of the combined sample. Despite the small number of females the t values for the sex dummy are all greater than two.

Holding constant age, experience, seniority, and college graduation, the estimated cost of being female is forty-four cents per hour in the random sample and is almost unaffected by the addition of establishment variables.[12] In the combined sample, the estimated cost of being female is higher when only individual variables are used. This of course reflects the absence of females in the public accounting firms, which pay higher wages for given individual characteristics. It is not clear whether the absence of women from our sample of accountants in public accounting firms reflects employer or employee preferences. Accountants in these firms do much of their work in the offices of clients, and women may not like the traveling that this involves.

We have run the regressions of table 7.5 omitting the observations for females. The results are so similar to those of table 7.5 that they are not presented.

12. In the random sample, the estimated difference between male and female wages per hour at work is 11 percent of the mean wage; in the combined sample (using individual variables only) it is 16 percent of the mean wage. These differentials are much smaller than the differential in median 1959 earnings between male and female accountants as shown in the 1960 census, which is more than one-third of the male earnings (see table 3.1). However, the annual earnings difference may involve rather substantial differences in weeks worked per year and hours worked per week between men and women. Census earnings also include the incomes of partners and proprietors of accounting firms which are probably on the average higher than salaries and go predominantly to men.

REGION

The method of dealing with the location of the establishment within the Chicago area used for the female clerical occupations was unsuccessful for accountants. Instead, we have used the method to be used in the blue-collar occupations. We have divided the area into three main contiguous regions or zones, which are shown in the map on page 96. The first of these regions, which we call the base region because we use it as the standard of comparison, includes the central business district (the Loop) and a compact area of the Near North Side of the city of Chicago in which much relatively light industry is located. The second region, which we call South, includes the South Side of the city of Chicago, the area of the city directly west of the Loop, the Indiana portion of the consolidated Statistical Area, and some industrial suburbs adjacent to Chicago on the west, particularly Cicero and Berwyn. This region includes the largest concentration of heavy industry in the area, especially basic steel and petroleum refining. The remaining region, which we call North and West, includes the far northern tip of the city of Chicago and the western and northern part of the area, including the cities of Joliet, Aurora, Elgin, and Waukegan.

In the regressions for accountants we use a dummy variable taking the value of one for the North and West region and zero for all other locations. This has a negative coefficient of nineteen cents for the random sample. The negative sign is characteristic of this region in most other occupations as well.

We do not present here any results for accountants using a distance variable. It is possible that distance in part depends on wages rather than the reverse—that is, high wage accountants may choose to live in the more distant and more expensive suburbs; the very coarse region variable included in these regressions did not seem to be an adequate control to rule out this interpretation. This issue will be discussed at greater length in chapter 11. For the combined sample, there is the additional reason for not using distance that accountants in public accounting firms often work away from their own offices.

INDUSTRY

Accountants are like the female clerical occupations in having a negative coefficient for establishments in trade and service (other than public accounting). Nondurable manufacturing has a positive coefficient but the t values of both the industry dummies are below two. (The reference base is durable goods and utilities.)

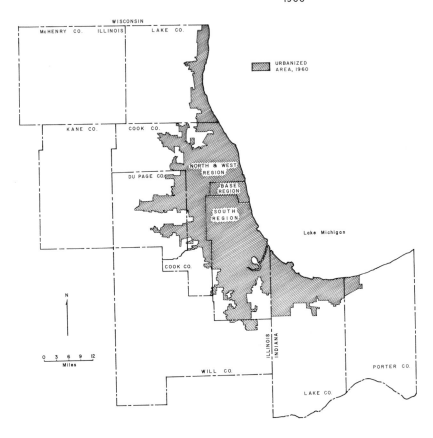

CHICAGO – NORTHWESTERN INDIANA
STANDARD CONSOLIDATED AREA,
BY REGIONS IN ANALYSIS –
1960

In the regression including establishment variables for the combined sample, a separate dummy was used for the public accounting firms. This had a positive coefficient of sixty-eight cents. This is much larger than the differential in mean wages between public accounting firms and others, which is only sixteen cents an hour. The remaining forty-six cents represents the extent to which on balance the public accounting firms get more "quality," as represented by the other variables in the regression, for the same wages. The most important elements in this advantage are the higher proportion of college graduates and CPAs and the absence of females in our sample of observations from public accounting firms.

It should be noted that the two establishment variables representing region and industry add rather little to the explanatory power of the model for the random sample of accountants. They raise the R^2 only from .404 to .444.

TESTS

Fifteen establishments in the random sample permitted us to administer to their accountants an intelligence test that forms part of the General Aptitude Test Battery of the United States Employment Service. Because of the small size of this subsample, we do

TABLE 7.6
Accountants: Regression Results for Test Score Subsample

Age	0.134
Age squared	−0.0012
Test score	0.015
	(2.68)
R^2	.285
Constant term	−1.242
Number of establishments	15
Number of individuals	64
Dependent variable:	
mean	3.84
standard deviation	0.72

NOTE: Females and Certified Public Accountants are excluded.

rather poorly in explaining wage variation within it. The results are shown in table 7.6. Five CPAs and three females have been omitted from the sample, since these groups seemed too small to control through the use of dummy variables. The test score is positively associated with wages and has a t value above two. No other variables except age and age squared contribute to the fit of the regression in the presence of test score.

TABULATING MACHINE OPERATORS

Our sample of tabulating machine operators (henceforth, for brevity, tab operators) is the smallest for our four white-collar occupations. It is also the occupation of all those in the study for which individual variables explain the largest part of the variance of wages (59 percent). Little more is added by establishment variables.

AGE AND SENIORITY

The mean age of tab operators is very close to that of typists and keypunch operators. However, the coefficients of age and age squared are closer to those of accountants. The value of an additional year of age at age twenty-five is two cents per hour, and the t value of the age function at age twenty-five exceeds five (see table 7.2).

The t values of seniority also fall about midway between the very high values for typists and keypunch operators and the more modest values for accountants.

The age-earnings functions for tab operators have rather large negative slopes and t values at age fifty, reflecting the low peak age and the relatively large coefficient of age squared. A tab operator of fifty with ten years of seniority is estimated to have little net gain from an additional year of service with his present employer, apart from general wage increases. The gain from one year of seniority, calculated from the regression including establishment variables, is an estimated 3.3 cents an hour; the cost of an additional year of age is 2.7 cents an hour. An example at age fifty with substantially more seniority would show an estimated net loss.

In many of the establishments in our sample, tabulating machine installations were being supplemented or replaced by electronic computer installations, creating opportunities for the most able tab operators to be trained for better jobs as programmers or computer operators. The promotion of the most able senior tab operators could account for the low age of peak earnings and the large negative slope of the age-earnings function beyond its peak.

EXPERIENCE AND SCHOOLING

As in the other white-collar occupations, we use a dummy for previous experience in the occupation. Its coefficient of thirty-eight cents and t value (above six) are larger than for the other three occupations. Unlike accountants, for whom experience and schooling had roughly equal coefficients, tab operators seem to gain far more from experience. The schooling variable that worked best was a dummy variable for high-school graduates, who made up 87 percent of the sample. On average, they earned an estimated fourteen cents an hour more than comparable nongraduates; the t value of this dummy was always somewhat below two.

SEX AND MARITAL STATUS

Females made up 21 percent of our sample of tab machine operators and earned an estimated thirty-eight cents an hour less than comparable males. Relative to the mean wage, this is a larger differential than that for female accountants (14 percent as compared with 11 percent). The t value is also much higher, perhaps reflecting the larger number of female observations for tab machine operators.

The difference in mean earnings between male and female tab operators was twenty-six cents an hour. This is smaller than the coefficient of thirty-eight cents largely because the average age and seniority of males is lower than that of females.

In the last two columns of table 7.7, we present results for male tab machine operators only; they are not appreciably different from those for both sexes combined. The proportion of wage variance explained drops only slightly, despite the absence of the powerful sex variable. Part of the slack is taken up by the marital status variable "single at hire." This dummy variable takes a value of one for all those not known to be married at hire, including those widowed and divorced. It is used only for groups of one sex, since we expect opposite signs for males and females. For males, a negative sign is expected on the grounds that married men, because of their family responsibilities, are thought to be steadier workers with lower turnover. For male tab operators we find the expected sign with a coefficient of thirteen cents and a t value of two, despite the fact that on average it was six years from the time of hire of male tab operators to the time when wages were measured. (Our data do not include current marital status.) The male tab operators who were single at hire are younger than average, and the inclusion of the marital status variable is responsible for about one-third of the drop in the coefficient of age between columns 2 and 4. When marital status is omitted, the coefficient of age is 0.070.

INDUSTRY AND REGION

For tab operators, we do not find a significant wage difference between trade and service industries and durable goods manufacturing. However, nondurable goods manufacturing pays an estimated nineteen cents an hour more for comparable tab operators than the other industries. This occurs despite the fact that about half our observations in nondurable goods are in apparel manufacturing, which is generally a low-wage industry. It is possible that nondurable goods establishments had not proceeded as far as others

TABLE 7.7

Regression Results for Tabulating Machine Operators

	Both Sexes		Males	
	Individual Variables Only	Including Establishment Variables	Individual Variables Only	Including Establishment Variables
Age	0.086	0.084	0.067	0.064
Age squared	−0.0011	−0.0011	−0.0009	−0.0009
Seniority[a]	0.342	0.377	0.365	0.394
	(8.07)	(8.81)	(7.72)	(8.28)
Experience (D)	0.381	0.407	0.358	0.366
	(6.34)	(6.84)	(5.39)	(5.61)
High-school	0.141	0.125	0.150	0.138
graduate (D)	(1.98)	(1.80)	(1.67)	(1.58)
Female (D)	−0.378	−0.330	------	------
	(6.70)	(5.70)		
Single at	------	------	−0.130	−0.136
hire (D)			(2.07)	(2.20)
Nondurable				
manufac-	------	0.192	------	0.204
turing (D)		(2.63)		(2.73)
North and				
west region	------	−0.092	------	------
(D)		(1.93)		
R^2	.586	.607	.562	.581
Constant term	0.570	0.570	0.994	0.998
Number of establish-				
ments	32	------	29	------
Number of individuals	216	------	170	------
Dependent variable:				
mean	2.728	------	2.784	------
standard devia-				
tion	0.498	------	0.490	------

NOTE: (D) Dummy variable
[a]Natural logarithm

in replacing tab installations with computers, thus downgrading the remaining tab operators, but we have no direct evidence on this point.

The North and West region has its usual negative sign, though the coefficient is much smaller than for accountants. When the female observations are omitted, the coefficient and t value for this variable both drop to very low levels, and the variable has been dropped from the regression shown in column 4 of table 7.7.

THE WHITE-COLLAR GROUP AS A WHOLE

Our models for the white-collar occupations explain from 44 to 61 percent of the variance in individual wages. The great bulk of this explanation is provided by the individual variables if they are entered first. The additional contribution of the establishment variables is 13 percent for typists, but only 3 to 6 percent in the other three occupations. However, these contributions would change if the two sets of variables had been entered in the reverse order.[13]

The results indicate that high wages are associated with a number of variables indicating higher employee quality, including experience, test scores, and schooling. The strongest association is with seniority, which we are inclined to view in part as an index of quality, although other interpretations are possible.

It is not possible to tell from these data whether quality differences are commensurate with the wage differences. As we measure them, quality differences explain only part of the variance in wages. However, we have not isolated all of the components of quality, and have not always been able to measure those isolated as well as we would like.

13. We are indebted to Professor John Pencavel of Stanford University for making this last point.

8

The Unskilled Occupations

MATERIAL HANDLERS

IN ALL THREE of the unskilled occupations—material handler, janitor[1], and janitress—our sample included substantial numbers of nonwhites. Tables 8.1 and 8.2 show the regression results for material handlers for whites and nonwhites separately and for all races combined. The number of observations in the combined regression exceeds the total for the other two because twenty-three persons whose race was not known are included only in the combined regression.

AGE AND SENIORITY

The material handlers are younger on the average than workers in the other unskilled occupations, with a slightly lower mean age for nonwhites than for whites. The peaks of the age-earnings functions are below the mean age in the combined regressions and the regressions for whites, but above the mean age for nonwhites (see table 8.3). The size of the age coefficients is very much larger for nonwhites; this may indicate that the more able nonwhite material handlers are less likely to be promoted than similar whites, so that at higher ages the remaining nonwhites are superior.

Seniority is again the most powerful variable in the regressions using only individual variables, and it remains powerful when establishment variables are added. Table 8.4 shows the value of selected amounts of seniority in cents per hour at work. The values are somewhat higher for nonwhites—for example, the value of ten years of seniority as estimated from regressions including only individual variables is fifty-seven cents an hour for nonwhites and forty-seven cents for whites.

1. The original regression analysis of earnings for material handlers and janitors was done by David P. Taylor in his unpublished doctoral dissertation "The Market for Unskilled Negro Males in Chicago" (March 1966). The results presented here differ somewhat from those in the dissertation because of improvements in the definition and form of certain of the variables included.

TABLE 8.1

Regression Results for Material Handlers Using Individual Variables Only

	All	White	Nonwhite
Age	0.018	0.0078	0.051
Age squared	−0.00029	−0.00017	−0.00065
Seniority[a]	0.214	0.198	0.237
	(11.79)	(9.72)	(6.05)
Experience (D)	0.144	0.131	—————
	(3.48)	(2.71)	
Previous job in Chicago (D)	—————	—————	0.158
			(2.78)
Schooling (years)	0.020	0.030	—————
	(3.34)	(4.44)	
Nonwhite (D)	−0.308	—————	—————
	(9.68)		
Spanish surname (D)	−0.152	−0.153	—————
	(2.10)	(2.17)	
Weight at hire 165 pounds or over (D)	0.047	0.033	0.075
	(1.75)	(1.06)	(1.40)
Single at hire (D)	−0.111	−0.103	−0.111
	(3.65)	(3.00)	(−1.71)
Distance to work (blocks)	—————	—————	0.0027
			(3.46)
R^2	.348	.264	.517
Constant term	1.658	1.798	0.694
Number of establishments	39	36	19
Number of individuals	550	394	133
Dependent variable:			
mean	2.408	2.482	2.200
standard deviation	0.384	0.349	0.419

NOTE: (D) Dummy variable
[a]Natural logarithm

TABLE 8.2

Material Handlers: Results of Regressions Including Establishment Variables

	All	White	Nonwhite
Age	0.011	0.0058	0.037
Age squared	−0.00016	−0.00010	−0.00047
Seniority[a]	0.188	0.169	0.222
	(14.07)	(11.00)	(7.83)
Experience (D)	0.050	0.045	—————
	(1.63)	(1.24)	
Previous job in Chicago (D)	—————	—————	0.086
			(2.03)

TABLE 8.2 (Continued)

	All	White	Nonwhite
Schooling (years)	0.019	0.023	-----
	(4.35)	(4.50)	
Nonwhite (D)	−0.130	-----	-----
	(4.90)		
Spanish surname (D)	−0.126	−0.143	-----
	(2.38)	(2.70)	
Weight 165 pounds	-----	-----	0.059
or over (D)			(1.47)
Single at hire (D)	−0.049	−0.056	-----
	(2.18)	(2.14)	
Printing and chemicals (D)	0.071	0.106	-----
	(2.49)	(2.91)	
Textiles, apparel,	−0.459	−0.438	−0.400
and paper (D)	(13.74)	(9.28)	(7.71)
Food manufacturing,	0.411	0.394	-----
utilities, and trade (D)	(14.38)	(13.42)	
North and West region (D)	−0.235	−0.251	-----
	(8.34)	(8.63)	
Percent nonwhite in area	-----	-----	−0.0044
of establishment			(2.47)
R^2	.655	.594	.735
Constant term	1.825	1.926	1.351

NOTE: (D) Dummy variable
[a]Natural logarithm

TABLE 8.3
Statistics Relating to the Age Functions for Material Handlers

Mean age	All	White	Nonwhite
	34.6	35.3	33.1
	Results of Regressions Using Individual Variables Only		
t value of age-earnings function at age			
25	1.08	−0.28	2.67
35	−1.40	−2.19	1.48
50	−4.59	−3.72	−2.12
Value of one more year at			
25	$ 0.003	$−0.001	$ 0.018
35	−0.003	−0.005	0.005
50	−0.012	−0.010	−0.014
Age of peak earnings	30.7	22.2	39.3

TABLE 8.3 (Continued)

Mean age	All 34.6	White 35.3	Nonwhite 33.1
	Results of Regressions Including Establishment Variables		
t value of age-earnings function at age			
25	1.23	0.33	2.74
35	−0.34	−0.74	1.55
50	−2.89	−2.08	−2.11
Value of one more year at			
25	$ 0.003	$ 0.001	$ 0.013
35	−0.001	−0.001	0.003
50	−0.005	−0.004	−0.011
Age of peak earnings	33.6	29.3	39.1

TABLE 8.4
Statistics Relating to the Value of Seniority for Material Handlers

	All	White	Nonwhite
Mean seniority (years)	5.3	5.7	4.9
	Results of Regressions Using Individual Variables Only		
Value of			
one year	$0.149	$0.137	$0.164
five years	0.384	0.354	0.424
ten years	0.514	0.474	0.568
one more year at five	0.033	0.030	0.037
one more year at ten	0.019	0.017	0.021
	Results of Regressions Including Establishment Variables		
Value of			
one year	$0.130	$0.117	$0.154
five years	0.337	0.303	0.398
ten years	0.451	0.405	0.533
one more year at five	0.029	0.026	0.034
one more year at ten	0.016	0.015	0.019

EXPERIENCE AND SCHOOLING

The experience variable used in the unskilled occupations differs from that used in the white-collar occupations. It is a dummy taking the value of one for any known previous civilian job in any occupation. It thus represents being accustomed to a work situation, and perhaps the ability of the employer to get references.

The experience dummy has a value of fourteen cents for the two races combined and thirteen cents for whites in table 8.1. When establishment characteristics are added, the coefficients and t values fall sharply, indicating that the lower wage establishments hire more inexperienced workers. The great majority (87 percent) of the workers in the sample had known previous experience.

For nonwhites, an alternative measure of experience worked substantially better than the experience dummy. This was a dummy taking a value of one if the worker had a known previous civilian job in the Chicago area. When the experience dummy is used in the nonwhite regression of table 8.1 in place of the job in Chicago dummy, its t value is only 1.85, as compared with 2.78, and the R^2 statistic falls from .517 to .501. If previous experience in a civilian job *outside* Chicago is entered as a separate dummy, it contributes nothing. These results suggest that employers of nonwhites are more concerned about checking references, which is much easier to do locally than at a distance. They may also be more concerned about the applicants' acculturation to urban life and work settings. In this connection, it should be pointed out that the origins of the nonwhites and whites who had not previously worked in Chicago are quite different. The whites were largely either new entrants to the labor force or had worked in other industrial areas in the North. The nonwhites were largely migrants from the South, and had often worked in nonindustrial jobs.

The best form of the schooling variable in the occupation was years of schooling. The mean number of years completed was 10.2, with a standard deviation of 2.5 for both whites and nonwhites. The coefficient for whites was three cents per year, so that the difference between eight years and twelve would amount to twelve cents per hour. For nonwhites separately the education variable does not contribute to the fit of the regression. Employers who seek formal schooling in their material handlers may be thinking in terms of possible promotion to more skilled jobs, and these possibilities are probably greater for whites than for nonwhites.[2]

2. As will be seen later, in the two other occupations where we run separate regressions by race, janitor and fork lift trucker, education also contributes to the regressions for whites and not to those for nonwhites. This is consistent with the results of other studies showing weaker relationships between years of schooling and earnings and between years of schooling and labor force participation for nonwhites. See Giora Hanoch, "Personal Earnings and Investment in Schooling," unpublished doctoral dissertation, University of Chicago, 1965, and William G. Bowen and T. A. Finegan, "The Economics of Labor Force Participation," (Princeton, N.J.: Princeton University Press, 1969), pp. 53–62.

COLOR AND ORIGIN

The regressions for all material handlers use two dummy variables for color and origin. The first takes a value of one for nonwhites and zero for whites; the second takes a value of one for workers with Spanish surnames (mostly of Mexican and Puerto Rican origin) and zero for others. The dummy for Spanish surname is also included in the regressions for whites.

The mean wage of nonwhites is $2.20 an hour, twenty-eight cents below the mean wage of all whites, and twenty-nine cents below the mean wage of whites other than those with Spanish surnames (the base group). The coefficient of the nonwhite dummy in the first column of table 8.1 is a negative thirty-one cents, indicating that only about two cents per hour can be attributed to differences between nonwhites and whites in the other characteristics that enter into the regression.

In the first column of table 8.2, the coefficient of the dummy variable for nonwhites is less than half as large as in table 8.1, showing that a large part of the gross differential comes about because nonwhites are employed in disproportionate numbers in the lower wage establishments.

The dummy for workers with Spanish surnames has a very similar negative coefficient (thirteen to fifteen cents) in all four regressions in which it appears. The t values are above two, although there are only twenty such workers in the sample. Since the addition of establishment characteristics does not substantially alter the coefficient, there appears to be less tendency for these workers than for nonwhites to be overrepresented in low wage establishments.

WEIGHT AND HEIGHT

Since the work of a material handler often requires physical strength, there is an advantage, within limits, to being tall and heavy. Some of our firms had explicit hiring standards for height and weight in this occupation, such as a minimum weight of 150 pounds and a minimum height of five feet ten inches. We tried both variables in different forms, and the one that worked best in a

---

Professor Bowen has suggested to us an explanation of these findings that supplements the one given in the text above. Since a much larger proportion of nonwhites than of whites have little formal schooling, lack of schooling is more likely among whites to be an index of other personal characteristics that make the worker less productive or a less desirable worker. Among nonwhites, lack of schooling is of a more random character, and there will be a higher proportion of unschooled nonwhites who nevertheless have native intelligence and initiative.

It is also possible that our results reflect the lower quality of nonwhite schooling for a given number of years.

majority of cases was a dummy variable for weight of 165 pounds and over.[3] This is approximately the mean weight of the men in the sample, and the dummy roughly divides the group into heavier and lighter than average. It seems more plausible than linear weight since the advantage (if any) of weighing 250 pounds rather than 200 should be less than that of weighing 180 pounds rather than 130.

The weight variable for material handlers never has a t value as large as two, though it contributes to the fit of all three regressions in table 8.1. The coefficient for nonwhites is about twice as large as for whites. When establishment variables are added, the weight variable no longer contributes to the fit of the regressions for all workers and for whites. This is consistent with weight being a hiring standard rather than a factor that leads to pay differentials within establishments.

MARITAL STATUS

A dummy variable for men who were single at the time of hire appears in all but one of the regressions of tables 8.1 and 8.2, and has a t value above two in four of them. The sign is negative as expected, reflecting the employer view that single men are in general less dependable than married men. The performance of this variable is unusually good in this occupation.

DISTANCE AND REGION

A distance variable improves the fit of the regression using only individual variables for nonwhite material handlers, but not for whites or for both groups combined. This difference may occur because the mean distance traveled to work was higher for nonwhites than for whites (sixty-four blocks as compared with forty-eight; there are eight blocks to the mile). The longer journey to work of nonwhites is in turn largely a result of residential segregation.

The linear form of the distance variable worked better for this group than the logarithmic form used in the clerical occupations.[4] A possible reason for this is that nonwhites are more heavily dependent on bus and elevated train transportation for long trips than are whites, and in these modes of transportation, the average speed does not increase with length of trip as it does in private automobiles or commuter railroads. The dependence on bus and elevated is in part

3. For nonwhite material handlers, linear weight gave somewhat better results than the dummy variable (t value 1.72). The dummy is used in table 8.1 for comparability and the reasons stated in the text.

4. Using the logarithmic form of the distance variable for nonwhite material handlers reduces the t value of the coefficient from 3.46 to 3.18 and the R^2 of the regression from .517 to .511.

a result of lower family income and in part a result of the concentration of nonwhite residence in the inner city.

The coefficient of the distance variable is twenty-seven-hundredths of a cent per hour per block traveled in one direction. This is more meaningful if expressed in dollars per eight-hour day per mile. This works out to about seventeen cents per day per mile, or to $1.38 for the average trip of eight miles (or round trip of sixteen miles).

The regressions of table 8.2 use two different ways of accounting for location through establishment variables. The regressions for all workers and for whites use the regional scheme described earlier in the regressions for accountants. The coefficients of the dummy variable for the North and West region have the expected negative signs, coefficients of about twenty-five cents an hour, and t values above eight.

For the nonwhites, there were too few observations in the North and West region to permit the use of the same model. The variable used instead is a continuous variable measuring the percentage of nonwhite population in the area of the establishment. By the area of the establishment is meant its immediate neighborhood if it is in Chicago, or suburb if it is outside, and all contiguous neighborhoods or suburbs. The variable is intended to measure the size of the nonwhite labor supply to the establishment. Since nonwhites often work in areas where they do not live, the contiguous areas are included to avoid anomalies. For example, Cicero had only four Negroes in its 1960 population, but it is adjacent to a heavily Negro area of Chicago (South Lawndale). It would therefore be unreasonable to use the percentage of nonwhites in Cicero alone to measure the supply of nonwhite labor to Cicero establishments.

Because of discrimination in employment and differential education and experience, white and nonwhite workers are not regarded as perfect substitutes. The expected sign of the variable for percentage of nonwhites in the area of the establishment is therefore negative—the larger the supply the lower the expected wage. In other terms, nonwhites who travel away from areas of nonwhite concentration can expect to find higher paying jobs. In this sense, the variable is a substitute for the distance variable of the nonwhite regression of table 8.1. The distance variable does not perform well when establishment variables are added, in part because it is correlated with some of the industry variables.

The mean value of the percentage nonwhite variable is 11.0 and the standard deviation is 13.2. The coefficient in table 8.2 is forty-four hundredths of a cent per hour per percentage point of nonwhite population. If we apply this to the range from zero to thirty-seven (two standard deviations above the mean) we get an estimated difference of sixteen cents an hour between wages of nonwhite material handlers in areas with little and with substantial local non-white labor supply.

INDUSTRY AND UNION

The analysis of industry variation in wages is more complicated in the blue-collar than in the white-collar occupations, both because of differences in work content among industries and because of industry wage contours reflecting such factors as collective bargaining and product market structure. For material handlers, the difference among industries in the heaviness of the work is especially important.

For the set of three industry dummies shown in the first two columns of table 8.2, the base industry is durable goods manufacturing. Nondurable goods manufacturing has been divided into three parts. The first, printing and chemicals, has moderately higher wages than the base (seven cents an hour for all workers, eleven cents for whites). The second, textiles, apparel, and paper products, is a conspicuously low wage sector, with earnings forty-six cents below the base group. The final sector, food manufacturing, has been combined with utilities and trade to form the highest wage sector, forty-one cents above the base group. This is the only result that seems surprising; it can be attributed to the particular characteristics of the firms in the sample. In particular, the trade group is dominated by a steel warehouse and two large furniture and appliance dealers, in all of which the work is especially heavy. The differentials mentioned in this paragraph are not, of course, the differences between the mean wages by industry, but differences remaining after the other factors entering the regression have been controlled.

In the regression for nonwhite material handlers, printing and chemicals did not differ significantly from the base, and the number of observations in food manufacturing and trade was too small to permit the use of separate dummies. These industries have therefore been added to the base. Against this new base, the dummy for textiles, apparel, and paper products has a negative coefficient of forty cents.

We attempted in a number of ways to use a unionism variable in the regressions for material handlers, and in all of these it had a negative sign. We believe that this is a result of some unidentified special characteristics of unionized firms in this sample, rather than a true effect of unionization, and therefore do not show these results in this chapter.

Because of the importance of industry and region, the addition of establishment variables substantially raises the percentage of wage variance "explained" by the material handler regressions—from 35 to 66 percent for all workers, from 26 to 59 percent for whites, and from 52 to 74 percent for nonwhites.

JANITORS AND JANITRESSES

The work of janitors (or porters) and janitresses (or charwomen) in business and industrial establishments is generally similar. However, there is some presumption that janitors do more heavy work, such as using floor-polishing machines, and that janitors are more likely to be employed in plants and janitresses in offices. In most of our analysis, we treat the two occupations separately. However, we also present some combined or pooled regressions in which the sexes are distinguished by means of a dummy variable (see tables 8.5 through 8.8). The pooled regressions are of interest largely in connection

TABLE 8.5
Regression Results for Janitors Using Individual Variables Only

	All	White	Nonwhite
Age	0.0054	0.0076	0.0013
Age squared	−0.0013	−0.00015	−0.00006
Seniority[a]	0.206	0.214	0.155
	(12.34)	(11.55)	(4.26)
Previous job in Chicago (D)	0.168	0.132	0.304
	(5.54)	(2.59)	(5.47)
Previous job not in Chicago (D)	-----	0.068	-----
		(1.09)	
High-school graduate (D)	0.114	0.172	-----
	(3.04)	(3.51)	
Nonwhite (D)	−0.077	-----	-----
	(2.48)		
Weight at hire 165 pounds or over (D)	0.079	0.045	0.162
	(3.03)	(1.43)	(3.49)
Distance to work over 70 blocks (D)	0.096	-----	0.165
	(3.32)		(3.56)
R^2	.317	.341	.376
Constant term	1.890	1.857	1.797
Number of individuals	473	314	153
Number of establishments	52	47	27
Dependent variable:			
mean	2.390	2.378	2.406
standard deviation	0.335	0.329	0.349

NOTE: (D) Dummy variable
[a]Natural logarithm

with differences in earnings by sex, and will be discussed largely in that context.

About one-third of both the janitors and janitresses in our samples are nonwhite (32 percent of the janitors and 31 percent of the janitresses). However, the janitress sample is too small (173 observations)

TABLE 8.6
Janitors: Results of Regressions Including Establishment Variables

	All	White	Nonwhite
Age	0.013	0.014	————
Age squared	−0.00017	−0.00019	————
Seniority[a]	0.202	0.207	0.173
	(12.76)	(11.47)	(7.04)
Previous job in Chicago (D)	0.151	0.097	0.211
	(5.50)	(2.87)	(4.59)
High-school graduate (D)	0.073	0.114	————
	(2.10)	(2.38)	
Nonwhite (D)	−0.090	————	————
	(3.31)		
Weight at hire 165 pounds	0.063	0.043	0.101
or over (D)	(2.69)	(1.49)	(2.73)
Food manufacturing (D)	0.404	0.322	0.445
	(9.12)	(5.36)	(7.53)
Other nondurable goods			
manufacturing, trade,	−0.106	−0.106	————
finance, and service (D)	(3.07)	(2.70)	
Transportation and utilities	0.135	0.111	0.253
(D)	(3.31)	(2.14)	(4.59)
South region (D)	0.119	0.125	0.224
	(3.58)	(3.62)	(3.73)
North and West region (D)	0.046	————	0.310
	(1.30)		(4.96)
Size of establishment	0.028	0.022	0.068
(hundreds of employees)[a]	(2.23)	(1.45)	(3.39)
R^2	0.465	0.439	0.628
Constant term	1.524	1.584	1.323

NOTE: (D) Dummy variable
[a]Natural logarithm

to permit separate regressions by race. Six janitors whose race is not known are included in the regressions for all janitors, but not in the separate regressions by race.

AGE AND SENIORITY

The janitors and janitresses in our sample are on the average older than material handlers. The mean age of janitors is forty-seven and of janitresses forty-eight. Among the janitors, the whites have a substantially higher average age than nonwhites (fifty as compared with forty-one). Since the age-earnings function is declining for both groups in this age range, and the standard deviations of age

TABLE 8.7

Regression Results for Janitresses and for Janitors and Janitresses Combined; Individual Variables Only

	Janitresses	Combined All	White	Nonwhite
Age	–––––	0.0023	0.0089	−0.0028
Age squared	–––––	−0.00008	−0.00013	−0.00003
Seniority[a]	0.234	0.208	0.216	0.193
	(9.54)	(14.09)	(13.38)	(6.08)
Experience (D)	0.067	–––––	–––––	–––––
	(1.12)			
Previous job in Chicago (D)	–––––	0.129	0.074	0.240
		(5.00)	(2.50)	(4.78)
High-school graduate (D)	–––––	0.083	0.167	–––––
		(2.51)	(3.98)	
Nonwhite (D)	−0.162	−0.094	–––––	–––––
	(3.70)	(3.50)		
Female (D)	–––––	−0.409	−0.365	−0.514
		(15.92)	(12.33)	(10.64)
Distance to work over 70 blocks (D)	–––––	0.055	–––––	0.128
		(2.17)		(3.10)
R^2	.362	.422	.447	.455
Constant term	1.537	2.004	1.833	1.972
Number of establishments	33	54	49	32
Number of individuals	173	646	434	206
Dependent variable: mean	2.018	2.291	2.284	2.293
standard deviation	0.316	0.369	0.360	0.387

NOTE: (D) Dummy variable
[a]Natural logarithm

are similar, this means that more of the nonwhites are in the preferred age range. (See table 8.9). For janitresses, age does not contribute to the fit of the regressions.

As usual, seniority is a powerful variable in all cases. For janitresses, it is one of only three individual variables that enter the regression in table 8.7. Differences in the value of seniority are small among all the regressions for unskilled occupations.

EXPERIENCE AND SCHOOLING

The dummy variable for previous job experience in the Chicago area, which was used for nonwhite material handlers, performs better than a general job experience dummy for all janitors and for

TABLE 8.8

Regression Results Including Establishment Variables for Janitresses and for Janitors and Janitresses Combined

	Janitresses	Combined All	White	Nonwhite
Age	————	0.0092	0.012	————
Age squared	————	−0.0001	−0.0002	————
Seniority[a]	0.166	0.204	0.204	0.177
	(7.91)	(14.96)	(13.20)	(8.10)
Previous job in Chicago (D)	————	0.114 (5.04)	0.073 (2.67)	0.159 (3.95)
High-school graduate (D)	————	0.069 (2.40)	0.127 (3.22)	————
Nonwhite (D)	−0.126 (3.74)	−0.099 (4.30)	————	————
Female (D)	————	−0.398 (17.37)	−0.393 (14.11)	−0.374 (9.45)
South region (D)	0.127 (3.42)	0.168 (6.30)	0.131 (4.64)	0.240 (5.07)
North and West region (D)	0.158 (3.24)	0.089 (3.03)	————	0.282 (5.50)
Food manufacturing (D)	————	0.318 (8.43)	0.243 (4.89)	0.382 (6.48)
Other nondurables, trade, finance, and service (D)	−0.365 (8.77)	−0.185 (6.80)	−0.177 (5.54)	−0.160 (2.77)
Transportation and utilities (D)	−0.238 (5.88)	————	————	0.085 (1.66)
Establishment size[a]	————	0.021 (2.06)	0.023 (1.89)	0.042 (2.27)
R^2	.629	.561	.531	.686
Constant term	1.815	1.687	1.674	1.546

NOTE: (D) Dummy variable
[a]Natural logarithm

nonwhite janitors. The coefficients and t values of the job in Chicago dummy are much higher for nonwhites than for all janitors, indicating again that employers place greater value on local experience for nonwhites.

For white janitors, there is very slight improvement in the fit of the regression when separate dummy variables are used for experience in Chicago and experience elsewhere, against a base of no experience. The dummy for experience elsewhere has a t value barely above one. For nonwhites, there is no evidence that employers prefer experience elsewhere to no experience at all.

One may ask why the local experience variable works better than the general one for all janitors when it does not for all material handlers. The difference probably lies in the origins of the whites in

TABLE 8.9
Statistics Relating to the Age-Earnings Functions for Janitors

Mean age	All	White	Nonwhite
	47.1	50.2	41.0
	Results of Regressions Using Individual Variables Only		
t value of function at age			
25	−0.31	0.07	−0.33
35	−1.84	−1.03	−0.98
50	−4.83	−4.11	−1.46
Value of one more year at			
25	$−0.001	$ 0.001	$−0.002
35	−0.004	−0.003	−0.003
50	−0.008	−0.007	−0.005
Age of peak earnings	21.1	26.0	a
	Results of Regressions Including Establishment Variables		
t value at age			
25	1.46	1.19	b
35	0.50	0.33	b
50	−2.90	−2.95	b
Value of one more year at			
25	$ 0.004	$ 0.004	b
35	0.001	0.001	b
50	−0.004	−0.005	b
Age of peak earnings	37.6	37.1	b

[a]Peak lies below range of observations
[b]Age variable not included in this regression

the two groups. The white janitors included many recent immigrants from Eastern Europe displaced by World War II and its aftermath. These people, like nonwhite migrants to Chicago, were unlikely to have had industrial jobs in other American labor markets and like the nonwhite migrants had an acculturation problem.

For janitresses, the general experience variable is the better of the two experience variables, though its t value is barely above one.

Only 9 percent of janitors and 13 percent of janitresses did not have known previous jobs, whereas 24 percent of janitors and 31 percent of janitresses did not have known previous jobs in Chicago. The schooling variable used for janitors is a dummy for completion of high school, which performs well in regressions for all janitors and for white janitors. It does not contribute to the regressions for nonwhites or for janitresses.

Only 15 percent of janitors were high-school graduates—13 percent of whites and 20 percent of the nonwhites—and only 12 percent of the janitresses were high-school graduates. The value of the coefficient of the high-school graduate dummy for janitors is somewhat greater than the value of the difference for material handlers between completing eight grades and twelve grades as estimated from the coefficient of the continuous schooling variable.

COLOR

The mean wages of nonwhite janitors ($2.406) were slightly higher than those of whites ($2.378). Nevertheless, the nonwhite dummy in the first regression of table 8.5 has a negative coefficient of eight cents an hour. In part this is because nonwhite janitors are of higher quality as indicated by their lower mean age and higher proportion of high-school graduates. In part it is because nonwhite janitors travel farther to work and the premium for distance enters the regression.

The addition of establishment variables slightly raises the coefficient and t value of the nonwhite dummy. Both this effect and the difference in mean wages suggest that nonwhite janitors, unlike nonwhite materials handlers, are if anything overrepresented in high wage establishments.

The difference in wages by color, after other variables are taken into account, is very much smaller for janitors than for material handlers. This smaller discrimination could be explained in several ways. Janitors are a group of workers who are often quite separate from other employees, frequently work at different hours, and are not often promoted to higher positions. The large number of displaced persons among white janitors also contributes to reducing the color differential.

For janitresses, the nonwhite dummy in the regression using individual variables only has a larger negative coefficient than in the corresponding regression for janitors. Since age, education, and distance do not enter the regression, the coefficient essentially measures wage differences between white and nonwhite janitresses of equal seniority.

116

WEIGHT

The same weight variable is used for janitors as for material handlers—a dummy for those whose weight at hire was 165 pounds or over. It contributes to the fit of all the janitor regressions, but has substantially higher coefficients and *t* values for nonwhites than for whites. This is similar to the pattern of results for material handlers. The performance of the variable is substantially better than in the material handler regressions, which is somewhat surprising.

We have no reason to believe that there is a preference for heavier janitresses, and have omitted the weight variable from regressions in which janitresses are included.

SEX

The difference in mean earnings per hour at work between janitors and janitresses in our sample is thirty-seven cents. The coeffi-

TABLE 8.10
Statistics Relating to the Value of Seniority for Janitors and Janitresses

	Janitors			Janitresses
	All	White	Nonwhite	
Mean seniority (years)	7.4	7.4	7.5	8.8
	Results of Regressions Using Individual Variables Only			
Value of				
One year	$0.143	$0.148	$0.108	$0.162
Five years	0.369	0.383	0.278	0.419
Ten years	0.494	0.513	0.372	0.561
One more year at five	0.032	0.033	0.024	0.036
One more year at ten	0.018	0.019	0.013	0.020
	Results of Regressions Including Establishment Variables			
Value of				
One year	$0.140	$0.143	$0.120	$0.115
Five years	0.361	0.370	0.310	0.298
Ten years	0.483	0.495	0.415	0.399
One more year at five	0.031	0.032	0.027	0.026
One more year at ten	0.018	0.018	0.015	0.014

117

cient of the dummy variable for females in the combined regression of table 8.7 is a negative forty-one cents. Some of the small difference between these figures is accounted for by the presence in this regression of the dummy variable for distance to work of more than seventy blocks, which applies to 32 percent of the janitors and only 25 percent of the janitresses. A second factor working to increase the differential as measured by the dummy variable is the smaller proportion of janitresses who had a previous known job in Chicago.

In the combined regressions for whites and for nonwhites of table 8.7, the negative coefficient of the dummy variable for females is substantially larger for nonwhites than for whites (fifty-one cents an hour compared with thirty-six cents). This difference undoubtedly reflects the larger relative supply of nonwhite females for low-skilled service jobs, caused by the higher labor force participation rates of nonwhite than of white females and by the greater willingness of nonwhites to accept this kind of work, perhaps because of habituation to it as cleaning women in private households.

When the establishment characteristics are added in table 8.8, the difference between the races in the size of the sex coefficient disappears. This result is unaffected by adding age to the nonwhite regression. It thus appears to indicate that nonwhite women are more heavily represented than nonwhite men in the lowest wage establishments.

DISTANCE AND REGION

The regressions using individual variables only for all janitors and for nonwhite janitors include a dummy variable for workers who travel to work more than seventy blocks (about nine miles). This gives a substantially better fit than the linear distance variable used for material handlers. For white janitors and for janitresses, no distance variable contributed to the fit. These groups typically live closer to their jobs. The mean distances are eighty blocks (ten miles) for nonwhite janitors, fifty blocks for white janitors, and fifty blocks for janitresses. Both the mean distance and the relative dispersion of distance are substantially higher for nonwhite janitors than for nonwhite material handlers, which may be related to the difference in the best form of the distance variable.

The coefficient of the distance dummy for nonwhite janitors is 16.5 cents per hour at work, or $1.32 per eight-hour day. The mean distance traveled by those who went more than 70 blocks is about 120 blocks. If we apply the linear distance coefficient for nonwhite material handlers to 120 blocks, we would get about 32 cents per hour at work, which indicates that the relation between distance and earnings is stronger for material handlers.

In the regressions including establishment variables the distance variable is replaced by dummy variables for the region in which the establishment is located. The percentage of nonwhite population in the area was also tried in the regression for nonwhite janitors, but does not work as well as the regional scheme.

The South region has its expected positive sign, reflecting the influence of concentrations of heavy industry. The North and West region is not significantly different from the base for white janitors, and is combined with the base region. For nonwhite janitors and for janitresses, it has a substantial positive coefficient. This is opposite to the usual pattern for this region, but is consistent with the positive sign for distance in the nonwhite janitor regression using individual variables. The North and West region has little nonwhite population, and much of it is far removed from the centers of nonwhite population and not readily accessible from them by public transportation. The nonwhites who work in this region must travel longer distances. Indeed, the variable for this region has a large negative simple correlation with our measure of percent nonwhite in the area of establishments employing nonwhite janitors, and a large positive correlation with the dummy variable for workers who travel over seventy blocks.

It should also be noted that the South region has larger positive coefficients for nonwhites than for whites, despite the concentration of nonwhite population in this region. This is probably the result of incomplete control for industry mix.

INDUSTRY AND UNION

The base industry for the set of industry dummies in columns 1 and 2 of table 8.6 is again durable goods manufacturing. Food manufacturing is identified by a separate dummy variable with large positive coefficients. The two largest establishments in our sample in this industry are both bakeries, where the duties of janitors include cleaning out ovens and where very high standards of cleanliness are essential. The high wages in this industry are thus clearly related to special job content.

Other nondurable manufacturing, trade, and service are combined into a dummy variable with a small (eleven-cent) negative coefficient. The remaining industry is transportation and public utilities, with a positive coefficient.

In the regression for nonwhite janitors "other nondurables, trade, finance, and service" is not significantly different from the base, and has been included in it. The coefficients of food and of utilities are higher in regressions for nonwhites than in those for whites, by more than could be explained by the change in the reference base (as can be seen by comparing the coefficients for white and for all janitors).

For janitresses, the food industry has few observations and does not have special job characteristics; it has therefore been included with other nondurables. The negative coefficient of nondurable goods, trade, finance, and service is very much larger for janitresses than for janitors. Transportation and utilities have a substantial negative coefficient for janitresses. We do not know why the difference in pay between janitors and janitresses should be especially large in this industry, which employs more than a third of the janitresses in our sample. In both occupations, the dummy variable for this industry is positively correlated with unionization, but the association is somewhat stronger for janitresses than for janitors.

Because transportation and utilities has opposite signs for janitors and janitresses, it does not differ appreciably from durable goods in the combined regression, and has been included with durable goods in the base. The food industry is again substantially positive, and "other nondurables, trade, finance, and service" is negative.

A unionism variable was tried in the regression for janitors and had a very small negative coefficient and very low t value. These results are presented in chapter 12. For janitresses, unionism is highly correlated with South region and with the utilities and transportation industry, and is omitted here for that reason.

SIZE OF ESTABLISHMENT

Janitor is the only occupation presented thus far in which the size of establishment has a positive sign and contributes to the fit of the regression. Size is measured as the natural logarithm of the number of employees in hundreds. Since the range of sizes is from one hundred to thirteen thousand, the linear form would make little sense—that is, one would expect a difference in size between 100 and 200 to have much more effect on earnings than one between 11,900 and 12,000.

Although size contributes to the fit of all the regressions in table 8.6, the coefficient and t value are substantially higher for nonwhites than for whites. Size does not help the regressions for janitresses.

The value of size differences in arithmetic units may be illustrated by the difference in earnings between an establishment of one hundred employees and one of one thousand employees implied by the coefficient of the natural logarithm of size. For all janitors, this difference is 6.5 cents an hour. For whites it is only 5 cents an hour, but for nonwhites, it is 15.7 cents.

The proportion of variance explained by individual variables is in general lower for janitors than for material handlers. It is somewhat higher for janitresses, despite the small number of individual variables that proved useful. The addition of establishment variables adds less to the explanatory power of the regressions for janitors and janitresses than for material handlers, perhaps because there is somewhat less variation in job content by industry.

9
The Semiskilled Occupations

THE THREE occupations considered in this chapter are fork lift trucker, punch press operator, and truck driver. For the first of these, separate analyses are presented by race and for the second, separate analyses by sex. For the last occupation, truck driver, we had little success in explaining wage dispersion and the presentation will be brief.

FORK LIFT TRUCKERS

Fork lift truckers had the largest proportion of nonwhites (35 percent) of any of the semiskilled occupations. Tables 9.1 and 9.2 show regression results for all fork lift truckers and for whites and non-

TABLE 9.1
Fork Lift Truckers: Results of Regressions Using Individual Variables Only

	All	White	Nonwhite
Age	0.037	0.042	0.026
Age squared	−0.00041	−0.00050	−0.00021
Seniority[a]	0.114	0.118	0.114
	(3.71)	(2.88)	(2.47)
High-school graduate (D)	0.119	0.187	─────
	(2.59)	(3.07)	
Nonwhite (D)	−0.157	─────	─────
	(3.57)		
Distance to work (blocks)[a]	0.028	0.037	─────
	(1.38)	(1.50)	
R^2	.127	.130	.194
Constant term	1.639	1.509	1.708
Number of establishments	30	27	20
Number of individuals	356	225	125
Dependent variable:			
mean	2.681	2.701	2.642
standard deviation	0.382	0.406	0.336

NOTE: (D) Dummy variable
[a]Natural logarithm

122

TABLE 9.2

Fork Lift Truckers: Results of Regressions Including Establishment
Variables

	All	White	Nonwhite
Age	0.036	0.047	-----
Age squared	−0.00037	−0.00047	-----
Seniority[a]	0.092	0.074	0.147
	(4.11)	(2.58)	(4.71)
High-school graduate (D)	0.071	0.105	-----
	(2.16)	(2.50)	
Nonwhite (D)	−0.156	-----	-----
	(5.02)		
Heavy durables (D)	0.535	0.610	0.432
	(16.17)	(13.79)	(7.38)
Nondurables and trade (D)	0.129	0.089	0.238
	(3.31)	(1.87)	(3.66)
South region (D)	0.169	0.126	0.209
	(5.81)	(3.35)	(3.85)
North and West region (D)	-----	-----	0.094
			(1.35)
R^2	.549	.599	.506
Constant term	1.432	1.236	1.959

NOTE: (D) Dummy variable
[a]Natural logarithm

whites separately. The amount of wage variance explained by the individual variables is much lower than for any of the occupations considered in chapters 7 and 8. For nonwhites, age and seniority are the only individual variables that enter the regression. Nevertheless, the R^2 of the regression for nonwhites in table 9.1 is higher than that of the other two regressions.

AGE AND SENIORITY

The relation between age and earnings is stronger for fork lift truckers than for the unskilled occupations, and the age of peak earnings is higher (see table 9.3). Nevertheless, the value of age is not large—about two cents per hour for an additional year of age at twenty-five. The peak age is especially high for nonwhites (sixty-three years). As with material handlers, the difference between whites and nonwhites in the peak ages could reflect a stronger tendency for whites in this occupation to be promoted. In the regression for nonwhites including establishment variables, the age variables raised the corrected standard error and have been omitted.

The value of seniority is substantially less for fork lift truckers than for the unskilled occupations (see table 9.4), and the t values of the seniority variable are lower than usual, though always above two. As with accountants, because of the rather high age of peak earnings the regressions may not be discriminating as well as usual between the effects of age and seniority and the age variable may be picking up more of the joint effects.

TABLE 9.3
Statistics Relating to the Age-Earnings Functions for Fork Lift Truckers

	All	White	Nonwhite
Mean age	35.6	34.6	37.3
Results of Regressions Using Individual Variables Only			
t value at age			
25	2.91	2.60	1.46
35	2.67	1.94	2.22
50	−1.25	−1.76	0.80
Value of one more year at			
25	$ 0.015	$ 0.016	$ 0.016
35	0.007	0.006	0.012
50	−0.005	−0.009	0.005
Age of peak earnings	44.2	41.7	63.3
Results of Regressions Including Establishment Variables			
t value at age			
25	4.48	5.19	a
35	4.82	5.56	a
50	−0.39	−0.12	a
Value of one more year at			
25	$ 0.017	$ 0.023	a
35	0.010	0.013	a
50	−0.001	−0.001	a
Age of peak earnings	48.5	49.6	a

[a]No age variables included in regression

The estimated value of seniority is almost identical for whites and nonwhites when only individual variables enter the regression. When establishment variables are added, the estimated value of seniority declines for whites and rises for nonwhites. This pattern suggests that low seniority whites and high seniority nonwhites are overrepresented in high wage establishments, perhaps because the nonwhites have less tendency to quit such establishments and less opportunity for promotion. A similar pattern is present for janitors (table 8.10), but is much less pronounced.

TABLE 9.4
Statistics Relating to the Value of Seniority for Fork Lift Truckers

	All	White	Nonwhite
Mean seniority (years)	8.6	7.7	10.4
	Results of Regressions Using Individual Variables Only		
Value of			
One year	$0.079	$0.082	$0.079
Five years	0.205	0.212	0.204
Ten years	0.274	0.284	0.273
One more year at five	0.018	0.018	0.018
One more year at ten	0.010	0.010	0.010
	Results of Regressions Including Establishment Variables		
Value of			
One year	$0.064	$0.051	$0.102
Five years	0.165	0.132	0.263
Ten years	0.220	0.177	0.352
One more year at five	0.014	0.011	0.023
One more year at ten	0.008	0.006	0.013

SCHOOLING AND EXPERIENCE

The best form of the schooling variable in this occupation was a dummy for completion of high school. The percentage completing high school was higher for whites (34 percent) than for nonwhites (26 percent). As in the unskilled occupations, the schooling variable performs well for all workers and for whites, but does not improve the fit for nonwhites.[1] The addition of establishment variables lowers the coefficient of the dummy for high-school graduation, but the *t* values remain above two.

Several forms of a variable indicating experience in previous jobs were tried for fork lift truckers, but none improved the results.

COLOR

The mean wage of nonwhite fork lift truckers is only six cents per hour lower than that of whites. However, the coefficient of the dummy for nonwhites in the first column of table 9.1 is a negative sixteen cents. The ten cents in excess of the difference in mean wages is explained by the higher average seniority and average age of the nonwhites (with the average age for both groups lying below the

1. For an interpretation of this difference, see the discussion of education of material handlers, chapter 8.

peak of the age-earnings function) and by the longer distance that nonwhites travel to work. A partial offset arises from the higher proportion of white high-school graduates. The size of the coefficient for color is unaffected by the addition of establishment variables but the t value is increased.

DISTANCE AND REGION

The logarithmic form of the distance variable gives the best fit in this occupation, implying some economies of scale in traveling longer distances. However, the relation of earnings to distance is very weak, with the t values substantially below two. In the nonwhite regression, distance does not contribute to the fit, although on the average nonwhites travel farther to work than whites.

For all fork lift truckers, the estimated value of traveling ten miles to work (eighty blocks) as compared with one block is 16.3 cents per hour at work, or \$1.30 for an eight-hour day.[2] As indicated by the low t value, this estimate is subject to substantial error. The estimated value is somewhat less than the value of the same distance for nonwhite material handlers, which is \$1.73 per day as estimated from a linear distance function.

In table 9.2, region replaces distance. For all workers and for whites, a separate dummy for the North and West region raises the standard error, and this region is combined with the base region (the Central business district and Near North Side). The coefficient for the South region has its usual positive sign, and is larger for nonwhites than for whites. The coefficient for North and West is positive for nonwhites, but the t value is below two. The sign may reflect distance traveled to work even though the distance variable itself did not perform well.

INDUSTRY AND UNION

This occupation contains no observations in public utilities or services. The most important wage differences are between the industries in durable goods manufacturing. The high wage sector is represented by the dummy variable "heavy durables"; it consists of SIC industries 33, 34, and 35 (primary metals, fabricated metal products, and machinery). The rest of durable goods is the base or reference group for the industry dummies. The most important industries in the base in this sample are electrical equipment and instruments. The coefficients of the dummy for heavy durables are all large, and are somewhat larger for whites than for nonwhites. Nondurable goods and trade are combined into a sector with a

2. The comparison with one block rather than with none is necessary because of the impossibility of taking the logarithm of zero.

rather small positive coefficient for whites and a larger positive coefficient for nonwhites. The high wage printing industry is well represented among the establishments in nondurable goods in this occupation.

A unionism variable had negative coefficients and t values greater than two in the fork lift regressions; runs including this variable are not presented here.

Because of the importance of the variables for industry and region, the R^2 for the regressions including establishment characteristics are very much higher than those for regressions including only individual variables.

PUNCH PRESS OPERATORS

Tables 9.5 and 9.6 present regression results for all punch press operators and for males and females separately. Because this occupation is confined to durable goods manufacturing, only fourteen establishments are represented and only limited use can be made of industry variables.

The regressions using individual variables only use an unusually small number of variables. Education and experience proved of no

TABLE 9.5
Punch Press Operators: Results of Regressions Using Individual Variables Only

	All	Male	Female
Age	-----	-----	0.012
Age squared	-----	-----	−0.00022
Seniority[a]	0.306	0.349	0.259
	(15.24)	(12.78)	(8.08)
Nonwhite (D)	−0.105	−0.134	−0.057
	(1.93)	(1.51)	(1.00)
Female (D)	−0.199	-----	-----
	(5.12)		
Distance to work (blocks)[a]	0.036	0.053	-----
	(1.76)	(1.70)	
R^2	.455	.483	.405
Constant term	1.974	1.839	1.902
Number of establishments	14	12	8
Number of individuals	303	183	120
Dependent variable:			
mean	2.591	2.642	2.512
standard deviation	0.434	0.490	0.318

NOTE: (D) Dummy variable
[a]Natural logarithm

127

TABLE 9.6

Punch Press Operators: Results of Regressions Including Establishment Variables

	All	Male	Female
Seniority[a]	0.200	0.270	0.179
	(10.68)	(10.12)	(10.33)
Nonwhite (D)	−0.150	−0.223	−0.082
	(3.29)	(2.77)	(2.27)
Spanish surname	−0.091	————	————
	(1.33)		
Female (D)	−0.500	————	————
	(12.70)		
Distance to work (blocks)[a]	0.032	0.054	0.031
	(1.86)	(1.98)	(2.11)
Heavy durables (D)	0.260	0.272	0.260
	(6.61)	(4.30)	(7.24)
South region (D)	0.480	————	0.356
	(10.61)		(10.26)
North and West region (D)	−0.169	−0.350	————
	(4.18)	(6.19)	
Incentive pay (D)	0.086	0.317	−0.120
	(2.32)	(5.38)	(3.48)
Establishment size[a]	————	0.105	————
		(3.71)	
R^2	.650	.623	.781
Constant term	2.035	1.525	1.753

NOTE: (D) Dummy variable
[a]Natural logarithm

help in explaining wage dispersion in this occupation as a whole, perhaps in part because of the highly repetitive character of the work and the wide use of incentive pay. Nevertheless, the individual variables explain from 40 to 48 percent of the variance.

AGE AND SENIORITY

This occupation contained some high wage establishments with both very high and very low average ages for males, so that the age-earnings function had implausible signs even in the absence of the seniority variable. The function was U-shaped rather than an inverted U. The age variables have been omitted from the regressions shown here for all punch press operators and for males only. For females, they have the expected signs and have been included.

Since age appears in only one of the six regressions for punch press operators, we have not included a table giving the t values of the age-earnings functions. For the regression for females in column

3 of table 9.5, the peak of the age-earnings function is at 27.1 years. The t values are 0.11 at age twenty-five, −0.82 at age thirty-five, and −2.11 at age fifty.

Seniority is once again powerful in all the regressions, with somewhat larger coefficients for males than for females. Table 9.7 shows the value of seniority translated from logarithmic units to years.

TABLE 9.7
Estimates of the Value of Seniority for Punch Press Operators

	Both sexes	Male	Female
Mean seniority (years)	8.8	8.1	9.9
	Results of Regressions Using Individual Variables Only		
Value of			
One year	$0.212	$0.242	$0.180
Five years	0.548	0.625	0.465
Ten years	0.734	0.837	0.622
One more year at five	0.047	0.054	0.040
One more year at ten	0.027	0.030	0.023
	Results of Regressions Including Establishment Variables		
Value of			
One year	$0.138	$0.187	$0.124
Five years	0.358	0.484	0.320
Ten years	0.479	0.648	0.429
One more year at five	0.031	0.042	0.028
One more year at ten	0.017	0.024	0.016

COLOR AND ORIGIN

Nonwhites made up 15 percent of the sample of punch press operators (10 percent of the males and 22 percent of the females). In table 9.5, color has a t value below two in all three regressions. For females, the coefficient is almost exactly the same size as its standard error, being larger only in the fourth decimal place. However, when establishment variables are added color has substantially larger coefficients and t values. This implies that nonwhites are overrepresented in the higher wage establishments and have lower earnings than the whites within establishments. The earnings differential is substantially larger for men than for women.

For males, nonwhites are heavily overrepresented in establishments having incentive pay; the dummy for such establishments has a large positive coefficient in the regression for males of table 9.6.

This accounts for the overrepresentation of nonwhites in high wage establishments and indicates the possibility of lower hourly earnings within an establishment without any racial discrimination in the pay structure. For women, the overrepresentation of nonwhites in establishments with incentive pay is less pronounced. The dummy for incentive pay has a negative sign in the regression for females; the overrepresentation of nonwhite women in high wage establishments arises because they are heavily overrepresented in the high wage South region.

A dummy variable for persons with Spanish surnames contributes to the fit of the regression for both sexes in table 9.6, where it has a negative coefficient of nine cents. This is somewhat smaller than the corresponding coefficient in the regressions for material handlers. The dummy for persons with Spanish surnames does not contribute to the regressions containing individual variables only; this suggests that Puerto Rican and Mexican workers in this occupation, like the nonwhites, are overrepresented in high wage establishments but earn less than their fellow workers.

SEX

In the first regression of table 9.5, the dummy variable for females has a negative coefficient of twenty cents an hour and a t value above five. The coefficient is raised to fifty cents and the t value to over twelve when establishment variables are added. This striking change occurs largely because of the very different regional distribution of men and women in this sample. Only 14 percent of the men, but 68 percent of the women, were in the high wage South region, whereas 36 percent of the men, but only 8 percent of the women, were in the low wage North and West region. Women were also overrepresented in heavy durable goods, a high wage sector.

The difference in mean wages between men and women is 13 cents an hour, which is smaller than either of the coefficients for the dummy variable. The difference between this figure and the twenty-cent coefficient of table 9.5 arises because women have higher average seniority than men.

The large differential between men and women, within establishments, implied by table 9.6 is probably related to differences in the heaviness of work. Punch presses vary considerably in size and in the heaviness of the stock to be punched, and men will tend to be used more frequently on the larger presses and to handle the heavier stock.

We will return to the discussion of sex differences in earnings in connection with incentive pay.

DISTANCE AND REGION

The logarithmic form of the distance to work variable contributes to the regressions for all punch press operators and for males only in table 9.5, though its t value never reaches two. The coefficient for males is substantially larger than for all workers. Rather surprisingly, the overall importance of distance is not reduced by the addition of establishment variables (including region). The variable contributes to the regression for females in table 9.6, and for the other two regressions its t value rises when establishment variables are added. The simple correlations between distance and the regional dummies are unusually low in this sample.

The dummy for the South region has its usual positive sign in this occupation and a very large coefficient; that for the North and West region has its usual negative sign. Because of the unequal distribution of the sexes, only one regional dummy can be used in each of the separate regressions by sex. For males, the South region is combined with the base region (the near North Side) and against this enlarged base the North and West region has a negative coefficient of thirty-five cents. For females, the North and West region is combined with the base, and with reference to this area, the South region has a positive coefficient of thirty-six cents.

INDUSTRY

The industry variable used is the same dummy for heavy durable goods used for fork lift truckers. Its reference base is the rest of durable goods.

The coefficients are very similar for all three regressions of table 9.6—twenty-six or twenty-seven cents an hour. For all punch press operators, the coefficient is about half the size of the corresponding coefficient for all fork lift truckers.

INCENTIVE PAY

More than half of the punch press operators in our sample received incentive pay (54 percent of the men and 58 percent of the women). It should be recalled that our dependent variable is measured differently for such workers; it is measured as average earnings per hour at work for a typical month, rather than for a single week, in order to even out any week-to-week fluctuation in earnings. Individual incentive rates are common for punch press operators because individual output can usually be measured accurately, and the pace of the operation is usually under the control of the individual worker, except in cases of breakdowns or shortages of stock. Incentive pay is treated as an establishment variable because we had only one establishment in the sample that paid some punch press operators time rates and others incentive rates.[3]

In the regression for all punch press operators that includes establishment variables, the dummy variable for incentive pay has a positive coefficient of nine cents an hour and a t value of two. However, the results are strikingly different for the two sexes separately. For men, the coefficient is a positive thirty-two cents an hour with a t value of five, for women the coefficient is a negative twelve cents an hour with a t value of three.

At first we found these results strange, but reflection has convinced us that they are plausible. An employer paying time rates cannot very well pay different rates to men and women for the same work. In many cases this would be a violation of union contracts, and in nonunion establishments it might invite union organization.[4] An employer with different kinds of equipment might establish different rates for different kinds, and assign men to the higher wage categories, but such opportunities would not be present everywhere.[5] In short, under time rates, if men are more productive than women they will tend to get lower wages per unit of output.

However, neither union contracts nor general mores prevent an employer from establishing uniform piece or incentive rates for men and women and letting differential output result in differential earnings. This is what our results suggest, for women on incentive pay earn less than women on time rates, whereas men on incentive pay earn substantially more than men on time rates.

This discussion also helps to explain why in the first regression of table 9.6 the dummy variable for females has a large negative coefficient. In part, this may represent differences in output between male and female workers doing the same kind of work and paid on an incentive basis.

ESTABLISHMENT SIZE

For all punch press operators and for females the logarithm of establishment size raises the corrected standard error of the regres-

3 In the one establishment that paid both time and incentive rates, the dummy variable for incentive pay distinguished between individuals, but was used only in the regressions that included establishment variables.

4 Our data refer to a period before the passage of the Civil Rights Act of 1964, which prohibits discrimination in employment by sex. The Equal Pay Act of 1963 was also not yet in effect.

5 Of the eight establishments employing women as punch press operators, six also employed men in the same occupation. In some of these, the men worked on a different kind of machine.

sion and has not been included. However, for males this size variable has a positive coefficient and a t value of almost four.

In the sample of males, establishment size has a positive correlation with a number of other variables with positive coefficients, including seniority, incentive pay, and the South region. The last of these is especially large. Since the South region dummy does not enter the regression for males, the size variable undoubtedly is also picking up much of any regional difference in wages between the South and base regions.

For females, the size variable has a negative correlation with the South region. It has a strong positive correlation with incentive pay, but for females incentive pay has a negative sign. As a result, the correlation between size and earnings is negative (the simple correlations between earnings and the natural logarithm of size are .38 for males —.37 for females, and .18 for both sexes combined).

The positive relationship between size and incentive pay is of some interest in its own right. It could be interpreted as indicating that incentive pay is a substitute for closeness of supervision, or as indicating that it does not pay to have an industrial engineering staff in a small establishment.

The regressions for punch press operators, like those for material handlers, "explain" more than three-fifths of the variance in earnings when establishment variables are included. The R^2 for female punch press operators in table 9.6 is the highest for any regression presented in this study.

TRUCK DRIVERS

The regressions results for truck drivers are by far the least successful of those for any of our twelve occupations, and are presented largely for completeness. The low R^2 of the two regressions shown in table 9.8 is probably related to the small size of the sample and to the small standard deviation of wages per hour at work (18.5 cents). This is by far the smallest for any of the twelve occupations; the next smallest is 28.1 cents for typists, the lowest wage occupation. The coefficient of variation (the standard deviation divided by the mean) is also smallest for truck drivers (5.8 percent). The next smallest is for tool and die makers (8.2 percent), the highest wage occupation.

The small dispersion of truck driver's wages in turn results from the way in which we defined the occupation and from the nature of collective bargaining for truck drivers. We excluded from the sample over-the-road truck drivers, since they are paid on a mileage basis and have substantial control over their hours. We therefore

TABLE 9.8

Regression Results for Truck Drivers

	Individual Variables Only	Including Establishment Variables
Seniority[a]	0.046	0.064
	(2.92)	(3.98)
Single at hire (D)	−0.058	————
	(1.51)	
Distance to work (blocks)[a]	0.022	0.018
	(1.38)	(1.20)
Nondurables or	————	0.210
nonmanufacturing (D)		(5.77)
North and West region (D)	————	−0.150
		(4.64)
R^2	.065	.228
Constant term	3.019	2.934
Number of establishments	19	————
Number of individuals	166	————
Dependent variable:		
mean	3.191	————
standard deviation	0.185	————

NOTE: (D) Dummy variable
[a]Natural logarithm

have no record of the earnings per hour. We also exclude driver-salesmen, such as milk-truck drivers, whose earnings are based in whole or part on sales commissions, and drivers of trucks of under three tons. The restrictions on size of firm (fifty employees minimum) kept out employees of small moving and express companies. We are left largely with what might be called local cartage drivers. Almost all such drivers in the Chicago area are represented by one of two teamster's locals, one affiliated with the International Brotherhood of Teamsters and the other independent, and these locals make association-wide wage agreements with associations of employers. Too few of the truck drivers in our sample were represented by other unions or by no union to permit the use of unionization as a variable in the analysis.

THE INDIVIDUAL VARIABLES

Seniority is the only individual variable to have a t value above two, and the individual variables as a group explain only 7 percent of the variance in truck driver wages. The value of seniority as shown in table 9.9, is estimated to be lower for truck drivers than for the occupations considered previously.

TABLE 9.9

Estimates of the Value of Seniority for Truck Drivers

	Individual Variables Only	Including Establishment Variables
Value of		
One year	$0.032	$0.044
Five years	0.083	0.114
Ten years	0.110	0.152
One more year at five	0.007	0.010
One more year at ten	0.004	0.006

NOTE: Mean seniority 9.6 years

Age is omitted because both age and age squared had the wrong signs—that is, the estimated age-earnings function is U-shaped. No measure of education or experience that we tried improved the results.

The dummy variable for men who were single at hire has the expected negative sign and a coefficient of five cents per hour, though the t value is well below two. The logarithmic distance function improves both regressions of table 9.8. In the first regression it has a coefficient very close to that for all fork lift truckers.

THE ESTABLISHMENT VARIABLES

Only three establishments in the truck driver sample were outside manufacturing. These have been combined with the six establishments in nondurable goods into a dummy variable with durable goods as its reference base. This has a positive coefficient of twenty-one cents and a t value above five.

The establishments in the central business district and Near North Side, our usual base region, had only nine employees in this occupation; the South region has therefore been added to the base. Against this base, the North and West region has a negative coefficient of fifteen cents an hour.

There is a strong negative correlation between establishment size and the dummy variable for nonmanufacturing and non-durables, which prevents both from being used in the same regression.

The regression including establishment variables explains 23 percent of the variance in truck driver earnings. Much of the rest could probably have been accounted for by data, which we did not collect, on the size and nature of the trucks driven.

10
The Skilled Occupations

WORKERS IN the two occupations considered in this chapter are all male, and almost exclusively white. Some of them are represented by craft unions, and a considerable number served an apprenticeship or had formal occupational training outside of secondary school.

MAINTENANCE ELECTRICIANS

Maintenance electricians were found in thirty-one establishments in our sample in a wide range of industries. The regression results are shown in table 10.1. Individual variables explain just over a fourth of the variance in wages; all the variables used explain just over two-fifths.

AGE AND SENIORITY

The mean age of maintenance electricians, 42.3 years, is higher than that in any of the semiskilled occupations. The statistics summarizing their age-earnings function are given in the first column of table 10.2. The age of peak earnings is second only to accountants when the regression contains no establishment variables. When establishment variables are added, the peak occurs at age fifty-one, the highest for any of the twelve occupations in the study. One reason for this high peak age is that there is little opportunity for promotion beyond maintenance electrician.

The seniority variable has a t value above six in both regressions of table 10.1. Column 1 of table 10.3 translates the value of seniority into arithmetic units for selected lengths of service.

SCHOOLING AND EXPERIENCE

In both the skilled occupations, measures of schooling and training make a strong showing. Three general kinds of measures were used: the length of formal schooling in years, the presence or absence at hire of previous experience in the occupation, and the presence or absence of formal apprenticeship or other formal occupational training, including courses in private trade schools.

TABLE 10.1
Regression Results for Maintenance Electricians

	Individual Variables Only	Including Establishment Variables
Age	0.031	0.032
Age squared	−0.00032	−0.00031
Seniority[a]	0.216	0.230
	(6.22)	(6.86)
Schooling (years)	0.055	0.040
	(4.46)	(3.45)
Experience and training (D)	0.204	0.185
	(3.30)	(3.20)
Distance to work (blocks)[a]	0.082	0.053
	(3.46)	(2.42)
Nondurable maniufacturing, trade, or service (D)	———	0.283 (3.82)
Transportation or utilities (D)	———	−0.153
		(1.93)
North and West region (D)	———	0.246
		(4.64)
Calumet region (D)	———	0.359
		(5.37)
Union (D)	———	0.260
		(4.01)
Establishment size[a]	———	0.072
		(2.89)
R^2	.276	.425
Constant term	1.456	1.068
Number of establishments	31	———
Number of individuals	275	———
Dependent variable:		
mean	3.639	———
standard deviation	0.433	———

NOTE: (D) Dummy variable
[a]Natural logarithm

The mean number of years of schooling for the electricians in the sample was 11.4, with a standard deviation of 2.0 years. In the regression including only individual variables each additional year of schooling is associated with 5.5 cents an hour of additional earnings, so that the difference between an electrician with two years less schooling than the average and one with two years more would be 22 cents an hour. The coefficient is reduced somewhat by the addition of establishment variables, but its *t* value remains above three.

This suggests that schooling is related to wage differences within establishments as well as between them.

Forty-five percent of the electricians in the sample had known previous experience in the occupation at the time of hire, 40 percent had formal training or apprenticeship, and 21 percent had both.

TABLE 10.2
Statistics Relating to the Age-Earnings Functions for Skilled Occupations

	Maintenance Electrician	Tool and Die Maker	
		Excluding Tool and Die Shops	Including Tool and Die Shops
Mean age	42.3	45.9	45.3
Results of Regressions Using Individual Variables Only			
t value at age			
25	1.97	1.38	1.94
35	2.18	0.73	1.54
50	−0.24	−2.86	−1.68
Value of one more year at			
25	$ 0.015	$ 0.009	$ 0.012
35	0.008	0.002	0.005
50	−0.001	−0.007	−0.005
Age of peak earnings	48.7	39.4	43.6
Results of Regressions Including Establishment Variables			
t value at age			
25	0.96	1.46	4.42
35	2.46	1.19	4.26
50	0.19	−1.30	−1.09
Value of one more year at			
25	$ 0.016	$ 0.007	$ 0.019
35	0.010	0.003	0.010
50	0.0003	−0.002	−0.002
Age of peak earnings	51.0	43.9	47.8

Neither experience alone nor training alone had an effect on earnings significantly different from that of having neither, but the combination of experience and training raises hourly earnings by twenty cents. The coefficient is reduced only slightly by the addition of establishment variables, suggesting that most of the effect of this variable is felt within establishments. Both experience and training are negatively associated with seniority, and in the case of experience the association is very strong. This may help to explain why these variables do not have the expected positive effect when entered separately.

TABLE 10.3
Estimates of the Value of Seniority for Skilled Occupations

	Maintenance Electrician	Tool and Die Maker	
		Excluding Tool and Die Shops	Including Tool and Die Shops
Mean seniority (years)	12.8	13.8	13.2
Results of Regressions Using Individual Variables Only			
Value of			
One year	$0.150	$0.137	$0.119
Five years	0.387	0.353	0.309
Ten years	0.518	0.473	0.413
One more year at five	0.033	0.030	0.027
One more year at ten	0.019	0.017	0.015
Results of Regressions Including Establishment Variables			
Value of			
One year	$0.159	$0.089	$0.083
Five years	0.412	0.231	0.214
Ten years	0.552	0.309	0.287
One more year at five	0.035	0.020	0.018
One more year at ten	0.020	0.011	0.010

DISTANCE AND REGION

The logarithmic form of the distance to work variable performs well for this occupation even after establishment variables, including region, are added to the regression. The coefficient is the largest for any occupation in which a continuous distance variable was used. The estimated value of traveling ten miles to work compared to that of no travel (one block) is thirty-six cents per hour at work, or $2.88 per eight-hour day. When establishment variables are included in the regression, the estimated value of traveling ten miles is twenty-three cents per hour at work.

The regional dummies used in this occupation differ slightly from those used in other occupations because there were substantial systematic differences in wages within the South region. The Illinois portion of the South region has been combined with the base region (the Near North Side) to form an enlarged base. A separate dummy, called Calumet region, identifies the Indiana portion of the South region.[1] This area contains a particularly high concentration of heavy industry, especially basic steel. The coefficient is a positive thirty-six cents with a t value above five. The dummy for the North and West region has a positive coefficient of twenty-five cents.

INDUSTRY AND UNION

Maintenance electricians are employed in a wide variety of industries. The base industry for the industry dummies is durable goods manufacturing.

Two industry sectors, nondurable goods manufacturing and trade and service, have higher wages than the base and have been combined in a single dummy variable with a positive coefficient of twenty-eight cents an hour. The dummy for the remaining sector, transportation and public utilities, has a negative coefficient of fifteen cents, with a t value of not quite two. The negative sign occurs because one of the large establishments in this sector is a railroad, where wages of electricians were conspicuously low. This situation, which results from some peculiarities of collective bargaining for railroad shopcrafts, received much attention in the shopcrafts wage dispute of 1967.[2]

A few of the maintenance electricians in our sample were represented by craft locals of the International Brotherhood of Electrical Workers. Others were represented by industrial locals of the same union, which represented the production workers in the same establishments. The craft locals included too few workers to be represented by a separate dummy variable, and the IBEW as a whole, including industrial locals, did not have an impact on wages ap-

1. The term Calumet area is commonly applied to this region, and is taken from the name of the river that flows through it.

2. The Emergency Board that considered this dispute made the following statement: "For thirty years unions have insisted on uniform cents per hour increases for all shopcraft employees. The result has been to compress severely the wage differentials between skilled and unskilled shopcraft employees and to widen the wage disparity between skilled workers in railroad shops and skilled workers in other industries." Report of the Emergency Board created under Executive Order 11324, 28 January 1967 as given in Bureau of National Affairs *Daily Labor Report* 10 March 1967, section F-1.

The mean earnings per hour at work in our railroad establishment were from $2.87 to $2.99. The earnings predicted for the same individuals by the regression shown in column 1 of table 10.1 were from $3.06 to $3.92. The mean negative residual for this establishment alone is much larger than the coefficient of the industry dummy in the regression of column 2, since the other large establishment in the industry (an electric utility plant) had top wages of $4.41 per hour at work and predominantly positive residuals.

preciably different from that of other unions. We have therefore used a single dummy variable for all unionized establishments, which included 81 percent of the workers in the sample. The coefficient of the union dummy is a positive twenty-six cents an hour with a t value of four.

ESTABLISHMENT SIZE

The establishment size variable, which contributed little to our results for the semiskilled occupations, is helpful in both the skilled occupations. The coefficient of the logarithmic size variable implies a difference in earnings of 16.6 cents per hour at work between an establishment of one hundred employees and one of one thousand employees.

TOOL AND DIE MAKERS

Tool and die makers are employed largely in metalworking industries, and particularly in SIC industry 3544, "special dies, tools, jigs and fixtures." The establishments in this industry, which we shall call tool and die shops, do job or custom work for other industries, and demand unusual versatility from their tool and die makers. One such establishment was drawn in our random sample. In addition, we took a supplementary nonrandom sample of three tool and die shops. It soon became apparent that wages in these shops were higher than those in other industries (the mean wages per hour at work of tool and die makers were $4.44 in tool and die shops and $3.99 elsewhere). We therefore did the regression analysis both including and excluding the tool and die shops, and did not make any distinction between the shop that was drawn in the random sample and the three in the supplementary sample. The relationship between the two samples is very similar to that between the two samples of accountants including and excluding public accounting firms.

Table 10.4 presents the regression results for both samples of tool and die makers. Individual variables explain about 30 percent of the variance in the sample excluding tool and die shops, and only 21 percent in the larger sample. When establishment variables are added, the R^2 for both samples is above .6.

AGE AND SENIORITY

Tool and die makers had a slightly higher average age than maintenance electricians—45.9 years excluding those in tool and die shops and 45.3 years including them. The second and third columns of table 10.2 give statistics relating to the age-earnings functions for the two samples.

141

The age of peak earnings is lower than that for maintenance electricians in both samples. The addition of establishment variables raises the age of peak earnings and in column 3 greatly improves the *t* values of the upward sloping portion of the age-earnings function. This is because the high wage tool and die shops, whose workers are slightly younger than those elsewhere (43.1 years compared with 45.9), are identified by a dummy in this regression.

The value of seniority in arithmetic units is shown in columns 2 and 3 of table 10.3. The coefficients of seniority are slightly smaller for tool and die makers than those for maintenance electricians, but most of the *t* values are higher.

SCHOOLING AND EXPERIENCE

The mean number of years of schooling in the sample excluding the tool and die shops was 11.4, with a standard deviation of 1.8; when tool and die shops are included the mean is 11.5 and the standard deviation is 1.6. The mean for the first sample is the same as that for maintenance electricians, although the dispersion is somewhat smaller.

The linear schooling variable works reasonably well in both samples, though both the coefficients and the *t* values are lower than for maintenance electricians. As with electricians, the schooling variable continues to work after the addition of establishment variables. Indeed, in the sample excluding tool and die shops the addition of establishment variables strengthens the showing of schooling.

The analysis of other training and of experience in this occupation proved to be rather difficult. In the tool and die shops 51 percent of the tool and die makers had served a formal apprenticeship or had occupational training outside secondary school; in the sample excluding tool and die shops, the corresponding figure is 39 percent. On the other hand, because most of the tool and die shops conduct their own apprenticeship programs, experience with other employers is less common. About a third of the tool and die makers in these shops (34 percent) had experience in the occupation with other employers, while this was true of exactly half the tool and die makers in other establishments.

In the sample excluding tool and die shops, formal training and experience seemed about equally valuable. The presence of either (or both) raised earnings about sixteen cents an hour relative to workers who had neither. Adding establishment characteristics lowers the coefficient slightly, but hardly affects the *t* value.

When the sample including tool and die shops is analyzed without establishment characteristics, a dummy for the presence of formal training serves in part to identify the tool and die shops, and is the training or experience variable that gives the best statistical results. Once the tool and die shops have been identified by an industry dummy, experience with another employer again contributes to the regression. So, too, does training without experience, though its t value is only 1.2 and the coefficient is about half as large as that of experience.[3] The smaller value of experience and training in the larger sample of establishments suggests that some workers move from the tool and die shops to other employers, who reward their special experience with wages above the average for the establishment. Evidence of this kind of movement was also obtained in some of our worker interviews. Young workers often prefer the job shops because of the higher wages and more frequent overtime, but may transfer to general industry later in search of greater job security.

MARITAL STATUS

In one of the four regressions of table 10.4, that including tool and die shops but without establishment variables, the fit is improved by including a dummy variable for men who were single at hire, which has the expected negative sign. This variable is negatively correlated with age, and since workers in tool and die shops are somewhat younger than those in other establishments it may in part be serving as a substitute for the tool and die shop dummy. When establishment variables are added, marital status is no longer helpful.

DISTANCE AND REGION

The logarithmic form of the distance variable works well in both of the regressions including only individual variables. The addition of establishment variables lowers the coefficient in the sample excluding tool and die shops and eliminates the contribution of the variable entirely in the larger sample. The estimated increase in earnings associated with traveling ten miles to work (as compared with one block) is seventeen cents per hour at work excluding tool and die shops and twenty-six cents including them, as estimated from the regressions without establishment variables. Per eight-hour day, the corresponding increases in earnings would be $1.36 and $2.08.

Only one region, South, was used in the analysis of both samples, with the North and West forming part of the reference base. The South region has almost identical positive coefficients of 31.2 and 31.4 cents in the two samples.

3. The dummy variables have been defined in such a way that no individual can be identified by both. The reference base is workers with neither known formal training nor known experience.

TABLE 10.4

Regression Results for Tool and Die Makers

	Excluding Tool and Die Shops		Including Tool and Die Shops	
	Individual Variables Only	Including Establishment Variables	Individual Variables Only	Including Establishment Variables
Age	0.024	0.017	0.029	0.040
Age squared	−0.00031	−0.00019	−0.00033	−0.00042
Seniority[a]	0.197	0.129	0.172	0.120
	(10.09)	(8.12)	(8.15)	(6.74)
Schooling (years)	0.018	0.020	0.029	0.018
	(1.80)	(2.63)	(2.49)	(2.29)
Training or	0.157	0.120		
experience (D)	(3.93)	(3.91)		
Training (D)	------	------	0.080	------
			(2.17)	
Training without	------	------	------	0.042
experience (D)				(1.20)
Experience (D)	------	------	------	0.087
				(2.54)
Single at hire (D)	------	------	−0.072	------
			(1.72)	
Distance to work	0.039	0.017	0.060	------
(blocks)[a]	(2.18)	(1.22)	(2.96)	
Tool and	------	------	------	0.772
die shop (D)				(12.72)
Other heavy	------	0.134	------	0.132
durables (D)		(3.12)		(3.01)
South region (D)	------	0.312	------	0.314
		(6.34)		(6.57)
Union–IAM (D)	------	0.142	------	0.140
		(3.26)		(3.98)
Union–other (D)	------	−0.201	------	−0.216
		(4.21)		(4.65)
Establishment	------	0.089	------	0.091
size[a]		(5.57)		(5.31)
R^2	.299	.607	.212	.645
Constant term	2.633	2.594	2.518	2.167
Number of				
establishments	17	------	21	------
Number of				
individuals	278	------	354	------
Dependent variable:				
mean	3.986	------	4.083	------
standard				
deviation	0.328	------	0.376	------

NOTE: (D) Dummy variable
[a]Natural logarithm

Heavy durable goods (primary metals, fabricated metals, and machinery) other than tool and die shops are identified by a dummy variable whose base is all other industries except tool and die shops. The bulk of the base is made up of electrical equipment and instruments and related products. The dummy has a positive coefficient of thirteen cents in both regressions including establishment variables. In the sample including tool and die shops, the dummy variable identifying these shops has a positive coefficient of seventy-seven cents with a t value of almost thirteen.

In the sample excluding tool and die shops, 26 percent of the workers are represented by the International Association of Machinists, 41 percent by other unions, and 33 percent by no union. Including the tool and die shops, the IAM represents 32 percent of the workers, other unions also represent 32 percent, and 36 percent have no union. Outside the tool and die shops, the IAM is often a separate craft unit representing only the toolroom workers.

In both regressions including establishment variables, the base group for the unionism variables is no union. Separate dummies are used for the IAM and for other unions. In both cases, the IAM dummy has a positive coefficient of fourteen cents and a t value above three. The dummy variable for other unions has a negative coefficient of twenty to twenty-two cents and a t value above four.

This suggests that industrial unions that include minority groups of tool and die makers have tended to compress skill differentials in their collective bargaining agreements.[4] Alternatively, it suggests that the nonunion firms have been more afraid of having the IAM organize their toolrooms than of having an industrial union organize the entire blue-collar work force. Of course, these explanations are compatible and may both be at work.

In addition, the establishments organized by industrial unions are larger than the average and are concentrated in the industry group "other heavy durable goods." The workers organized by industrial unions are less likely than those in either the IAM shops or the nonunion shops to have served a formal apprenticeship. This kind of intercorrelation among independent variables casts doubt on the reliability of the coefficient of "other unions."

ESTABLISHMENT SIZE

The establishment size variable contributes substantially to both of the regressions containing establishment variables, with t values

4. Evidence from employer interviews supporting this view was presented in chapter 4.

above five. The estimated difference in earnings per hour at work between an establishment with one hundred employees and one with one thousand is twenty-one cents in both samples of establishments.

11
Summary of Findings
for Individual Variables

IN THE PRECEDING four chapters we have tried to present the best model of the determinants of wage dispersion for each of our twelve study occupations, and in many cases for subsamples of these occupations. In doing this we have not used the same variables, or the same form of a given variable, for every occupation. This has undoubtedly made it difficult for readers with an interest in a particular variable, such as education or color, to form any overall impression of how that variable was performing across the twelve occupations as a whole.

In this chapter and the following one, we focus on the principal independent variables and compare them across occupations. In order to reduce the duplication involved, we observe the following ground rules: (a) In this chapter, we consider the performance of individual variables when establishment variables are not present, and we say no more about the ways in which they are affected by the addition of establishment variables to the regressions. (b) In both this chapter and the following one, we present results for the occupations as a whole, and do not, in general, review results for subsamples of occupations by sex or color or for samples in which the randomly chosen establishments have been supplemented by adding others. The exception to this rule is the marital status variable, which in occupations including both sexes was never used on the occupation as a whole. (c) Where useful, we add to the results of our best models results from other models not previously presented that include the variable in question. (d) We omit independent variables relevant to fewer than three occupations. In all the tables of chapters 11 and 12 that present regression coefficients, the source of an observation is a regression model previously presented for the occupation as a whole, unless another source is indicated in a footnote. An additional summary of the contribution of variables to wages as estimated from the "best" regression equations is given in an appendix to chapter 12. It supplements this chapter as well in that a comparison of the importance of individual variables in the presence of establishment variables is included.

AGE

The quadratic age-earnings function was used in the best models for nine of the twelve occupations, as shown in table 11.1. In one additional occupation, janitress, this form produces the expected signs of the coefficients, but does not contribute to the fit of the regression. In the two remaining occupations, truck driver and punch press operator, the signs were the opposite of those expected. However, the use of dummy variables in an attempt to achieve a better form of the age-earnings relation in these occupations was also unsuccessful.

The choice of the quadratic form for age was based on successful uses of this form to approximate the age-earnings profile in a num-

TABLE 11.1

Comparative Statistics on Age-Earnings Functions

Occupation	Coefficient of		Age of Peak Earnings (Years)	Value of One Year Older at Age 25 (Percentage of Mean Wage)	t Value at Age 25
	Age[a]	Age Squared[a]			
Typist	0.020	−0.00026	38.0	0.3	3.33
Keypunch operator	0.016	−0.00021	38.0	0.2	2.43
Accountant	0.108	−0.0011	49.7	1.3	4.44
Tab operator	0.086	−0.0011	38.6	1.1	5.45
Material handler	0.018	−0.00029	30.7	0.1	1.08
Janitor	0.0054	−0.0013	21.1	[b]	−0.31
Janitress[c]	0.0084	−0.000068	[d]	[d]	[d]
Fork lift trucker	0.037	−0.00041	44.2	0.6	2.91
Punch press operator	[e]	[e]	[e]	[e]	[e]
Truck driver	[e]	[e]	[e]	[e]	[e]
Maintenance electrician	0.031	−0.00032	48.7	0.4	1.97
Tool and die maker	0.024	−0.00031	39.4	0.2	1.38

[a]Dependent variable is dollars per hour at work.
[b]Negative, absolute value less than 0.05.
[c]Coefficients shown are those of age variables added to janitress regression of table 8.7.
[d]Values not shown where age variables did not contribute to the regression.
[e]Values not shown where age variables did not have the expected signs.

ber of earlier studies,[1] and on the general shape of age-earnings profiles derived from census data on which no fixed functional form had been imposed.[2] We never had any reason to abandon this original choice.

Our models differ from the earlier uses of quadratic age-earnings functions in that we also include a separate variable for seniority (the natural logarithm of years of continuous service with the present employer in any occupation). It will be recalled from the discussion in chapter 7 that age and seniority are positively correlated, and that we are able to distinguish between them through the use of different functional forms. This distinction rests on the fact that some older workers have low seniority, and these workers in particular bear the wage disadvantages associated with age. These disadvantages arise on two accounts. First, particularly in the manual occupations, they are undoubtedly related to declining physical vigor. Second, in those occupations that constitute the lower rungs of a promotional ladder, remaining in the occupation to an advanced age is an index of low quality as perceived by the employer, certainly in terms of criteria for promotion and perhaps in terms of performance on the present job.

Table 11.2 presents the simple correlation coefficients between age in years and the natural logarithm of seniority. There is a substantial range of values of this statistic, from .31 for tool and die makers to .70 for accountants. This would seem to be an inverse measure of mobility among employers in the older age groups. Of particular interest for the interpretation of the age variable is that the three occupations in which the age variable performs poorly are not those with the highest correlations between age and seniority. They rank fourth, sixth, and eleventh among the twelve occupations in order of these correlation coefficients. This suggests that these really are occupations in which age is of less relevance to earnings than in the others. For punch press operators this may be because of the importance of incentive pay, and for truck drivers because of the importance of the union wage scale.

Table 11.3 presents some data on earnings by age for the United States for 1959 for the occupations most closely related to those in this study. These age-earnings profiles differ from our own age-

1. See, for example, Leonard W. Weiss, "Concentration and Labor Earnings," *American Economic Review* 56 (March 1966): 106, and George J. Stigler, *The Theory of Price*, 3d ed. (New York: The Macmillan Co., 1966), pp. 295–96.

2. See, for example, Gary S. Becker, *Human Capital* (New York: National Bureau of Economic Research, 1964), pp. 138–44; Giora Hanoch, "Personal Earnings and Investment in Schooling," *Journal of Human Resources* 2 (Summer 1967); and Herman P. Miller, *Income Distribution in the United States* (Washington: Government Printing Office, 1966), pp. 154–55.

TABLE 11.2

Simple Correlations between Age and the Natural Log of Seniority

Typist	.591
Keypunch operator	.501
Accountant	.696
Tab operator	.678
Material handler	.581
Janitor	.501
Janitress	.433
Fork lift trucker	.608
Punch press operator	.589
Truck driver	.606
Maintenance electrician	.563
Tool and die maker	.306

earnings functions in several respects. First, several of the occupations are much more broadly defined. "Office machine operators" includes operators of a number of machines other than keypunch; "electricians" includes construction electricians; "janitors and por-

TABLE 11.3

Median Earnings of Experienced Labor Force by Age, U.S., Selected Occupations, 1959

Sex and Occupation	Age						
	14–17	18–24	25–34	35–44	45–54	55–64	65 & over
Males							
Accountants and auditors	a	$3661	$5993	$7375	$7615	$7012	$5202
Electricians	a	3295	5886	6302	6216	5922	5299
Toolmakers and diemakers and setters	a	4761	6480	6816	6545	6430	5719
Truck drivers and deliverymen	$579	2513	4434	4853	4580	4167	2565
Janitors and porters	544	1446	2872	3328	3229	3138	1874
Laborers, n.e.c.	582	1878	3509	3716	3561	3412	2144
Females							
Office machine operators	876	2672	3383	3567	3660	3664	3439
Typists	719	2331	3111	3110	3257	3326	3036
Charwomen	527	750	1075	1311	1495	1574	1145

SOURCE: Census of Population, 1960 Subject Reports, Occupational Characteristics, table 31
aMedian not shown in source where base is less than 1,000

ters" includes apartment janitors; "truck drivers and deliverymen" includes over-the-road drivers and driver salesmen, and "laborers, n.e.c." is a much broader category than material handlers. Second, the data refer to annual—not hourly—earnings and include part-time and part-year workers. This is undoubtedly a major reason for the low earnings in the age group fourteen to seventeen years. Among the other differences are that the earnings recorded in the census data need not have been earned in the person's current occupation as of the census week.

In part because of these differences the peak of the age-earnings functions in our study falls in the decade of peak earnings in the census data in only two of the seven occupations for which comparisons can be made between tables 11.1 and 11.3. These two are accountant and tool and die maker. In one occupation, electrician, the peak of our function comes at an age above the peak decade of the census earnings. This may reflect a decline of overtime hours with age, especially for construction electricians and self-employed maintenance electricians; such a decline would affect annual earnings more than hourly earnings. For the remaining four occupations, the census earnings peak at a substantially higher age than our functions do. In the male occupations, janitor and material handler, this is most likely to be the result of our separate control for seniority. In the female occupations there is the additional reason that younger women, many of whom have responsibilities for children, are more likely to be part-time or part-year workers, which lowers annual earnings more than hourly earnings. It should be noted that in all three of the female census occupations, the peak annual earnings are in the age class fifty-five to sixty-four.

All five of the blue-collar male occupations in the census data have their peak earnings in the age class thirty-five to forty-four. Accountant and auditor, the occupation with the highest earnings, has its peak earnings in the age class forty-five to fifty-four.

The data in table 11.1 show a much stronger tendency among the male occupations for high mean earnings to be associated with a high age of peak earnings. The only large difference in ranks is for tool and die makers, who rank first in hourly earnings in our sample and fourth in age of peak earnings. The Spearman coefficient of rank correlation between mean earnings and age of peak for the male occupations with entries in column 3 of table 11.1 is .71, which is significant at the 10 percent level on a two-tail test for seven observations. There are weaker positive associations between mean earnings and the entries in the last two columns of the table on the relative size of the net coefficient and the significance of the function, both at age twenty-five.

The finding that age is more strongly associated with earnings in the high wage occupations is hardly a surprising one. In general, the high wage occupations place a higher premium on experience and wisdom and a lower value on physical vigor than low wage occupations do, and we have not included any occupations, such as mathematician, in which mental abilities reach their peak at an early age.

SENIORITY

It will come as no surprise to readers of the four preceding chapters to learn that seniority is the only variable included in the regressions for all twelve occupations in the same form, and that in most of them it has the highest t value of all the independent variables. Column 1 of table 11.4 compares the coefficients of the natural logarithm of seniority across these occupations. The t value is above ten in six of the twelve occupations, and above four in all but two of them.

Table 11.4 also addresses itself to a question first raised in chapter 7. It will be recalled that our dependent variable is wages per hour at work, and that this is above the stated wage per payroll hour because it attaches an explicit value to paid vacations and holidays. Since most establishments base the length of paid vacations on seniority, our choice of dependent variables builds in some correlation between seniority and wages that would not be present for the stated wage per payroll hour.

To obtain the last two columns of table 11.4, the final regression models including only individual variables have been rerun using wages per payroll hour as the dependent variable, and the coefficients of seniority and the R^2 statistics have been presented here. In every case, the coefficient and t value of seniority and the R^2 are lower when the dependent variable is wage per payroll hour. However, in only one case (truck drivers) does the t value fall below two—in this occupation vacation pay seems to be the only element of compensation related to seniority. In all other cases the reduction in the coefficient of seniority is rather small—of the order of one-sixth to one-third of the original value—and it is smaller the higher the original value. The change in the R^2 statistic is proportionately smaller, ranging from about one-fifth of the original value where this was lowest to less than 2 percent of the original value.

Comparison of tables 11.2 and 11.4 supports a hypothesis that has been suggested earlier: that the seniority variable performs least successfully where it is most highly correlated with age. The Spearman coefficient of rank correlation between the entries in table 11.2 and the t values in the first column of table 11.4 is $-.51$, which with twelve observations is significant at the 10 percent level on a two-tail test. The three occupations with the lowest t values for the seniority variable are among the four with the highest simple correlations between age and seniority.

TABLE 11.4
Coefficients for Seniority Variable (Natural Logarithms) with Alternative Dependent Variables

	Dependent Variable Wage per Hour at Work		Dependent Variable Wage per Payroll Hour	
	Coefficient of Seniority	R^2	Coefficient of Seniority	R^2
Typist	0.164 (11.52)	.333	0.132 (9.84)	.274
Keypunch operator	0.230 (14.00)	.492	0.198 (12.61)	.444
Accountant	0.259 (4.21)	.404	0.190 (3.38)	.384
Tab operator	0.342 (8.07)	.586	0.296 (7.55)	.577
Material handler	0.214 (11.79)	.348	0.172 (10.08)	.311
Janitor	0.206 (12.34)	.317	0.162 (10.62)	.273
Janitress	0.234 (9.54)	.362	0.190 (8.33)	.306
Fork lift trucker	0.114 (3.71)	.127	0.074 (2.57)	.100
Punch press operator	0.306 (15.24)	.455	0.245 (13.67)	.411
Truck driver	0.046 (2.92)	.065	0.0057 (0.40)	.040
Maintenance electrician	0.216 (6.22)	.276	0.137 (4.24)	.212
Tool and die maker	0.197 (10.09)	.299	0.127 (7.23)	.199

We should also remind the reader at this point of the major issue in the interpretation of the seniority variable. Our inclination is to regard it in large part as a measure of experience on the job or, to use Gary Becker's terminology, of training specific to the employer. The success of the logarithmic form of the variable can be viewed as supporting this interpretation. In arithmetic units the value of seniority increases at a decreasing rate, giving a curve that looks like the learning curves for individuals or groups that are shown in the standard textbooks of industrial psychology. The alternative explanation is that wage increases based on seniority are institutionally determined for such purposes as maintaining morale, and have no relation to individual productivity. The success of the logarithmic form is not necessarily inconsistent with this interpretation. For example, the morale-building function of periodic wage increases could be most important for short-service employees, who are the most likely to quit. Or in each establishment, the rates could advance linearly with seniority until the ceiling of a range was reached, and when these kinked functions were aggregated across establishments, the kinks would occur at different levels and the aggregate might be well approximated by the logarithmic form.[3]

One might expect some further help in the interpretation of the seniority variable to be derived from examining the value of seniority as a percentage of the mean earnings in the occupation. Such a comparison across occupations is shown in table 11.5, based on the estimated value of five years of seniority in each occupation. The range of values is quite large—from 22 percent of the mean earnings to 3 percent. Unfortunately, no clear pattern emerges, since the extreme values at both ends are for quite dissimilar occupations.

EXPERIENCE

The experience variable is closely related to seniority, and to some extent is a substitute for it. Seniority measures experience with the

TABLE 11.5
Estimated Value of Five Years Seniority as Percentage of Mean Earnings (Dollars per Hour at Work)

Typist	14.6
Keypunch operator	18.7
Accountant	11.8
Tab operator	22.5
Material handler	15.9
Janitor	15.4
Janitress	20.8
Fork lift trucker	7.6
Punch press operator	21.2
Truck driver	2.6
Maintenance electrician	10.6
Tool and die maker	8.9

3. We are indebted to William G. Bowen for suggesting the first of these two possibilities, and to Professors Peter Doeringer of Harvard University and Myron Joseph of Carnegie-Mellon University for independently suggesting the second, which we find ingenious though not fully persuasive.

present employer, whereas the experience variable measures experience with previous civilian employers.

In our early work with this variable, we used measures of the length of previous experience, especially for the most skilled occupations. Such variables, which took considerable effort to construct, proved consistently to be somewhat less successful than dummy variables that measure simply the presence or absence of known previous experience.[4]

We use the term "known experience" because in some cases workers may have had experience that was not recorded in their personnel records. Such experience may or may not have been known to the employer at the time of hire. It should also be mentioned that our experience variables measure the effect of experience on wages not at the time of hire, but at a time that is on average later by the mean seniority of the workers in the occupation. This interval can be expected to attenuate the effects of experience with previous employers, since during the interval the present employer accumulates direct evidence on the employee's performance.

Table 11.6 compares the coefficients of the dummy variables for experience across occupations. Some form of experience variable has a *t* value above two in seven of the twelve occupations, and is included in the final model for two more because it improves the fit of the regression and has the expected sign. Three different dummies are used: (*a*) *occupational experience*, which is experience with a previous employer in the present occupation (not necessarily the occupation in which the worker was first hired by the present employer); (*b*) *general experience*, which is previous experience in any civilian occupation, and excludes only new entrants to the civilian labor force and those whose prior experience is unrecorded; (*c*) *experience in Chicago*, which is general experience in the Chicago area, and excludes both new entrants to the civilian labor force and experienced migrants.

The first of these forms, occupational experience, is used in six of the eight cases in which an experience variable was successful, and the other two are used in one case each, both in unskilled occupations.

It will be recalled that in the final models for the two skilled manual occupations experience was combined with training in a single variable. However, table 11.6 shows the results of alternate

4. The results of using measures of the length of previous experience can be illustrated by the case of accountants. If the natural logarithm of the number of calendar quarters of occupational experience is substituted for the dummy variable for experience in the regression of column 1, table 7.5, its coefficient is 0.094 and its *t* value is 3.00. The R^2 statistic falls from .404 to .403. Although the continuous variable is inferior, the difference in this case is very small.

models for these occupations in which experience is entered separately, so as to permit comparison with other occupations.

In some occupations we tried a fourth form of dummy variable for experience: experience in some related occupation, such as

TABLE 11.6
Comparison of Coefficients of Dummy Variables for Experience

Occupation	Type of Experience	Coefficient (Dollars per Hour at Work)	t Value	Coefficient as Percentage of Mean Earnings
Typist	Occupational	0.062	2.88	3.1
Keypunch operator	Occupational	0.177	7.37	8.0
Accountant	Occupational	0.301	3.06	7.7
Tab operator	Occupational	0.381	6.34	14.0
Material handler	General	0.144	3.48	6.0
Janitor	In Chicago	0.168	5.54	7.0
Janitress	General	0.067	1.12	3.3
Fork lift trucker	In Chicago[a]	0.023	0.53	b
Punch press operator	Occupational	c	c	c
Truck driver	Occupational	c	c	c
Maintenance electrician	Occupational[d]	0.102	1.78	2.8
Tool and die maker	Occupational[e]	0.156	3.34	3.9

[a]Results using a general experience variable were even poorer than those shown.
[b]Not computed where variable did not contribute to the regression.
[c]Values not shown where variable did not have the expected sign.
[d]From a regression that differs from that of table 10.1, column 1 in that experience was entered separately with no variable for training. The R^2 statistic for this regression was .255. Training without experience was not included because it did not have the expected sign.
[e]From a regression that differs from that of column 1 of table 10.4 in that training and experience without training were entered separately. The R^2 statistic for this regression is the same as for the regression in table 10.4 (.2994) but since this regression contains one more variable, the standard error corrected for degrees of freedom is very slightly higher (0.2782 as compared with 0.2777).

bookkeeper for accountant or machinist for tool and die maker. The related experience could be entered as a separate dummy if there were enough observations, or added to occupational experience to form a broader experience variable. Our results with related experience were never quite successful. When it was entered as a separate variable, it had low *t* values and slightly worsened the fit of the regression.[5] When it was added to occupational experience to form a broader experience variable, the results were again inferior.[6]

As table 11.6 indicates, the value of previous occupational experience as a percentage of the mean wage is in general higher for the white-collar than for the blue-collar occupations. Three of the four coefficients for white-collar occupations are above 7 percent of the mean wage, whereas none of the coefficients of occupational experience for blue-collar occupations is as high as 4 percent of the mean wage. The relative values of the general experience variables for the unskilled occupations in general fall between the ranges of the white-collar and the more skilled blue-collar occupations. The differences for unskilled workers between a general experience variable and an experience in Chicago variable is usually not large.[7]

SCHOOLING

We use the term "schooling" in this study rather than the broader term "education" to describe variables that measure the number of years of formal schooling completed. Our choice is intended to remind the reader that this is only one aspect of education. In particular, we do not have any variables that measure the quality of schooling or the worker's performance in school as measured by grades received, test scores, or recommendations. We did collect data on the location of the school last attended, but in the end no use was made of them.

5. For example, if a dummy variable for related experience as a bookkeeper is added to the regression of column 1, table 7.5, its coefficient is 0.116, but its *t* value is only 0.93, and it raises the corrected standard error of the regression from 0.6267 to 0.6268.

6. For example, in the case of tool and die makers if "occupational and related experience" (where experience as a machinist is considered related) is substituted for occupational experience in the regression for which the experience coefficient is reported in table 11.6, the new coefficient is 0.067 with a *t* value of only 1.37. This regression included a variable for training without any occupational or related experience. The R^2 statistic falls from .299 to .286, with the same number of variables.

7. For material handlers, if separate dummies for experience in Chicago and experience elsewhere are substituted for general experience in the regression in the first column of table 8.1, they both have *t* values above two, but the coefficients differ very little (0.149 for experience in Chicago and 0.123 for experience elsewhere). Combining them reduces the corrected standard error of the regression from 0.3130 to 0.3128.

For janitors, if general experience is substituted for experience in Chicago in the regression of the first column of table 8.5 the coefficient is 0.147 and the *t* value is 3.09. The R^2 falls from .317 to .286 with the same number of variables.

For janitresses, if experience in Chicago is substituted for general experience in the regression of column 1, table 8.7 its coefficient is 0.026 and its *t* value is 0.60. The R^2 statistic falls from .362 to .359 with the same number of variables.

In our early work with the unskilled occupations we constructed a dummy variable called "unfamiliarity" which made use of the location of schooling. It identified those workers who had neither gone to school in Chicago nor had a previous job in Chicago and therefore were presumably recent migrants at the time of hire. This variable performed very well, having the expected negative sign and t values that were sometimes above four. However, even better results were obtained from the pure experience variables, including the dummy for a previous job in Chicago, which groups migrants and new entrants to the labor market in its reference base.

Because of the strong interest in recent years in the economics of education, we report our results with schooling variables, including the unsuccessful ones, in greater detail than usual. It should be clear that regressions run within tightly defined occupations are not relevant to the measurement of the private economic return to schooling, since one of the main avenues by which schooling affects incomes is by opening access to higher income occupations and by altering the tastes and knowledge that guide occupational choice. The returns to education within occupations should therefore be substantially lower than those for all occupations taken together. Our measures are relevant to a related but narrower issue: given that a person is in a particular occupation in a particular labor market, how much are his earnings raised by additional schooling?[8]

Table 11.7 compares the coefficients of both linear and dummy schooling variables across occupations.[9] All of the dummy variables include people with the specified amount of schooling completed *or more*, against a reference base of people with less schooling. The coefficients identified by asterisks are included in the models presented in chapters 7 through 10. The other coefficients, except as noted, are the result of using a different form of the schooling variable in the same regression, or of adding a schooling variable to the model previously presented if none was included.

Table 11.8 gives data on the amount and dispersion of schooling in each occupation and compares the coefficients of linear schooling and of high-school graduate dummies as percentages of the mean earnings in the occupation. These data are of help in interpreting table 11.7.

8. For another study with a similar focus, see Bruce W. Wilkenson, "Present Values of Lifetime Earnings for Different Occupations," *Journal of Political Economy* 74 (December 1966); 556–72. Wilkenson uses 1961 Canadian census data to estimate discounted present values of different amounts of schooling within census occupations.

9. As noted in chapter 5, schooling was originally collected in intervals rather than by single years. The linear variable is formed by assigning midpoints to class intervals of more than one year. This may help to explain why the linear variable frequently does not work as well as a dummy variable.

TABLE 11.7

Comparisons of Coefficients of Schooling Variables

Occupation	Coefficients and t Values of Schooling Variables				
	Linear (Years Completed)	Dummies Attended High School	High-School Graduate	Attended College	College Graduate
Typist	0.012 (1.21)	————	0.014 (0.44)	0.038* (1.41)	————
Keypunch operator	a	————	a	a	
Accountant	0.042 (1.56)	————	————	————	0.282* (3.03)
Tab operator	0.027 (1.52)	————	0.141* (1.98)	————	————
Material handler	0.020* (3.34)	0.062 (1.80)	0.084 (2.76)	————	————
Janitor	0.0077 (1.51)	0.051 (1.75)	0.114* (3.04)	————	————
Janitress	a	a	a	————	————
Fork lift trucker	0.018 (2.07)	0.054 (1.17)	0.119* (2.59)	————	————
Punch press operator	0.0050 (0.69)	0.028 (0.74)	0.0014 (0.029)	————	————
Truck driver	a	a	a	————	————
Maintenance electrician	0.055* (4.46)	0.272 (3.55)	0.201 (3.84)	————	————
Tool and die maker	0.018* (1.80)	0.115b (1.96)	0.018 (0.51)	————	————

*Included in model previously presented.
aNot shown where coefficient is negative.
bAlthough this dummy variable has a higher t value than linear education, it was not used in chapter 10 because the reference base is less than 10 percent of the sample.

Schooling variables entered the final models for eight of the twelve occupations. In three cases the linear form was most successful and in five a dummy variable worked better. In the remaining four cases, the coefficients and t values were close to zero in either form, and in two of these the coefficients were consistently negative. Three of the four occupations where schooling variables did not work are unskilled or semiskilled blue-collar occupations with low mean years of schooling. The fourth, keypunch operator, has a mean of almost twelve years of schooling, but the smallest standard deviation of any of the occupations. There is in general a tendency for higher means to be associated with smaller standard deviations, suggesting that as the educational requirements of an occupation

TABLE 11.8

Comparative Statistics on Schooling

Occupation	Number of Years Completed		Percentage of High-School Graduates	Coefficients as Percentage of Mean Earnings	
	Mean	Standard Deviation		Linear (Years Completed)	Best Dummy Variable
Typist	12.2	1.1	88.0	0.6	1.9
Keypunch operator	11.9	1.0	80.2	a	a
Accountant	14.4	1.8	c	1.1	7.2
Tab operator	12.4	1.3	86.6	1.0	5.2
Material handler	10.3	2.5	36.5	0.8	3.5
Janitor	8.6	2.8	15.4	0.3	4.8
Janitress	8.5	2.6	11.6	a	a
Fork lift trucker	10.1	2.5	30.6	0.7	4.4
Punch press operator	9.4	2.6	20.8	b	b
Truck driver	10.5	2.0	31.3	a	a
Maintenance electrician	11.4	2.0	58.9	1.5	5.5
Tool and die maker	11.4	1.8	60.4	0.5	2.9

aNot shown where sign is negative.
bNot shown where t value is less than one.
cNot computed.

rise, hiring standards for schooling become more strictly defined and observed.

Where one form of the schooling variable worked well, alternate forms often worked reasonably well also. However, the linear form is markedly inferior to the dummy variable for accountant and janitor. The three occupations where the linear form works best are in the central range of percentages of high-school graduates, one-third to two-thirds, so that a high-school graduate dummy would split the group nearly in half. The dummies are in general more successful when they separate a smaller group from the rest.

Our results do not show much of the "completion bonus" or "scalloping" effect often shown in estimates of the rate of return to education. This effect indicates especially high returns to completing a stage of education, such as high school or college, as opposed to starting a stage and dropping out. Four of our eight best forms are dummies for completing such a stage (college for accountant, high school for tab operator, janitor, and fork lift trucker). However, the three linear best forms and the dummy variable for "attended college" in the case of typist do not suggest a completion bonus. Perhaps this is merely because we do not have enough observations in some of the relevant cells.

The relative gain in earnings per year of school completed is shown in the fourth column of table 11.8 for the eight cases in which a linear schooling variable had a coefficient larger than its standard error. These range from 0.3 percent of mean earnings per year of school in the case of janitor to 1.5 percent for maintenance electrician. Where a dummy is the better form, the percentage increase in earnings obtained by applying the relative increase per year of schooling to a range of two standard deviations of years of schooling is smaller than the relative increase shown for the dummy variable. Where the linear form is better, the percentage increase estimated for two standard deviations of years of schooling exceeds the relative increase for the best dummy.

The relative increases in earnings for the best dummy variable run from 1.9 to 7.2 percent, with all but two above 3 percent. These, of course, are not rates of return, among other reasons because no account has been taken of costs. They are simply the amount by which earnings per hour at work within an occupation increase for certain levels of educational attainment, holding constant the other variables that enter the regression. These other variables include a number not usually held constant in rate-of-return estimates.

TRAINING

Our only successful uses of a variable measuring formal training other than in secondary school or college have been reported in chapter 10 for the two skilled manual occupations. In addition, for each of the four white-collar occupations, we tried a dummy variable designating people with formal training outside secondary school or college—that is, in a private commercial or secretarial school or data processing school. The proportion of workers having such training ranged from 5 percent for typists to 25 percent for accountants. In no case did the variable have a *t* value as high as one.

COLOR AND ORIGIN

Table 11.9 shows the coefficients of dummy variables for color and origin in the seven occupations in which we had enough nonwhites or people with Spanish surnames to attempt the use of a separate variable. All of these coefficients have been presented previously except the three unsuccessful ones, and all but one of them have the expected negative sign.

TABLE 11.9

Comparison of Coefficients of Dummy Variables for Color and Origin

Occupation and Variable	Percentage of Workers in Minority Group	Coefficient and t Value	Coefficient as a Percentage of Mean Earnings
Typist, nonwhite	2.7	−0.096 (1.56)	−4.8
Keypunch operator, nonwhite	4.2	−0.010[a] (0.17)	[b]
Material handler, nonwhite	24.2	−0.308 (9.68)	−12.8
Material handler, Spanish surname	3.6	−0.152 (2.10)	−6.3
Janitor, nonwhite	32.3	−0.077 (2.48)	−3.2
Janitor, Spanish surname	5.7	0.037[c] (0.63)	[b]
Janitress, nonwhite	30.6	−0.162 (3.70)	−8.0
Fork lift trucker, nonwhite	35.1	−0.157 (3.57)	−5.9
Punch press operator, nonwhite	15.2	−0.105 (1.93)	−4.1
Punch press operator, male, nonwhite	10.4	−0.134 (1.51)	−5.2
Punch press operator, Spanish surname	5.6	−0.045[d]	[b]

[a]Coefficient of nonwhite dummy added to the regression of column 2, table 7.1.
[b]Not shown where variable does not contribute to the fit of the regression.
[c]Coefficient of dummy for Spanish surname added to the regression of column 1, table 8.5. When establishment variables are added to the regression, the coefficient of this dummy becomes −0.061 (t value 1.15), suggesting that Latin janitors are overrepresented in high wage establishments.
[d]Coefficient of dummy for Spanish surname added to the regression of column 1, table 9.5.

The negative coefficients for nonwhites range from 3 to 13 percent of the mean earnings in the occupations.[10] The negative coefficient for material handlers with Spanish surnames is well below that for

10. The relative earnings differentials shown in tables 11.9, 11.10, and 11.11 are similar to what Gary Becker calls "market discrimination coefficients." If we use the symbols W for white wages, N for nonwhite wages and T for the wages of both groups taken together, Becker's measure is $\frac{W-N}{N}$ and ours is $\frac{W-N}{T}$. The use of T here puts these relative differentials on the same base as other kinds of relative wage differences discussed in this chapter. See Gary S. Becker, *The Economics of Discrimination* (Chicago: Univ. of Chicago Press, 1957), pp. 6–10 and table 12.

nonwhite material handlers, but it is within the range of coefficients for nonwhites in other occupations.

The earnings of nonwhites and Latin-Americans are lowered by at least three different kinds of discrimination, past and present. The first is discrimination in the amount and quality of schooling they have received. The second is the smaller likelihood of their finding steady employment in a particular occupation for given levels of education. The third is the receipt of lower earnings per hour within an occupation for given education. The coefficients of our dummy variables for color and origin in principle measure only the third of these kinds of discrimination. The second is eliminated because the dependent variable is defined as earnings per hour of work and because the observations are restricted to employed workers. The first is in part eliminated by the inclusion of years of schooling among the independent variables, at least where there is a discernible positive relation between schooling and earnings. That part of the first kind of discrimination that relates to the quality of schooling remains entangled in the final estimate.

Although our estimates of wage differences by color are adjusted for years of schooling, age, seniority, and experience, there are other aspects of worker quality we cannot take into account. Employers may have higher hiring standards for Negroes than for whites with respect to these qualities, and if this is true, our estimates of "pure" wage discrimination are biased downward.

Since establishment data on wages have seldom been collected by color or origin, most previous estimates of discrimination in earnings have been based on census data on annual earnings. As we mentioned earlier, these earnings have not necessarily been earned in the occupation in which the worker was classified at the time of the census. They also reflect the frequency of part-time and part-year work, and to some extent therefore reflect the second kind of discrimination mentioned above, differential access to employment and regularity of employment.

We can use census earnings statistics in two ways to make comparisons with our coefficients for color. Within the Chicago area, we can estimate relative differences between white and nonwhite earnings by occupation, with no control for age or education.[11] Some such estimates are shown in table 11.10, for the occupations most nearly comparable to those in table 11.9. In some cases, the occu-

---

11. The reason for describing these figures as estimates is that the census data are given as *median* incomes for nonwhites and for both color groups combined. The median for whites is estimated by assuming that $E_N N + E_W W = E_T T$, where E_N is the median income of nonwhites, and N is the number of nonwhites with earnings, and similarly for the other groups. This equation is not in fact correct for medians, except for distributions where the medians happen to be the same as the means (see, for example, W. A. Wallis and H. V. Roberts, *Statistics, A New*

TABLE 11.10

Estimates of Differences in Annual Earnings between Whites and Nonwhites in Selected Occupations, Chicago Area, 1959

Sex and Occupation	White Earnings Minus Nonwhite Earnings as Percentage of Overall Median	Percentage Working 50–52 Weeks in 1959	
		Total	Nonwhite
Males			
Operatives and kindred workers	20.4	66.0	59.7
Service workers, except private household	23.8	67.6	62.5
Laborers, except farm and mine	6.3	47.5	45.8
Females			
Secretaries, stenographers, and typists	11.6	67.9[a]	62.5
Charwomen	2.9	59.6	54.0

[a]Weighted mean of separate percentages for secretaries, stenographers, and typists.
Estimated from data in Census of Population, 1960, vol. 1, part 15, table 124. For methods, see text.

pations shown in table 11.10 are very broad, because the census data are classified by a coarser occupational classification for nonwhites than for all workers, and the two classifications sometimes correspond only at the level of the major occupation group.

The second kind of census data on earnings by color are available only for males and apply to the North and West regions of the United States. These permit control by major occupation group, years of school completed, and age.[12] Table 11.11 shows relative differences in earnings for the major occupation groups in which the male occupations of table 11.10 fall, for the two levels of schooling most important in our sample in these occupations.

Most of the relative wage differentials shown in tables 11.10 and 11.11 are larger than the most closely corresponding entries in table

---

Approach [Glencoe, Illinois, 1956] p. 217). Our assumption therefore amounts to assuming that the median equals the mean. Where both means and medians of earnings distributions of workers in these occupations are available, the means are consistently above the medians. However, the differences are generally small, and hence the errors in our estimates should not be serious.

12. Similar data are available for a somewhat finer occupational breakdown for the United States as a whole, but the finer breakdown is not helpful for the particular occupations of interest here.

11.9. The exceptions occur when the census occupations are defined rather narrowly, as in the case of charwomen and nonfarm laborers. Where the census occupation covers a broad range of skills, as with male service workers, the relative wage differentials in the census data are large even in the presence of control for age and years of schooling. This is undoubtedly because nonwhites are overrepresented in the lowest paid and underrepresented in the best paid detailed occupations within the occupation group.

The last two columns of table 11.10 demonstrate an additional reason for the tendency of the census differentials to be larger than ours. In every case, a smaller proportion of nonwhites than of whites had worked fifty to fifty-two weeks in 1959. In general, this seems less important than the breadth of the occupational categories.

The greatest puzzle that arises in comparing the three tables dealing with wage differentials by color is the narrowness of the differential for nonfarm laborers in table 11.10, as compared with table 11.11 and with the nonwhite material handlers in table 11.9. The most probable explanation for this is the great importance in the Chicago area of two high wage industries, construction and basic steel, as employers of laborers, and probably of nonwhite laborers. Together, these two industries employ more than one-fourth of the nonfarm laborers in the Chicago area. Since construction labor is heavy outdoor work, and since steel mills are located in the parts

TABLE 11.11
Relative Differences between White and Nonwhite Mean Annual Earnings by Age, North and West, 1959 for Selected Occupation Groups and Educational Attainments

Major Occupation Group and Years of School Completed	White Minus Nonwhite Mean Earnings as Percentage of Mean for All Races by Age			
	25–34	35–44	45–54	55–64
Operatives and kindred workers				
High school, 1–3 years	22.0	19.5	17.1	14.7
Elementary, 8 years	16.9	18.8	14.8	13.8
Service workers, including private household				
High school, 1–3 years	30.3	25.4	25.1	16.2
Elementary, 8 years	27.9	18.9	21.7	14.8
Laborers except farm and mine				
High school, 1–3 years	17.6	18.7	16.9	2.5
Elementary, 8 years	16.1	14.3	12.0	9.1

SOURCE: Computed from Census of Population, 1960. Subject Reports, Occupation by Earnings and Education, table 2.

of the area close to concentrations of Negro residence, both may have a higher ratio of nonwhite laborers to all laborers than other industries do.

The importance of basic steel in table 11.11, which includes all of the United States except the South, would be much lower than in table 11.10. In table 11.9, neither construction nor basic steel is represented among our material handlers. Construction is outside our universe of establishments, and basic steel does not appear in the sample for this occupation, since the duties of laborers in the steel industry are broader and more varied than material handling.

No comparisons between our estimates and census data are possible for workers with Spanish surnames. The census does not give any earnings data for such workers.

Before closing this section, we should mention one unsuccessful attempt to use an origin variable. A dummy variable for foreign-born workers was included in some of our early regressions for tool and die makers. Some employers had praised the skill of some of their tool and die makers who had been trained in Europe, particularly Germany, and we therefore expected the variable to have a positive sign. Instead, it had a negative one, apparently because foreign-born workers had a very high average age, and the dummy variable interacted with the negative term of the quadratic age-earnings function.[13]

SEX

Three of our occupations contained enough workers of both sexes so that females could be identified by a dummy variable.[14] In addition, a fourth occupation containing both sexes was created by pooling observations for janitors and janitresses. Table 11.12 summarizes the results for the sex variable. All of the coefficients are negative in sign as expected; three are in the neighborhood of forty cents an hour and the fourth (punch press operator) is about half as large as the others. However, it may be recalled from chapter 9 that in this occupation women were overrepresented in high-wage establishments, and that when establishment variables are added to

13. If a dummy for foreign born is added to the regression of column 1, table 10.4, its coefficient is −0.056 and its t value is 1.16. For the sample including tool and die shops the coefficient is about twice as large in absolute value and the t value is above 2.

14. A further discussion of the sex dimension of wage differentials in our study occupations appears in Mary T. Hamilton's unpublished doctoral dissertation "A Study of Wage Discrimination by Sex: A Sample Survey in the Chicago Area," University of Pennsylvania, December 1969. In addition to examining the pure differentials attributable to sex, she considers possible interaction between the sex dummy and other variables.

the regression the coefficient for the dummy variable for females becomes a negative fifty cents with a *t* value above twelve.

Comparison of tables 11.12 and 11.9 suggests that within our occupations, differences in pay based on sex are in general larger than those based on color or origin. Only one of the coefficients in table 11.9 is larger in absolute size than the smallest of the four coefficients in table 11.12.

TABLE 11.12
Comparison of Coefficients of Dummy Variable for Females

Occupation	Percent Female	Coefficient and *t* Value	Coefficient as Percentage of Mean Wage (Both Sexes)
Accountant	6.1	−0.440 (2.49)	−11.2
Tab operator	21.3	−0.378 (6.70)	−13.9
Punch press operator	39.6	−0.199 (5.12)	−7.7
Janitor and janitress	26.8	−0.409 (15.92)	−17.9

Although the coefficients of table 11.12 come from regressions that control for age, seniority, education, and experience where these are significantly related to wages, there may be other factors affecting the relative performance of men and women that we have not been able to measure. In particular, we have no data on the frequency of absence from work or tardiness, which are factors sometimes mentioned by employers as objective reasons for preferring male employees. For the manual occupations, men also have an advantage in their ability to do heavy work.

MARITAL STATUS

The marital status variable was never included in regressions including both sexes, because we expected opposite signs for men and women. Employers tend to prefer married men on the ground that they are "steadier" and less likely to quit. They tend to prefer women who do not have responsibility for small children, on the ground that the illness of the children may cause the mother to be absent from work. We cannot distinguish such women in our sample, but women who were single at hire are less likely to have child care responsibilities than those who were married, widowed, or divorced. One firm in our sample stated that it did not hire married women, and female employees who got married were put at the

TABLE 11.13

Comparison of Coefficients of Dummy Variable "Single at Hire" in Regressions for Males

Occupation	Percent Single at Hire	Coefficient and t Value	Coefficient as Percentage of Mean Wage of Males
Accountant	39	−0.134[a] (1.42)	−3.4
Tab operator	59	−0.130 (2.07)	−4.7
Material handler	48	−0.111 (3.65)	−4.6
Janitor	30	−0.039[b] (1.33)	−1.6
Fork lift trucker	41	−0.037[c] (0.81)	[d]
Punch press operator	36	0.110[e] (1.99)	[f]
Truck driver	17	−0.058 (1.51)	−1.8
Maintenance electrician	36	0.035 (0.70)	[f]
Tool and die maker	37	0.051 (1.32)	[f]

[a]From a regression similar to column 1, table 7.5, for male accountants only. The number of individuals in this regression is 214 and the R^2 is .389. The marital status variable is added and the dummy variable for females is omitted.

[b]From a regression that adds marital status to the regression of column 1, table 8.5. This variable was not used in that regression because of interaction with the age variable.

[c]From a regression that adds marital status to the regression of column 1, table 9.1.

[d]Not shown where variable does not contribute to the fit of the regression.

[e]From a regression that adds marital status to the regression of column 2, table 9.5.

[f]Not shown where variable does not have the expected sign.

bottom of the list for promotional seniority. Another did not hire married women and until shortly before the time of our visit had discharged female employees who got married.

Table 11.13 compares the results of the variable "single at hire" for the nine male occupations. In six of the nine cases the variable has the expected negative sign and in one of the others the coefficient is not appreciably different from zero. Five of the six negative cases contribute to the fit of the regressions, and two have t values larger than two. On the whole, the regressions support the view that em-ployers prefer married men, though they do not support it very strongly. A major factor that prevents a more conclusive test of the hypothesis is the typically high correlation of marital status with age.

TABLE 11.14
Coefficients of Dummy Variables for Marital Status at Hire in Regressions for Female Workers

Occupation and Variable	Percent in Group	Coefficient and t Value	Expected Sign
Typist, married	36	0.019 (0.64)	negative
Typist, widowed or divorced	9	0.022 (0.51)	negative
Keypunch operator, married	43	−0.002 (0.05)	negative
Keypunch operator, widowed or divorced	10	−0.050 (1.12)	negative
Janitress, single	32	0.029 (0.67)	positive
Punch press operator, female, single	30	−0.054 (1.07)	positive

Table 11.14 compares the results of dummy variables for marital status of women. None of these results have been presented previ-ously, but all are obtained by adding marital status variables to regressions presented in earlier chapters. Here the variables are uniformly unsuccessful. They have the expected sign in only half the cases, and in all cases the t values are well below two. This seems to indicate that policies against hiring married women are not reflected in wage differences. We might have gotten better results if we had been able to collect data on the presence or ages of children of fe-male employees.

DISTANCE

An individual variable measuring the distance from home to work was included in the regressions for each of our occupations. The hypothesis that led us to include it was that establishments which—because of their size or their isolation from residential areas—must draw workers from a long distance will probably have to pay a pre-

TABLE 11.15

Comparison of Coefficients of Distance Variables

Occupation	Mean Distance to Work (Blocks)[a]	Coefficients and t Values		
		Natural Logarithm	Linear (Blocks)	Dummy (Over 70 Blocks)
Typist	47.0	0.018 (1.89)	——————	—————
Keypunch operator	51.9	0.035 (3.09)	——————	—————
Accountant	80.2	0.121[b] (2.55)	——————	—————
Tab operator	63.6	0.049[c] (2.38)	——————	—————
Material handler	52.2	d	d	d
Janitor	60.1	0.018[e] (1.26)	0.00060[e] (2.16)	0.095 (3.32)
Janitress	49.6	0.0043[f] (0.20)	d	d
Fork lift trucker	66.2	0.028 (1.38)	——————	—————
Punch press operator	50.3	0.036 (1.76)	——————	—————
Truck driver	71.9	0.022 (1.38)	——————	—————
Maintenance electrician	66.8	0.082 (3.46)	0.0013[g] (3.03)	—————
Tool and die maker	62.1	0.039 (2.18)	0.00046[g] (1.56)	—————

[a]Eight blocks to the mile; sum of north-south and east-west distances.

[b]Coefficient from a regression that adds logarithmic distance variable to the regression of column 1, table 7.5. The R^2 of this regression is .421.

[c]Coefficient from a regression that adds logarithmic distance to the regression of column 1, table 7.7. The R^2 of this regression is .597.

[d]Not shown where sign is negative.

[e]Coefficients from regressions similar to column 1 of table 8.5, but with continuous distance variables instead of a dummy.

[f]Coefficient from a regression that adds a logarithmic distance variable to a regression similar to the regression of column 1, table 8.7.

[g]Substitutes linear for logarithmic distance in regression shown in chapter 10.

mium wage.[15] Table 11.15 compares the cofficients of the distance variables, including four not previously presented.

The distance variable was omitted from the regressions for accountants and tab operators as shown in chapter 7, even though it improved the regressions, because in these occupations we were particularly worried about the direction of causation. For male white-collar workers, we felt that higher earnings might lead to a change of residence toward more distant and desirable suburbs or neighborhoods, and in particular that this might partly explain the large coefficient of distance for accountants.[16] This is of less concern for the female workers, who are often second earners in the family and whose earnings will therefore have less influence on location of the family's residence. It is also of less concern for the manual workers, whose dispersion of earnings is smaller than that of accountants and tab operators, and who are more likely to be held in particular neighborhoods by discrimination in the housing market or by ties to ethnic groups or neighborhood organizations.[17] The consideration that prompted the omission of the distance variables for accountants and tab operators in chapter 7—the reluctance to claim that we explain more of the dispersion in wages than we really do— is not relevant here, where we are examining the association between distance and earnings as such.

The other coefficients in table 11.15 that were not previously presented are the coefficients of the continuous distance variables for janitors. These have lower *t* values than the dummy variable used

15. For an earlier and more complete statement of this hypothesis, see William Goldner, "Spatial and Locational Aspects of Metropolitan Labor Markets," *American Economic Review* 45 (March 1955): 111–28.

16. For further discussion of this point, see note 18 below.

17. It may be recalled from chapters 8 and 9 that in the three occupations in which our sample includes substantial numbers of nonwhites (janitors, material handlers, and fork lift truckers), we find that nonwhites travel farther to work than whites. This we interpret as arising largely from racial segregation in housing, though discrimination in employment could also be a contributing factor.

This conclusion is somewhat different from that of J. R. Meyer, J. F. Kain, and M. Wohl in their book *The Urban Transportation Problem* (Cambridge, Mass.: Harvard Univ. Press, 1965). These authors divide the Chicago area into rings, which are separated by concentric circles around the central business district, and into sectors, which are separated by lines radiating outward from the central business district. They note that nonwhites live in rings closer to the rings in which they work than whites do, but more frequently change sectors in traveling to work. They conclude that "it is difficult to estimate whether this cross-haulage more than offsets the shorter travel distances of Negro workers who are employed in the central zones" (p. 155). Our results suggest that it does. However, results within occupations may differ from those across occupations, since nonwhites are severely underrepresented in the highly paid occupations in which average distance to work tends to be greater.

in table 8.5, but can more easily be used to estimate the value of travel time.

The distance variable has the expected positive sign and contributes to the fit of the regression in ten of the twelve occupations. One of the two exceptions is material handlers, where for nonwhites separately the coefficient was positive with a t value above three.

In ten of the occupations, the logarithmic form of the distance variable gave a good fit, and usually was the only form tried. It seems consistent with economies of scale in both money and time reflected in the greater speed and lower cost per mile of longer trips. Table 11.16 illustrates these economies in time with data from the Chicago Area Transportation Study. The only occupation in which the logarithmic form was less successful than others is janitors, where both a dummy and a linear form gave better fits than the logarithmic form.

Most of the coefficients of table 11.15 are in units of the natural logarithm of city blocks. To make these easier to understand, table

TABLE 11.16

Speed of Travel by Mode by Airline Trip Length (All Figures in Miles per Hour)

Airline Trip Length in Miles	Automobile Driver	Suburban Railroad	Elevated-Subway	Bus
0– 1.9	5.3	3.4	2.8	3.2
2.0– 3.9	8.4	5.8	5.5	5.2
4.0– 5.9	10.6	9.7	7.3	6.6
6.0– 7.9	12.0	10.4	8.6	7.6
8.0– 9.9	13.6	10.9	9.8	8.5
10.0–11.9	14.6	13.1	10.5	10.3
12.0–13.9	15.6	12.7	11.3	11.9
14.0–15.9	17.1	14.2	13.0	11.4
16.0–17.9	18.3	16.4	a	a
18.0–19.9	18.9	15.8	a	a
All trips	11.1	14.4	8.9	6.2

SOURCE: Chicago Area Transportation Study, Final Report, Vol. 2, Data Projections, July 1960, table 46.
NOTE: "Speed of travel" denotes airline journey speed, or elapsed time from door to door divided by airline trip length.
"Mode" denotes priority mode. Where two or more modes were used by a traveler, the mode of travel in the linked trip is defined as the mode having highest priority in the following list, taken in the following order: (1) suburban railroad, (2) elevated-subway, (3) bus, (4) auto driver, (5) auto passenger.
a Insufficient data.

11.17 converts them into dollars per eight-hour work day for a standard trip of ten miles one way (the sum of the north-south and east-west distances). The use of a standard trip for comparison purposes of course suppresses the differences between occupations in the average length of trips shown in column 1 of table 11.15.

The ten occupations in table 11.17 are those with positive distance coefficients larger than their standard errors. The estimated additional earnings associated with the standard ten-mile trip (as compared with a trip of one block) vary from only thirty-eight cents in the case of janitors to $4.24 for accountants. These are still the extreme observations when expressed as a percentage of mean daily earnings in the occupation: 2 percent for janitors and 13.5 percent for accountants.

The last column of table 11.17 expresses the added earnings associated with a trip of ten miles each way in dollars per hour of estimated travel time after deducting the estimated money costs of the trip. The methods of estimation are discussed in the appendix to this chapter. In four of the ten occupations, the added earnings are less than the estimated direct costs of travel. In the other six, the implied compensation for travel time ranges from fifteen cents an hour in the case of keypunch operators to $2.33 an hour for ac-

TABLE 11.17
Additional Earnings Associated with a Distance to Work of Ten Miles

Occupation	Dollars per Eight-Hour Work Day	Percentage of Mean Earnings	Dollars per Hour of Estimated Travel Time[a] (After Deducting Direct Costs)
Typist	0.62	3.8	[b]
Keypunch operator	1.21	6.9	0.15
Accountant	4.24	13.5	2.33
Tab operator	1.73	7.9	0.53
Janitor	0.38[c]	2.0	[b]
Fork lift trucker	0.98	4.6	[b]
Punch press operator	1.25	6.0	.18
Truck driver	0.79	3.1	[b]
Maintenance electrician	2.87	9.9	1.35
Tool and die maker	1.38	4.3	0.27

[a]Estimated travel time is 1.39 hours (round trip).
[b]Direct costs (estimated at one dollar per day) exceed amount in first column.
[c]Estimated from coefficient of linear variable shown in table 11.15.

countants.[18] The two substantial figures, those for accountants and for maintenance electricians, are respectively 60 percent and 37 percent of mean earnings per hour at work.

The much smaller implied value of commuting time for the other occupations, including the four zero or negative implied values, may be the result of the crudity of our estimates. However, one should keep in mind that in our study not all of the value of commuting time is necessarily reflected in earnings. Commuters can also be compensated for their time by savings in the cost of housing and the nonpecuniary income associated with preferred residential locations.

CONCLUSIONS

The principal conclusions that emerge from this summary are that within most of our occupations hourly earnings are positively associated with seniority, previous experience, education, and distance from work, and with age up to some maximum age. Hourly earnings are lower for women than for men, and lower for nonwhites and people with Spanish surnames than for whites in general. None of these results is at all startling, but the estimates given here disentangle them from one another so that the sizes of the separate effects emerge more clearly than they do in larger bodies of wage data.

APPENDIX: ESTIMATING THE VALUE OF COMMUTING TIME

This appendix explains the estimates of the value of commuting time that appear in the last column of table 11.17. The first estimate to be explained is the estimated direct cost of travel of one dollar per day. The cost of a ten-mile trip by bus or subway was estimated at twenty-five cents, the basic fare of the Chicago Transit Authority in 1963. The cost by suburban railroad was assumed to be fifty

18. This figure for accountants permits a comparison that assists in the interpretation of our distance variables. Thomas E. Lisco has estimated the value of commuting time for commuters from Skokie to the Loop in his unpublished doctoral dissertation at the University of Chicago, "The Value of Commuters' Transportation Time: A Study in Urban Transportation" (June 1967). His analysis is based on choice of mode of travel to work by people whose residences and whose workplaces were all in the same small areas. For these suburban Chicago area commuters whose median family income was $10,000 a year, he estimates a value of commuting time of $2.53 to $2.67 an hour. If this median income was earned by one earner working 2,000 hours a year, it would equal $5.00 an hour, somewhat above the mean hourly earnings of our accountants, which were $3.93. The value of commuting time would be 51 to 53 percent of these hourly earnings. Our estimate of the value of commuting time for accountants is 59 percent of their hourly earnings. The closeness of the two estimates suggests that despite the fears expressed earlier, little of the value of our distance variables reflects the influence of earnings on choice of residence in terms of distance from work, since this was roughly constant in Lisco's study.

cents. The operating cost by private automobile was assumed to be six cents per passenger mile, based on 1.5 passengers per car, an average speed of thirteen miles per hour, and an average charge of seventy-five cents per car for parking.[18] Of course, many of our workers park free, and others pay much more. The costs for each of these modes were weighted by the data from table 2.4 showing means of transportation used in getting to work in the census week of 1960. The use of constant weights ignores the complication that, even for a trip of given distance, workers in the higher paying occupations would tend to use the expensive modes (auto and rail) more frequently than workers in the lower paying occupations. The average cost for all modes was forty-nine cents per one-way trip, which was rounded upward to fifty cents.

The second element of the estimates is the estimated average time of 1.39 hours per day. This was derived from table 11.16. However, the distances shown in that table are airline distances. This would be the same as our distance for a trip that was all in one direction along an east-west or north-south street. Where the trip is half in one of these directions and half in the other, our distance is still ten miles, but the airline distance falls to 7.1 miles. The estimate assumes a case halfway between these extremes: 2.5 miles in one direction and 7.5 in the other, for an airline distance of 7.9 miles. The average door-to-door speeds for this distance were derived by interpolation from table 11.16; they are 12.8 miles per hour by auto, 10.6 miles per hour by railroad, 9.2 miles per hour by rapid transit, and 8.0 miles per hour by bus. These were weighted by the same census weights used for direct cost to get an average door-to-door speed of 11.4 airline miles per hour, or 0.69 hours for an airline trip of 7.9 miles. The speeds given above are greater than the average speeds for all bus and rapid transit trips, which are on average shorter than our standard trip, and less than average speeds for all rail trips, which tend to be longer than our standard trip.[20]

19. See D. S. Berry, et al., *The Technology of Urban Transportation* (Evanston Ill.: Northwestern Univ. Press, 1963), p. 18. These authors show a figure of 6.3 cents per passenger mile for an eight-mile trip at an average speed of fifteen miles per hour, with 75 cents for parking.

20. See J. R. Meyer, J. F. Kain, and M. Wohl, p. 134. This work shows data from the Chicago Area Transportation Study giving the average lengths and door-to-door speeds of trips shown below:

Rapid transit	7.2 miles,	9.1 m.p.h.
City bus	4.0 miles,	6.4 m.p.h.
Suburban bus	4.6 miles,	7.8 m.p.h.
Rail	13.5 miles,	15.5 m.p.h.

12

Summary of Findings
for Establishment Variables

THIS CHAPTER compares the results for establishment variables across the twelve study occupations, as the last chapter did for the individual variables. All the comparisons are for the random samples as a whole, and not for subsamples by sex or color, or for the supplementary samples of accountants or tool and die makers. As we mentioned in chapter 6, two important sets of establishment variables, those for location and industry, do not have "expected signs" from theory or from substantial bodies of previous research. In these cases, results have not been omitted for wrong sign in chapters 7 through 10, so that more of the material presented here has been previously presented.

In this chapter, as in the last, coefficients in the tables are drawn from the tables of chapters 7 through 10 unless otherwise indicated. Multicollinearity and interaction are a more important problem among establishment variables than among the individual variables, in part because we have a smaller number of establishments than of individuals. For this reason, we present a number of results in this chapter in the form of coefficients that are larger than their standard errors, but have not been presented before because of multicollinearity. In each such pair of interrelated variables, it is the one that has been presented earlier that we regard as the more fundamental or the more reliable. When the remaining variable of the pair is presented here, its meaning should be regarded as unclear even if the t value is large.

LOCATION

Dummy variables for location were used in ten of the twelve occupations. In the two female clerical occupations, a variable for nonresidential neighborhoods was used instead. These results were shown in chapter 7 and will not be reviewed here. Results of alternate regressions using the regional dummies are presented instead for comparison.

Table 12.1 compares the coefficients of the regional variables for the twelve occupations. The regions used were defined in chapter 7,

TABLE 12.1

Comparison of Coefficients of Dummy Variables for Regions

Occupation	South Region		North and West Region	
	Coefficient and t Value	Percentage of Mean Wage	Coefficient and t Value	Percentage of Mean Wage
Typist	0.007[a] (0.28)	[b]	−0.027[c] (1.35)	−1.3
Keypunch operator	0.015[d] (0.48)	[b]	−0.050[d] (2.14)	−2.3
Accountant	−0.122[e] (1.03)	−3.1	−0.188 (2.00)	−4.8
Tab operator	−0.089[f] (1.47)	−3.3	−0.092 (1.93)	−3.4
Material handler	0.026 (0.97)	[b]	−0.235 (8.34)	−9.8
Janitor	0.119 (3.58)	5.0	0.046 (1.30)	1.9
Janitress	0.127 (3.42)	6.3	0.158 (3.24)	7.8
Fork lift trucker	0.169 (5.81)	6.3	−0.002 (0.06)	[b]
Punch press operator	0.480 (10.61)	18.5	−0.169 (4.18)	−6.5
Truck driver	[g]	[g]	−0.150 (4.64)	−4.7
Maintenance electrician	0.359[h] (5.37)	9.9[h]	0.246 (4.63)	6.8
Tool and die maker	0.312 (6.34)	7.8	−0.027 (0.76)	[b]

[a]From a regression that substitutes regional variables for the nonresidential neighborhood dummy in column 3, table 7.1, and omits nondurable manufacturing.

[b]Not shown where variable does not contribute to fit of regression.

[c]From a regression like that described in note a, but with South region added to the reference base.

[d]From a regression that substitutes regional variables for the nonresidential neighborhood dummy in column 4, table 7.1.

[e]From a regression that adds South region to column 2, table 7.5. South region was not used in chapter 7 because it is highly correlated with trade and service industries.

[f]From a regression that adds South region to column 2, table 7.7. Not used in chapter 7 because it is highly correlated with trade and service industries.

[g]Variable not used; too few establishments in the South region.

[h]Variable is Calumet region only (Lake and Porter Counties, Indiana). When the South region as a whole is used instead, the coefficient is 0.062, with a t value of 0.77.

pp. 95 and by the map on p. 96. The base region always includes the Near North region and the central business district (the Loop) if it has any employment in the occupation. In addition, if one of the two other regions does not enter the regression, as indicated by the footnotes, it is added to the base for the remaining region.

The most consistent result in table 12.1 is that the South region is a high wage region for blue-collar occupations. It has a positive sign in all seven of the blue-collar occupations in which it was used, and both the coefficient and the t value are substantial in five of these. In one of the remaining two, maintenance electricians, the coefficient becomes large if the region is restricted to include only the Calumet (Indiana) portion, and the balance is added to the base.

We ascribe this result to the concentration of heavy industry, particularly basic steel and petroleum refining, in the South region. A similar configuration of wages within the Chicago area was noted in a much earlier study.[1] The pattern does not seem to extend to the white-collar occupations. In the two of these where the coefficient of the dummy for South region is larger than its standard error, the sign is negative.

The North and West region has a coefficient larger than its standard error in ten of the twelve occupations. In seven of these, the sign is negative, including all four of the white-collar occupations. Of the three blue-collar occupations with positive coefficients, two, janitor and janitress, are low-skilled occupations in which the employment of nonwhites is substantial. The North and West region is the farthest from the heavy concentrations of Negro residence, and the separate regressions by color for janitors (Table 8.6) show that the positive coefficient for the occupation as a whole results entirely from the much larger positive coefficient in the regression for non-whites. In the regression for whites, the coefficient was not shown in table 8.6 because it did not contribute to the regression, but if the variable is added it has a negative sign.

The positive coefficient for maintenance electricians is more difficult to explain. This occupation does not fit well into the pattern of regional wage contours that fits the other blue-collar occupations. A possible explanation is that in our sample, the low wage industry transportation and utilities is underrepresented in the North and

---

1. George Seltzer, "Pattern Bargaining and the United Steelworkers," *Journal of Political Economy* 59 (August 1951): 319–31. Seltzer studied negotiated wage rates of steel fabricators and miscellaneous manufacturers organized by the United Steelworkers for the period 1946–50. He reports that in 1950 about half the units in subdistrict 31-2 (the Calumet area) paid the minimum plant rates of the key bargain in basic steel. In subdistrict 31-4, the west side of Chicago, less than 5 percent of the units paid key-bargain minimum plant rates; the deviations were predominantly downward (pp. 328–29).

West region, and there may be some interaction between the regional and industry variables.

The whole wage pattern described by the regional variables might be roughly described as a wage gradient that is lowest in the northwest corner of the Chicago area and highest in the southeast. This gradient is related to the pattern of location of employment and residences, since the North and West region has a heavier concentration of residential neighborhoods and the South and East region has a heavier concentration of nonresidential areas.[2] For the female clerical occupations, as we have seen, this pattern is most clearly reflected in wages if the nonresidential neighborhood variable is used explicitly, and defined on the basis of a small area. For the male occupations, the broader regions work better, but are consistent with the same underlying forces operating with a wider scope.

INDUSTRY

For a number of reasons the results for the industry variables are the hardest of all our results to summarize across occupations. The industry variables reflect a variety of differences among establishments, including the detailed content of the work, the atmosphere of the workplace, and the nature of the product market (for example, how competitive it is, and whether or not it is regulated). Our sample of establishments has differing industry composition from one occupation to another because not all occupations are found in all industries. In most cases the sample of establishments is too small to permit detailed classification of industries; we have therefore worked with one-digit industries and with groupings of two-digit industries.

Table 12.2 compares the results for the industry variables to the extent that they are comparable. The three unskilled blue-collar occupations have been omitted from the table. The special status of the food industry for janitors, and the division of nondurable goods into high and low wage portions for material handlers, make these occupations noncomparable with the others. The results for janitresses have been made as comparable as possible with those for janitors, and this makes them hard to compare with the remaining occupations.

The column headed "heavy durables" in table 12.2 refers to the two-digit industries 33, 34, and 35—primary metals, fabricated metals, and nonelectrical machinery. Where an entry appears in this column, the reference base for the industry dummies is other durable goods manufacturing (in our sample largely electrical equipment

2. This relationship shows up very clearly in the simple correlations between the variables for region and nonresidential neighborhoods in our samples of typists and keypunch operators.

179

TABLE 12.2
Comparison of Coefficients of Industry Variables

Occupation	Heavy Durables	Nondurables	Trade, Finance, or Service	Transportation or Utilities
Typist	*	−0.097 (3.80)	−0.195 (10.03)	−0.026*a (0.72)
Keypunch operator	*	−0.029*a (0.78)	−0.096 (3.98)	−0.021*a (0.39)
Accountant	*	0.198 (1.53)	−0.169 (1.68)	0.074*a (0.42)
Tab operator	*	0.192 (2.63)	−0.034*a (0.60)	−0.177*b (2.40)
Fork lift trucker	0.535 (16.17)	0.129 (3.31)		c
Punch press operator	0.260 (6.61)	c	c	c
Truck driver	*	0.210 (5.77)		
Maintenance electrician	*	0.283 (3.82)		−0.153 (1.93)
Tool and die maker	0.134 (3.12)	*	c	c

*Included in the reference base for the unstarred variables.
aDoes not contribute to fit of regression.
bNot used in chapter 7 because of high positive correlation with dummy variable for females.
cNot represented in the sample.

and instruments and related products) except that in the case of tool and die makers, two nondurable goods establishments with five individuals in the occupation have also been included in the base. If there is no entry in the column "heavy durables" the reference base is all durable goods manufacturing.

In the three occupations in which heavy durable goods have been treated as a separate industry, the sign of the dummy is positive. The size of the coefficient varies from thirteen cents for tool and die makers to fifty-four cents for fork lift truckers. The positive coefficient is not a direct reflection of the higher proportion of female workers in other durable goods, since in two of the three occupations there are no females in the sample, and in the third the regression includes a dummy variable for females.

The industry trade, finance, and services has a negative coefficient in all four of the white-collar occupations, and in three of these the coefficient is larger than its standard error. However, in the blue-collar occupations, trade and services are combined with other industries in groups that have positive coefficients.

The coefficient for transportation and utilities is negative in both of the cases in which it is larger than its standard error. This industry was also represented by a separate dummy variable in the regressions for janitors and janitresses, where it had a positive coefficient for janitors and a substantial negative one for janitresses.

Except in the female clerical occupations, nondurable manufacturing has a positive sign or is included in a group with a positive sign whenever it is represented in the sample. This suggests that the high wage component of nondurables—printing, chemicals, and food —is more important than the textile, apparel, and paper component in most of our samples.

No very significant generalizations emerge from this review of the industry variables. Clearly, industry characteristics have an important effect on wages, but the precise nature of this effect is not the same from one occupation to another, and our sample was not well designed for studying it in depth.

UNIONIZATION

Both common sense and a substantial body of statistical evidence suggest that trade unions raise the wages of the workers covered by collective bargaining agreements. We therefore expected our dummy variables for unionization to have positive signs, and in general have not presented them previously when they did not. However, there are two reasons why the expectation of a positive sign is not as strong in this study as in some others. The first is that we are adding a unionization variable to regressions that already include a number of measures of worker quality. Under these circumstances, a coefficient that did not differ significantly from zero could be interpreted in two rather different ways. First, it could mean that the union had not had any effect on relative wages, where relative wages are defined as wages in the union establishments relative to those in nonunion establishments. Second, it could mean that the union had raised relative wages, but that union employers had succeeded in using these higher wages to attract a superior work force, so that the difference in relative wages was offset by differences in worker quality. In general, one would not expect this offset to be complete in the sense that unionization does not raise unit labor costs, for in this case it should have paid the employer to offer higher wages and get better workers before he was unionized. However, if the offset is incomplete but substantial we might be unable to detect the remaining effect.

The second reason we might not expect to find a positive sign is that the Chicago area is substantially unionized, despite the rather large number of nonunion establishments in our sample. In an area with a strong trade union movement, nonunion establishments in industries employing blue-collar workers will be strongly influenced by the threat of unionization in determining their wage levels.[3] In some cases, the price of remaining nonunion may be to offer union wages; management could nevertheless prefer the resulting situation to being organized because it had greater discretion in nonwage aspects of industrial relations, or because it could operate when union establishments were on strike.

The argument of the last two paragraphs does not mean that we should accept negative coefficients as representing the effects of unionization. These seem more likely to result from peculiarities of our sample or chance correlations of unionization with other independent factors affecting the level of wages.

Table 12.3 summarizes the results of unionization variables in eleven of our twelve occupations. In the twelfth, truck drivers, we had too few nonunion establishments to permit the use of a unionization variable. Several forms of the unionization variable were tried in the course of our work, and those used in table 12.2 are those that were generally the most successful. For white-collar workers the form used is "union in the establishment," a dummy that takes the value of one if the production and maintenance workers in the establishment are organized (whether or not the white-collar workers themselves are), and zero if there is no union in the establishment or if there is a union covering only certain craft workers such as electricians or toolroom workers. This gave better results than a dummy for unionization of the workers in the occupation itself only, since white-collar workers were organized in only a few of our establishments. The results of this variable suggest the presence of some spillover of union effects to nonunion white-collar workers in the organized establishments, but these results are hardly conclusive. For typists, keypunch operators, and accountants, the coefficients are positive and larger than their standard error, but are suspect because of high correlation among the independent variables. The coefficient for tab operators is negative, but there is high correlation between the union variable and the dummy variables for industries.

For both typists and keypunch operators, there are substantial positive correlations between the variable indicating that there is a union in the establishment and the variable for nonresidential

3. Evidence on this point from employer interviews was presented in chapter 4.

TABLE 12.3

Comparison of Coefficients of Unionism Variables

Occupation and Variable	Percentage of Sample in Group Designated by Variable	Coefficient and t Value	Coefficient as Percentage of Mean Wage
Typist, union in establishment	42.7	0.054[a] (2.09)	2.7
Keypunch operator, union in establishment	47.1	0.053[b] (1.65)	2.4
Accountant, union in establishment	58.3	0.182[d] (1.74)	4.6
Tab operator, union in establishment	59.7	−0.093[e] (1.88)	−3.4
Material handler, union	64.5	−0.048[f] (2.10)	−2.0
Janitor, union	70.8	−0.0006[g] (0.02)	[c]
Janitress, union	76.3	0.218[h] (5.65)	10.8
Fork lift trucker, union	74.4	−0.104 (2.96)	−3.9
Punch press operator, union	52.5	−0.275[i] (4.37)	−10.6
Maintenance electrician, union	81.5	0.260 (4.01)	7.1
Tool and die maker, IAM	25.5	0.142 (3.26)	3.6
Tool and die maker, other unions	41.0	−0.201 (4.21)	−5.0

[a]From a regression that adds union and omits nondurable manufacturing from regression of column 3, table 7.1. Not used in chapter 7 because of the high negative correlation between union and trade and services industry and the high positive correlation between union and nonresidential neighborhood.

[b]From a regression that adds union to column 4, table 7.1.

[c]Not shown where variable does not contribute to fit of regression.

[d]From a regression that adds union and omits nondurable manufacturing from column 2, table 7.5. Not used in chapter 7 because of high negative correlation between union and trade service industry.

[e]From a regression that adds union to column 2, table 7.7.

[f]From a regression that adds union to column 1, table 8.2.

[g]From a regression that adds union to column 1, table 8.6.

[h]From a regression that adds union to column 1, table 8.7. Not used in chapter 8 because of high positive correlations between union and transportation and utilities industry.

[i]From a regression that adds union to column 1, table 9.6, and omits Spanish surname.

183

neighborhoods; these correlations are larger than those between unionization and the variable for trade and service industries. This suggests that even in a relatively compact area like the Chicago area, unions are less likely to organize the employers not located in the major concentrations of employment.

For the blue-collar occupations shown in table 12.3, the variable "union" is a dummy that takes the value of one if the workers in question are covered by a collective bargaining agreement and zero otherwise. In most cases, these workers are part of a unit that covers all production and maintenance employees, but in a few cases they are part of a separate unit covering just their own occupation. This last situation is most common in the two skilled occupations. For tool and die makers, as was explained in chapter 10, we have used different variables to distinguish the International Association of Machinists and all other unions.

In the six cases in which the single variable "union" is used for a blue-collar occupation, it has a substantial positive coefficient twice, a substantial negative coefficient three times, and a coefficient that is almost exactly zero in the sixth case. In the two occupations with the largest negative coefficients, there are high correlations between the unionization variable and other independent variables. For punch press operators, unionization is positively correlated with the number of females in the occupation and with the use of incentive pay. Adding the unionization variable substantially changes the coefficients of these variables. For fork lift truckers, unionization is positively correlated with the dummy variable for South region and for nondurable goods and trade.

The coefficients of the two unionization variables for tool and die maker are taken from column 2 of table 10.4. Since they were discussed at some length in chapter 10, the discussion will not be repeated here.

On the whole, we do not regard our study as contributing anything of importance to the literature on the influence of unions on earnings. The small size of our establishment sample and the importance of the indirect effects of unions by way of the threat of organization severely limit the usefulness of our data for estimating the impact of the union.

ESTABLISHMENT SIZE

At the outset of our study, we expected establishment size to have an important effect on the level of wages—so important that we stratified our sample of establishments by size. The data on which this expectation was based are average hourly earnings by establishment size within industries. An excellent example of such data is given in table 12.4, which is taken from a recent article by Professor Richard A. Lester.

Table 12.5 summarizes our results for the variable that measures establishment size, which is the natural logarithm of the total number of employees in hundreds. As we have mentioned earlier, the logarithmic form of this variable gives better fits than the linear form, and also has greater intuitive appeal. It seems likely that an increase in establishment size from 100 to 200 employees would have more impact on the wage level than one from 11,000 to 11,100.

As column 1 of table 12.5 illustrates strikingly, our original expectation was not correct. Establishment size has a coefficient larger than its standard error in only six of the twelve occupations, and in three of these its sign is negative. The size and t values of the negative coefficients are about the same as those of the positive ones. On the whole, then, we find no positive relationship between establishment size and wages within occupations after allowing for the influence of the other variables that enter the regressions. Within the same geographic area, otherwise similar establishments of different sizes do not generally pay different wages for workers having the same characteristics.

What then explains the striking difference between the results of tables 12.4 and 12.5? For one thing, table 12.4 includes data for cities of different sizes. There is undoubtedly a positive correlation between city size and establishment size, and as Victor Fuchs has shown clearly, there is a very substantial positive relation between city size and average hourly earnings even after other variables such as sex, color, and education have been taken into account.[4] Thus one probable reason why our data do not show a stronger relation between establishment size and earnings is that they are all from the same metropolitan area. A second major difference is that the data of table 12.4 are for all production and maintenance workers taken together, whereas ours are for individual occupations. Part of the relation between establishment size and average hourly earnings in table 12.4 could arise from a tendency for occupation mix to differ systematically by establishment size, with larger establishments having a higher proportion of more skilled and more specialized occupations.

The factors just mentioned relate to the way in which we defined the domain from which our observations were drawn. This is the whole explanation of our failure to find a positive relation between wages and establishment size in four of our occupations, as indicated

4. Victor R. Fuchs, *Differentials in Hourly Earnings by Region and City Size, 1959*, Occasional Paper 101 (New York: National Bureau of Economic Research, 1967).

TABLE 12.4

Indexes of Wages per Man-Hour by Size of Manufacturing Establishment, 1954

Industry	Number of Employees						1,000* and Over	Wages per Man Hour Used as Base
	10–19	20–49	50–99	100–249	250–499	500–999		
All industries	73	73	74	77	81	87	100	$2.16
Food & kindred products	64	67	71	77	85	92	100	2.08
Meatpacking, wholesale plants	72	74	79	85	88	97	100	2.10
Pulp, paper & products	79	82	87	95	100	104	100	1.91
Lumber & wood products	65	70	73	76	83	88	100	1.99
Furniture & fixtures	83	82	81	80	78	85	100	1.91
Chemicals & products	70	70	74	83	91	96	100	2.22
Petroleum & coal products	73	77	77	83	89	94	100	2.60
Rubber products	71	68	70	77	83	84	100	2.26
Stone, clay, & glass products	70	71	75	81	85	89	100	2.17
Pressed & blown glassware	83	78	82	91	88	91	100	1.96

Industry	10–19	20–49	50–99	100–249	250–499	500–999	1,000* and Over	Wages per Man Hour Used as Base
Primary metal products	76	78	82	86	91	93	100	2.35
Fabricated metal products	80	81	83	85	88	94	100	2.34
Transportation equipment	79	81	84	87	90	96	100	2.26
Electrical equipment	79	79	81	81	86	90	100	$2.01
Iron & steel forgings	76	87	89	93	93	97	100	2.50
Nonferrous foundries	80	81	82	86	95	99	100	2.30
Aircraft engines	97	99	96	98	99	97	100	2.15
Radios & related products	87	82	82	88	90	91	100	1.81
Textile mill products	101	98	96	99	97	98	100	1.41
Apparel & related products	96	92	88	80	77	83	100	1.55
Men's & boys' suits & coats	112	97	97	100	98	98	100	1.62

*Generally calculated by combining size categories above 1,000.

Source: Calculated by Richard Lester from data in Census of Manufactures, 1954, vol. 1, chap. 3. See Richard Lester, "Pay Differentials," Industrial Relations 7 (October 1967): 59.

TABLE 12.5

Comparison of Coefficients of Natural Logarithm of Establishment Size

Occupation	Coefficient and t Value	Difference in Wage between Sizes 100 and 1,000	Simple Correlation With:	
			Wage	Log Seniority
Typist	0.0008[a] (0.095)	[b]	.09	−.07
Keypunch operator	−0.002[c] (0.19)	[b]	.15	.01
Accountant	−0.054[d] (1.43)	[k]	.12	.31
Tab operator	−0.00006[e] (0.003)	[b]	−.08	−.07
Material handler	−0.083[f] (7.57)	[k]	−.36	−.09
Janitor	0.028 (2.23)	0.065	.16	.28
Janitress	−0.002[g] (0.10)	[b]	.48	.38
Fork lift trucker	0.0008[h] (0.06)	[b]	−.14	.13
Punch press operator	0.001[i] (0.06)	[b]	.18	.21
Truck driver	−0.068[j] (4.87)	[k]	−.34	.55
Maintenance electrician	0.072 (2.89)	0.166	.25	.22
Tool and die maker	0.089 (5.57)	0.21	.36	.24

[a]From a regression that adds establishment size to column 3, table 7.1, and omits nondurable manufacturing.

[b]Not shown where variable does not contribute to the fit of the regression.

[c]From a regression that adds establishment size to column 4, table 7.1.

[d]From a regression that adds establishment size to column 2, table 7.5, and omits nondurable manufacturing.

[e]From a regression that adds establishment size to column 2, table 7.7.

[f]From a regression that adds establishment size to column 1, table 8.2.

[g]From a regression that adds establishment size to column 1, table 8.8.

[h]From a regression that adds establishment size to column 1, table 9.2.

[i]From a regression that adds establishment size to column 1, table 9.6, and omits Spanish surname.

[j]From a regression that adds establishment size to column 2, table 9.8.

[k]Not shown where dependent variable does not have expected sign.

by the four negative simple correlations shown in the third column of table 12.5. In other cases, the explanation lies in the effect of the other variables in the regressions. For example, the simple correlation between wages and establishment size for accountants is positive, but when the other variables are in the regression, the coefficient of size becomes negative.

One of the most important of the variables in these regressions is seniority. Since there is in general a negative relation between turnover and establishment size, one might expect larger establishments to have employees with greater average seniority, and hence higher wages for a given wage structure by length of service. The last column of table 12.5 gives the simple correlation coefficients between the natural logarithm of seniority and the natural logarithm of establishment size for each occupation. The proposition stated about the relation between seniority and establishment size is supported by these coefficients; nine of the twelve are positive, including seven of the eight for the blue-collar occupations covered by table 12.4. All the negative correlations are small, whereas many of the positive ones are quite large. This suggests that the seniority variable in our regressions is catching some wage differences that might have been caught by establishment size if it had been entered first, and that establishment size would then have been more likely to have had a positive sign.

CONCLUSIONS

Of the four main sets of establishment variables included in our analysis, only one, location, produces a reasonably systematic pattern of results when compared across occupations. The other three—industry, unionization, and establishment size—tend to give results that differ substantially from one occupation to another and that often disappoint expectations. In part this is because the establishment variables reflect institutional differences, and institutions do not always present neat patterns. But it remains likely that there are more consistent patterns of establishment characteristics in the Chicago labor market than we have reported, and that we have missed them because we sampled too few establishments.

APPENDIX

The following tables are presented in order to afford the reader a concise summary of the regression results for each occupation and to facilitate comparisons across occupations.

Tables 12.6 and 12.7 indicate the contribution in dollars to wages per hour at work of each variable as estimated from the regression

TABLE 12.6
Contribution of Variables to Wages as Estimated from Regression Equations with Individual Characteristics (Dollars per Hour at Work)

Variable	Value of:	Typist	Keypunch Operator	Accountant	Tab Machine Operator	Material Handler	Janitor
Age:	One year older at mean age for occupation	.003	.003	.019	.015	−.003	−.007
Seniority:	One more year at mean years for occupation	.031	.046	.022	.044	.031	.023
Education:	One more year					.020	
	High-school diploma				.141		.114
	Some college or more	.038					
	College degree			.282			

Experience—Training:						
Previous job					.144	
Previous job in Chicago						
Occupational experience	.062	.177	.301			
Occupational experience or formal training				.381		
Occupational experience and formal training						.168
CPA			1.176			
Distance from Work:						
One more mile at mean distance for occupation	.003					
71 blocks or over		.005				
Weight: 165 pounds or over at hire					.047	.096
Marital status: Single at hire					−.111	.079
Color or origin: Nonwhite	−.096				−.308	
Spanish surname					−.152	−.077
Sex: Female			−.440	−.378		
Mean wage per hour at work:	2.013	2.205	3.926	2.728	2.408	2.390
Standard deviation	.281	.302	.799	.498	.384	.335
Coefficient of variation	13.9%	13.7%	20.4%	18.2%	16.0%	14.0%

TABLE 12.6 (Cont.)
Contribution of Variables to Wages as Estimated from Regression Equations with Individual Characteristics (Dollars per Hour at Work)

Variable	Value of:	Janitress	Fork Lift Trucker	Punch Press Operator	Truck Driver	Maintenance Electrician	Tool and Die Maker
Age:	One year older at mean age for occupation		.007			.004	−.004
Seniority:	One more year at mean years for occupation	.023	.011	.030	.004	.015	.013
Education:	One more year						
	High-school diploma		.119				
	Some college or more					.055	
	College degree						.018

	(1)	(2)	(3)	(4)	(5)	(6)
Experience—Training:						
Previous job	.067					
Previous job in Chicago						
Occupational experience						
Occupational experience or formal training						.157
Occupational experience and formal training					.204	
CPA						
Distance from Work:						
One more mile at mean distance for occupation		.003	.005	.002	.009	.005
71 blocks or over						
Weight: 165 pounds or over at hire						
Marital status: Single at hire	−.162	−.157				
Color or origin: Nonwhite			−.105	−.058		
Spanish surname						
Sex: Female			−.199			
Mean wage per hour at work:	2.018	2.681	2.591	3.191	3.639	3.986
Standard deviation	.316	.382	.434	.185	.433	.328
Coefficient of variation	15.7%	14.3%	16.8%	5.8%	11.9%	8.2%

TABLE 12.7

Contribution of Variables to Wages as Estimated from Regression Equations with Individual and Establishment Characteristics (Dollars per Hour at Work)

Variable	Value of:	Typist	Keypunch Operator	Accountant	Tab Machine Operator	Material Handler	Janitor
Age:	One year older at mean age for occupation	.005	.004	.018	.014	−.000a	−.003
Seniority:	One more year at mean years for occupation	.028	.042	.021	.048	.028	.023
Education:	One more year						
	High-school diploma				.125	.019	.073
	College degree			.254			
Experience— Training:	Previous job	.051	.175	.332	.407	.050	
	Previous job in Chicago						.151
	Occupational experience						
	Occupational experience or formal training						
	Occupational experience and formal training						
	CPA			1.073			
Distance from Work:	One more mile at mean distance for occupation						
Weight:	165 pounds or over at hire					.049	.063
Marital status:	Single at hire	−.094					
Color or origin:	Nonwhite					−.130	
	Spanish surname					−.126	−.090

		C1	C2	C3	C4	C5	C6
Sex:	Female			−.432	−.330		
Location:	Nonresidential neighborhood	.117	.116				.119
	South region						
	Calumet region						
	North and west region			−.188	−.092	−.235	.046
Industry:	Nondurable goods manufacturing	−.097		.198	.192		.404
	Food manufacturing						
	Textiles, apparel, or paper					−.459	
	Printing or chemicals					.071	
	Transportation or utilities						
	Trade, service, or finance	−.195	−.096	−.169			.135
	Nondurables, trade, service, or finance						
	Nondurables or nonmanufacturing						
	Food manufacturing, transportation, utilities, trade, service, or finance					.411	
	Nondurables except food, and trade, service, or finance						
	Heavy durables						
Union:	Occupation organized						
	Occupation organized by IAM						
	Occupation organized—not by IAM						−.106
Pay Arrangement:	Incentive						
Establishment Size:	100 more employees at mean size for occupation						.001

aAbsolute value less than .0005

195

TABLE 12.7 (Cont.)

Contribution of Variables to Wages as Estimated from Regression Equations with Individual and Establishment Characteristics (Dollars per Hour at Work)

Variable	Value of:	Janitress	Fork Lift Trucker	Punch Press Operator	Truck Driver	Maintenance Electrician	Tool and Die Maker
Age:	One year older at mean age for occupation					.005	−.001
Seniority:	One more year at mean years for occupation		.009			.016	.008
Education:	One more year	.016	.009	.019	.006	.040	.020
	High-school diploma		.071				
	College degree						
Experience—Training:	Previous job						
	Previous job in Chicago						
	Occupational experience						
	Occupational experience or formal training						.120
	Occupational experience and formal training					.185	
	CPA						
Distance from Work:	One more mile at mean distance for occupation			.005	.002	.006	.002
Weight:	165 pounds or over at hire						
Marital status:	Single at hire						
Color or origin:	Nonwhite	−.126	−.156	−.150			
	Spanish surname			−.091			

196

Sex:						
Female			−.500			
Location:						
Nonresidential neighborhood		.169				
South region	.127		.480			
Calumet region					.359	.312
North and west region	.158				.246	
Industry:						
Nondurable goods manufacturing			−.169	−.150		
Food manufacturing						
Textiles, apparel, or paper						
Printing or chemicals						
Transportation or utilities	−.238					
Trade, service, or finance					−.153	
Nondurables, trade, service, or finance	−.365	.129				
Nondurables or nonmanufacturing					.283	
Food manufacturing, transportation, utilities, trade, service, or finance				.210		
Nondurables except food, and trade, service, or finance						
Heavy durables						
Union						
Occupation organized		.535	.260		.260	.134
Occupation organized by IAM						.142
Occupation organized—not by IAM						−.201
Pay Arrangement						
Incentive			.086			
Establishment Size:						
100 more employees at mean size for occupation					.002	.002

TABLE 12.8

Proportion of Variance in Wage per Hour at Work Explained by Regression Equations

	Individual Variables Only	Including Establishment Variables	Coefficient of Variation in Wage per Hour at Work
Typist	33.3%	47.4%	13.9%
Keypunch operator	49.2	55.5	13.7
Accountant	40.4	44.4	20.4
Tab machine operator	58.6	60.7	18.2
Material handler	34.8	65.5	16.0
Janitor	31.7	46.5	14.0
Janitress	36.2	62.9	15.7
Fork lift trucker	12.7	54.9	14.3
Punch press operator	45.5	65.0	16.8
Truck driver	6.5	22.8	5.8
Maintenance electrician	27.6	42.5	11.9
Tool and die maker	29.9	60.7	8.2

equations. The relationships between the dollar values presented here and the regression coefficients which are given earlier in the study depend on the mathematical form of the variable in the equation. If the form is linear, such as years of education, the value of an additional year is constant over the range and is equal to the coefficient. Similarly, if the variable is a zero, one dummy showing the absence or presence of some characteristic, the value is given directly by the coefficient. However, if the form is nonlinear, the value of additional units is not constant over the range. For these variables (age, seniority, the first form of the distance variable, and size), the values of additional units have been computed at the occupational means.

Table 12.8 gives for each occupation the coefficient of determination (R^2) for the "best" equations using individual variables only and those including establishment variables. The coefficients of variation in wage per hour at work have also been included to indicate the relative wage dispersions. As we pointed out earlier, the increase in the proportion of variance explained with the inclusion of establishment variables is generally larger for the blue-collar occupations than for the white-collar group.

13

The Search for
New Workers and New Jobs

THIS CHAPTER consists of three parts. In the first, we discuss the ways
in which the workers in our sample found their present jobs. In the
second, we illustrate the relation between wage levels and the extent
to which employers need to search for new workers. In the third, we
analyze the experience of some of the workers in our sample who
changed jobs, in terms of the length of time between jobs and the
change in wages from the old job to the new. The first section is
essentially a description of the search process, while the second two
are different ways of exploring the interrelations between job search
and wage determination.

How Workers Found Their Jobs

We recorded how each worker in the sample found his present job
whenever this information was available, which it was in the majority of cases.[1] The present job is defined as a period of continuous
employment (that is, of unbroken seniority) with the present employer in any occupation and in any establishment. If the worker
had transferred to the sample establishment from another establishment of the same employer, we recorded the source of his job in
the first establishment when it was known. If he had been rehired
after formally severing an earlier employment relationship, for example by quitting, we treated the rehire as a separate job source.

The known job sources, other than rehires, are considered in two
groups: informal and formal. The informal sources are those that
do not involve the use of any outside organization or agency to

1. This section draws freely on two published papers that are in part preliminary
reports on this phase of our study: Albert Rees, "Information Networks in Labor
Markets," *American Economic Review* 56 (May 1966): 559–66 and Eaton H.
Conant, "The Evaluation of Private Employment Agencies as Sources of Job
Vacancy Data," in *The Measurement and Interpretation of Job Vacancies*, A Conference of the National Bureau of Economic Research (New York: National
Bureau of Economic Research, 1966), pp. 519–47. The statistics given here differ
from those in the earlier publications in two respects: the sample used here is
restricted to the random sample of establishments after the deletion of observations discussed in chapter 6, and the percentages are based on the total number
in this sample, whereas in "Information Networks" the occasional percentages
given were based on the number for whom the source was known.

arrange a contact between the employer and the job applicant. These include referrals by present employees, referrals by other employers and by friends or other individuals, and gate applications. A gate application is one in response to a "help wanted" sign posted on the employer's premises or one initiated by the applicant without any referral at all.

The principal formal sources are the two state employment services in the area (Illinois and Indiana), private employment agencies, newspaper advertisements, trade unions, and schools and colleges. Of these, the private agencies and newspapers usually involve an explicit cost to the hiring employer. The others, like the informal sources, do not.

The data on job source are presented in table 13.1. The most striking feature of the table is the difference in the use of formal sources between the white-collar and the blue-collar occupations. In three of the four white-collar occupations, formal sources are more important than informal, and in the fourth they are of almost equal importance. In contrast, for the blue-collar occupations informal sources are three or four times more important than formal sources. The percentage of unknowns is also much higher for the blue-collar occupations. It seems probable that informal sources are more likely not to be recorded than formal ones, and the small proportion of unknowns for the white-collar occupations reinforces this expectation. If anything, then, the relative importance of informal sources for blue-collar workers is understated by the percentage distributions. The greater importance of formal sources for white-collar workers is undoubtedly related to the relative tightness of the white-collar labor market in the Chicago area throughout the postwar period.

INFORMAL SOURCES

By far the most important informal source in all occupations is employee referral. Three of our establishments told us that they paid bonuses to present employees for referrals who were hired; in one case the bonus was fifty dollars per hire. Several employers listed employee referrals as their preferred source of recruitment. The few cases in which employers told us that they preferred not to use referrals were cases in which they were trying to upgrade their work force or in which they had been having difficulties with cliques.

The strong employer preference for employee referrals requires some explanation in view of the general hostility of labor economists to unorganized markets and to informal channels of transmitting market information. It is often asserted in the literature on labor markets that the organized markets for commodities or securities are models of well-functioning markets and that the state employment

TABLE 13.1
Percentage Distribution of Sample by Job Source

Job Source	Typist	Keypunch Operator	Accountant	Tab Operator
Informal sources				
Employee referral	23.0	26.2	17.5	22.2
Other informal referral[a]	2.0	3.7	6.6	1.9
Gate application	3.4	7.9	4.8	1.9
Total informal sources	28.4	37.8	28.9	26.0
Formal sources				
State employment service	0.9	1.1	2.6	0.5
Private agency	20.5	8.7	16.7	12.5
Newspaper ad	10.1	15.9	19.7	13.0
School or college[b]	1.1	10.3	6.6	6.0
Union	0.2	––	––	––
Other formal sources[c]	0.5	0.3	––	0.5
Total formal sources	33.3	36.3	45.6	32.5
Rehires	5.0	10.3	5.7	4.2
Unknown	33.4	15.6	19.7	37.5

Job Source	Material Handler	Janitor	Janitress	Fork Lift Trucker
Informal sources				
Employee referral	38.4	34.0	29.5	32.9
Other informal referral[a]	1.8	1.7	2.9	5.9
Gate application	3.6	6.8	3.5	3.9
Total informal sources	43.8	42.5	35.9	42.7
Formal sources				
State employment service	1.5	2.1	1.2	0.6
Private agency	2.7	1.7	1.2	1.7
Newspaper ad	2.0	2.5	5.2	3.7
School or college[b]	––	––	––	––
Union	2.0	2.5	0.6	0.3
Other formal sources[c]	––	0.6	2.3	0.3
Total formal sources	8.2	9.4	10.5	6.6
Rehires	3.8	4.2	19.1	8.1
Unknown	44.2	43.8	34.7	42.7

TABLE 13.1 (continued)

Job Source	Punch Press Operator	Truck Driver	Maintenance Electrician	Tool and Die Maker
Informal sources				
Employee referral	28.7	22.9	26.9	24.5
Other informal referral[a]	2.3	5.4	3.6	3.2
Gate application	2.6	6.0	8.0	8.3
Total informal sources	33.6	34.3	38.5	36.0
Formal sources				
State employment service	1.7	0.6	0.4	0.7
Private agency	1.7	— —	1.1	— —
Newspaper ad	6.6	0.6	5.5	7.9
School or college[b]	0.3	— —	— —	0.4
Union	— —	4.8	0.7	0.7
Other formal sources[c]	— —	— —	0.7	— —
Total formal sources	10.3	6.0	8.4	9.7
Rehires	11.2	8.4	5.5	11.9
Unknown	44.9	51.2	47.6	42.4

[a]Includes referrals by other employers and contacts initiated by present employer.
[b]Includes private trade schools, which account for all school placement of tab operators and 33 of 39 for key punch operators. Colleges account for 14 of 15 school placements of accountants.
[c]Includes churches, welfare agencies, and professional associations.

services provide the closest analogies to such organized markets in the labor sector.[2] This view seems to us to give insufficient weight to the distinction between extensive and intensive search in a market. Extensive search occurs when one gets a price quotation from one additional buyer or seller; intensive search occurs when a potential

2. For example, a recent edition of a leading textbook in labor economics includes this passage: "Recent studies have also underlined the rather haphazard character of labor mobility and the serious structural defects in labor markets. One can say, indeed, that labor markets are less adequate than any other type of factor or product market in the economy. If one thinks of degrees of perfection in competition measured along some sort of rating scale, the organized stock or commodity exchange would come closest to one end of the scale while labor markets would stand at the opposite pole." Shortly afterward, the author adds "central to any effort to improve labor market efficiency is the system of public employment offices." Lloyd G. Reynolds, *Labor Economics and Labor Relations*, 4th ed. (Englewood Cliffs, N.J.: Prentice-Hall, 1964), pp. 375 and 382.

buyer or seller obtains additional information about the quality or character of the commodity or service in question from a buyer or seller whose quotation is already in hand. The formal organization of markets is of greatest use when the item being traded is highly standardized and the important unknown aspect of the transaction is the exact price, to be determined through extensive search. The greater the variance in the quality or nature of the item or service to be traded, the greater are the inherent obstacles to the formal organization of markets, and the larger the amount of intensive search that may be needed. Both workers and jobs are of course subject to wide variation in quality and character in many dimensions.

Employee referrals are very well suited to providing qualitative information to both parties. An employer who is satisfied with his work force is likely to get new employees similar to those he already has. He may feel that the reputation of his present employees is to some extent at stake when they make referrals, and that they will therefore have an incentive to recommend people who in their judgment would do well.

From the point of view of the applicant, the employee referral also has important advantages. He can get many kinds of information accurately from a present employee that could not be known with any certainty to an employment service or agency—for example, information about the fairness and attitudes of supervisors. If he accepts a position, he will have a friend in the establishment who can help him learn his way around.

Of course, not all job seekers have access to informal sources, and those who are most disadvantaged, such as Negroes and recent migrants to the area, will have less access to them than others. A special tabulation of our job source data for material handlers and janitors by color shows that the nonwhite workers in these occupations found their present jobs through formal sources twice as often as whites.

All this is not to say that extensive search is not also important in labor markets, or that there is not still a major role to be played by formal sources. However, we do not feel that the findings of this and many similar studies about the importance of informal sources reveal something to be deplored.

Among the informal sources other than employee referrals which turned up in our interviews there were several that suggested ingenuity on the part of employers. For example, one small firm hired its accountants through the public accounting firm that audited its books. A distributor of furniture and home appliances hired warehousemen through moving and storage companies, whose slack season coincided with his busy season.

FORMAL SOURCES

The most striking aspect of the data on the use of formal sources is the relative unimportance of the two state employment services. In no occupation were as many as 3 percent of the workers known to have found their jobs through the employment service; in several cases this source was less than 1 percent of the total. Accounting for the unknowns might raise these percentages somewhat, but there is little reason to believe that it would increase the importance of the employment service relative to other job sources. In eleven of the twelve occupations, newspaper ads were a more important source than the employment service, in most cases by substantial margins. In the white-collar occupations, where formal sources as a group are most important, both newspaper ads and private employment agencies were many times as important as the employment service.[3]

Our interviews with employers provide some insight into the poor showing of the employment service. Many of them stated that they do not use it, for a variety of reasons. One reason sometimes given was that the employment service refers too many Negroes. This reason was advanced by some employers who, despite fair employment practices acts, did not hire Negroes, but it was also advanced by others. One company whose work force was 40 percent Negro stated that it did not use the employment service because nine out of ten referrals were Negro.

The most important reason for not using the employment service was poor screening. Particularly for white-collar jobs, the employers in our sample tended to feel that private agency screening was better than that of the employment service, or that the private agencies had a better pool of applicants. We also encountered some complaints of overreferral. An extreme example is that of a firm in retail trade that wanted two high-school graduates for work in its credit department. The employment service made forty referrals, of whom half were not high-school graduates. Some of the rest were overqualified and would not accept the job.

3. The United States Employment Service has estimated that in 1965 the employment service in the Chicago SMSA had a penetration rate of 11.8 percent (that is, its placements accounted for 11.8 percent of new hires). This is substantially above the figures for our study occupations, and may suggest that the employment service was improving its performance through time. Our data refer to placements over a long period ending in 1963. The Employment Service estimates are based on administrative statistics for placements, and on estimates of total new hires that may be subject to substantial error. The Employment Service estimates include, and ours exclude, employment in private households, an area in which the service makes many short-term placements. The source of the estimate given above is a letter to the authors from Frank H. Cassell, then director of the U.S. Employment Service, dated 22 November 1966.

In contrast, some of the employers we interviewed were well satisfied with the employment service and used it regularly. These tended to be the employers in the suburbs who used suburban rather than central-city employment service offices. Perhaps this is because the suburban offices had a better and more homogeneous pool of applicants. However, we also have the impression that counselors in the suburban employment service offices have a better understanding of employer requirements, and that this in turn is related to lower turnover of counselors in the suburban offices.

Private agencies were very important in all four white-collar occupations, and much less important for blue-collar workers. For white-collar jobs, it was the standard practice in the Chicago area at the time of our study for the employer to pay the fee, which was generally about two-thirds of the monthly salary. In blue-collar occupations, agency fees were usually paid by the worker, and often he was charged a fee to register with the agency before he was referred to an opening.

In the period August–December 1962, there were 291 private employment agencies in the Illinois portion of the Chicago area, according to the records of the Illinois Division of Private Employment Agencies. Only 36 of these were large enough to receive an average of more than two hundred employer job orders per month; 126 received fewer than forty orders per month.[4] There is a somewhat greater degree of specialization among private agencies than exists in the organization of the state employment services, both because some agencies are narrowly specialized to certain occupations, such as data processing occupations, and because in the city of Chicago the Illinois State Employment Service has only one central office for each major occupational group, whereas some private agencies are located in neighborhoods outside the central business district.

Many of our employers reported satisfaction with the referrals from private agencies; these tended to be the smaller employers who had less capacity to do extensive screening within their own personnel departments. Other employers had various complaints against the private agencies. Many complained of high turnover of agency counselors and of being pestered by phone calls from agencies. Some complained of "pirating"—a practice in which agencies approach workers they have previously placed and try to place them with a new employer to earn another fee. For obvious reasons, the employers consider this unethical. Employers with complaints against one agency often transfer their business to another one rather than to

4. See Conant, p. 536 for the complete distribution and comments on possible sources of error in these data.

some entirely different source; this is, of course, seldom a possible line of response to dissatisfaction within the system of public employment service offices.

The figures for newspaper advertisements in table 13.1 combine newspapers of several different types. Some firms advertised in the metropolitan papers, particularly the *Chicago Tribune*. Others used suburban or neighborhood papers or foreign language papers. Yet others used different kinds of papers in recruiting for different occupations. The use of local and foreign-language papers may have been designed to discourage Negro applicants (firms who wanted to encourage such applicants sometimes advertised in a Negro paper, such as the *Chicago Defender*). Another reason for the use of local papers was to draw applicants from the immediate vicinity of the establishment, in the hope that this would reduce absenteeism, tardiness, or turnover of those hired. Foreign-language papers were used especially for skills that are heavily represented in certain ethnic groups.

There is a rough tendency for the use of newspaper advertising to rise with the skill level of the occupation. Among the white-collar occupations, typists were least often recruited by ads and accountants most often; among the blue-collar occupations, tool and die makers were most often recruited through ads.

Schools and colleges were important only in three of the white-collar occupations: keypunch operator, tab operator, and accountant. In the first two cases, all or most of the referrals were from private proprietary data processing schools. In the case of accountants, all but one of the referrals were from colleges.

There were only three occupations in which any employees were recruited from public high schools, and this source did not account for as much as 2 percent of the total in any occupation. The unimportance of public schools in the recruiting of new clerical employees is in sharp contrast with the pattern in the Boston area.[5] Those employers who reported to us that they recruited from high schools almost always mentioned suburban high schools. The Chicago vocational high schools as of 1963 did not seem to be active in the placement of their graduates.

The use of unions as a source of recruitment is unimportant except in the case of truck drivers, where the union accounts for almost 5 percent of the sample. Among the sources included in "other formal," the most important is charitable and welfare agencies. These accounted for a total of eleven workers in six occupations;

5. See George P. Shultz, "A Non-Union Market for White Collar Labor," in *Aspects of Labor Economics* (Princeton, N.J.: Princeton Univ. Press for the National Bureau of Economic Research, 1962).

churches accounted for two workers, and professional associations for only one.

The total pattern of recruitment is varied and perhaps even untidy. Yet its variety may be a strength rather than a weakness, in offering alternatives both to workers and employers. Greater rationalization might be possible, for example through the use of electronic data processing in the state employment services, but this would not and should not mean that the employment service would take over the entire placement function in the market.

THE COSTS OF SEARCH IN CLERICAL OCCUPATIONS

We mentioned in chapter 1 the hypothesis advanced by George Stigler that search and wages are substitutes for the employer—that is, that an employer who offers low wages will have to engage in more than a usual amount of search to fill his job vacancies.[6] In this section, we present a test of this hypothesis using data for our two female clerical occupations.[7] These occupations were chosen because they are those with the highest turnover of employees and therefore those in which employers have to do the most recruiting. They are also the occupations in which the most use is made of formal sources.

Two variables are used to measure the cost of search to the employer: the percentages of workers hired between 1 January 1961 and 30 June 1963 through newspaper advertisements and through private employment agencies. In the Chicago market for clerical workers ads and agencies are the two job sources that always involved an explicit cost to the employer. In addition, the use of ads may involve relatively high implicit costs within the employing firm, since workers who respond to ads have not been screened.

The reader should be warned that the means of the source variables used in table 13.2 cannot be obtained from table 13.1. The restriction of the time period used in defining the source variables to two and one-half years produces a mean that is higher than that for all workers hired through these sources. For typists, the mean percentage hired through ads since January 1961 was 13.8, as compared with 10.1 in table 13.1; the corresponding percentages for agencies are 26.3 and 20.5. For keypunch operators, the percentage hired through ads since January 1961 was 17.1, compared with 15.9 in the whole sample and the corresponding percentages hired through agencies were 10.7 and 8.7. These differences could arise in

---

6. See George J. Stigler, "Information in the Labor Market," *Journal of Political Economy* 70 (October 1962; supplement): 94–105.
7. This section draws heavily on the previously published work of Joseph C. Ullman, especially his article "Interfirm Differences in the Cost of Search for Clerical Workers," *The Journal of Business* 41 (April 1968): 153–65.

TABLE 13.2

Regressions Including Job Source Variables for Typists and Keypunch Operators

	All Industries		Excluding Trade and Service	
	Typist	Keypunch Operator	Typist	Keypunch Operator
Age	0.019	0.016	0.020	0.015
Age squared	−0.00023	−0.00019	−0.00024	−0.00016
Seniority[a]	0.151	0.210	0.141	0.191
	(11.82)	(13.57)	(8.21)	(8.39)
Experience (D)	0.051	0.172	0.057	0.178
	(2.66)	(7.72)	(2.31)	(5.63)
Nonwhite (D)	−0.092	——————	——————	——————
	(1.68)			
Nonresidential	0.124	0.117	0.070	0.072
neighborhood (D)	(6.70)	(4.71)	(2.93)	(1.74)
Nondurable goods	−0.095	——————	——————	——————
(D)	(3.46)			
Trade or service (D)	−0.194	−0.092	——————	——————
	(9.23)	(3.84)		
Percentage hired	0.00041	−0.0013	−0.0035	−0.0019
through ads	(0.81)	(2.48)	(4.92)	(2.91)
Percentage hired	−0.00052	0.0014	−0.0015	−0.00020
through agencies	(1.90)	(2.80)	(4.52)	(0.27)
R^2	.480	.576	.474	.457
Constant term	1.512	1.552	1.486	1.648
Number of establishments	56	41	42	29
Number of individuals	557	378	354	236
Dependent variable:				
mean	2.013	2.205	2.084	2.265
standard deviation	0.281	0.302	0.281	0.283

NOTE: (D) Dummy variable
[a]Natural logarithm

several ways. Among these are a possible rising trend in the use of ads and agencies or a trend toward better record keeping, resulting in fewer unknown sources among the recent hires. The most probable cause is higher turnover in firms that rely most heavily on formal sources, which would result in their having a larger proportion of their total work force hired recently.

The job source variables are, in our earlier terminology, establishment—not individual—variables. The hypothesis being tested is that low wage firms engage in more costly search, and not that the particular individuals hired through high-cost sources receive a lower wage.

The results of our test of this hypothesis are presented in table 13.2. The first two regressions are the regressions of columns 3 and 4, table 7.1, with the source variables added. The higher R^2 statistics in table 13.2 should not be regarded as indicating an improvement in our ability to explain wage dispersion, for at least two reasons. First, the regressions of table 13.2 include some source variables that do not have the expected signs or whose coefficients are smaller than their standard errors; these would have been excluded under the rules we were applying in chapter 7. Second, and more important, although wage per hour at work is still the dependent variable in the new regressions, we do not view the causal relationship as running from the source variables to wages. Rather, the firm is viewed as choosing either a low wage, high search strategy or a high wage, low search strategy; in this sense the wage level and the amount of search needed are simultaneously determined.

The Stigler hypothesis leads us to expect negative signs for both of the job source variables. However, in the regression for typists the percentage hired through ads has a positive sign, though its coefficient is smaller than its standard error. In the regression for keypunch operators, the percentage hired through agencies has a positive sign and a t value above two.

The key to these unexpected results appears to lie in the characteristics of the insurance companies in the clerical samples. The insurance companies are in general low wage employers of clerical workers and some of them are very large. In the keypunch sample, the three largest insurance companies employed 114 of the 378 workers in the sample. Two of these three hired almost entirely through ads, since they were large enough to do their own screening. In the case of typists, smaller insurance companies were also important, and these tended to hire through agencies. The insurance companies as a group employed 152 of the 557 workers in the sample, and 115 of these workers were in the three largest companies.

The last two columns of table 13.2 give the results of regressions in which all establishments in trade, finance, and service industries have been removed from the sample. For keypunch operators, these consist entirely of insurance companies; for typists they include establishments in other trade, finance, and service industries with a total of twenty-seven workers in the occupation. When the trade and service establishments are omitted, the dummy variables for non-whites and for nondurable goods manufacturing no longer contribute to the regression for typists, and have been omitted. The dummy variable for nonresidential neighborhoods is considerably less successful than before. However, the improvement of the performance of the source variables is very great. In the typist regression both source variables now have the expected negative sign and t values greater than four. In the keypunch regression, the performance of both variables is improved, though not so dramatically as for typists. The percentage hired through agencies now has a negative sign, but is not appreciably different from zero. The results for the samples excluding trade, finance, and service establishments thus support the Stigler hypothesis in three tests out of four, and do not contradict it in the fourth.

A short calculation will suggest better than the regression coefficients by themselves the size of the wage differences associated with differences in the sources of employees. In the sample excluding trade, finance, and service, the mean percentage of typists hired through ads since January 1961 was 10.0 and the mean percentage hired through agencies was 23.8. If we compare these with a hypothetical establishment that hired half its typists through ads and the other half through agencies, the regression coefficients indicate that this hypothetical firm would have an average wage eighteen cents an hour lower than the mean of the sample for employees of equal age, seniority, and experience. Of this difference, fourteen cents would be associated with the greater reliance on ads, where both the coefficient and the difference between the average and assumed percentages are larger than for agencies. The estimated wage for this hypothetical firm, $1.90 per hour, is slightly above the actual average wage per hour at work for typists at the two large insurance companies that relied most heavily on ads.

THE EXPERIENCE OF JOB CHANGERS

For many of the workers in our sample, the personnel file contained information on the last job the worker held before being hired by his present employer. Usually this included his last wage on his previous job, his reason for leaving the job, and the date at which his last job ended. From these data we could calculate how long he was out of work between jobs, though not whether this period represented unemployment or temporary withdrawal from the labor force. We could also measure the wage change between his last job and his starting job with his present employer.

We attempted to do regression analysis to see what factors determined the number of months the worker was out of work and what determined the change in wages between jobs. In general, this analysis was unsuccessful and is not presented here. The reasons for the lack of success are of two sorts. First, the sample of job changers was much smaller than that of all workers, both because some of our workers had no known previous job and because for some who did, not all the information needed for the analysis was in the personnel record. Second, the job changes took place at very different times and under different labor market conditions. We could control for one aspect of this difference, the over-all rate of unemployment in the Chicago area at the date the worker left his last job, but we did not succeed in controlling for the change in wages within the occupations during the varying periods that workers were out of work.

Despite these difficulties, two factors emerged from the regression analysis as clearly related to the experience of job changers: age and reason for leaving. An analysis of these factors using descriptive statistics is given in tables 13.3 through 13.7. Even for this kind of analysis, it was necessary to omit some of the occupations with the smallest samples, and to combine observations for some closely related occupations. The occupation refers to the worker's occupation in 1963, and is not necessarily that of his last job, nor of his first occupation with his present employer.

The sample of job changers used in this section has been restricted in several ways. The nature and purpose of these restrictions should be explained briefly before we turn to the results. First, only those persons are included who ended their last job in or after 1952. The original purpose of this restriction was related to the availability of data on the unemployment rate in the Chicago area. However, it also serves to eliminate those who changed jobs during World War II and the immediate postwar years, when labor shortages would have shortened the time between jobs and raised the probability of getting a new job at a higher wage. This would make these observations noncomparable with those for later years in an analysis that does not include an unemployment variable. The sample also excludes those who were between jobs for more than eighteen months. The few workers excluded by this rule were likely to have been out of the labor force rather than unemployed for at least part of the period, and their inclusion could raise the mean number of months out of work by a substantial amount. For similar reasons, we exclude those who left their last job because of illness or to enter military service, and we exclude women who left their last job for family reasons (usually marriage or pregnancy). The two men who left their last job for family reasons have been included in the category "other reasons." In short, the sample of job changers is intended to represent the experience of those who were most likely to have looked for a new job as soon as they left the old one, without an intervening period of withdrawal from the labor force. Thus months out of work as used in this section is intended to approximate unemployment experience.

TABLE 13.3
Wage Comparisons for Job Changers by Reason for Job Change

Reason	Keypunch Operators and Typists			Janitors		
	Wage Increase	No Change	Wage Decrease	Wage Increase	No Change	Wage Decrease
Voluntary moves						
Quit for better job	61	12	17	23	1	6
Quit, too far to travel	13	6	15	—	—	4
Quit, other reasons	62	8	28	9	—	12
Total	136	26	60	32	1	22
Involuntary moves						
Laid off, plant shutdown or relocation	7	3	14	4	—	8
Laid off, reduction in work force	33	6	40	34	3	51
Discharged	1	1	2	—	—	—
Total	41	10	56	38	3	59
Reason unknown	30	7	15	14	—	9
Total, all reasons	207	43	131	84	4	90

Reason	Material Handlers and Fork Lift Truckers			Tool and Die Makers and Maintenance Electricians		
	Wage Increase	No Change	Wage Decrease	Wage Increase	No Change	Wage Decrease
Voluntary moves						
Quit for better job	48	2	19	12	2	11
Quit, too far to travel	—	—	4	1	2	2
Quit, other reasons	29	—	23	6	7	14
Total	77	2	46	19	11	27
Involuntary moves						
Laid off, plant shutdown or relocation	4	—	15	—	—	4
Laid off, reduction in work force	69	5	95	14	7	33
Discharged	3	1	3	—	—	2
Total	76	6	113	14	7	39
Reason unknown	32	—	8	10	2	15
Total, all reasons	185	8	167	43	20	81

The wage variable used in this section is average hourly earnings as stated in conventional payroll records, and not earnings per hour at work. This is because we lacked information about the vacation and holiday policies of the worker's previous employer.

Table 13.3 shows the direction of wage change by reason for move for the four occupational groups considered in this section: typists and keypunch operators, janitors, material handlers, and fork lift truckers, and maintenance electricians and tool and die makers. In each of the four occupational groups a majority of those who changed jobs involuntarily experienced a wage decrease. In contrast, in three of the four groups a majority of those who changed jobs voluntarily started their new jobs at a higher wage. The exception is maintenance electricians and tool and die makers. This result may be influenced by voluntary moves of tool and die makers from job shops to other industries, which often involved a reduction in hourly rate but more stable or less demanding work.

The wage decreases associated with involuntary moves are a larger proportion of the total in the case of plant shutdown or relocation than in the case of layoffs for reductions in work force, though the small size of the first group cautions against putting much weight on this result. The result is, of course, to be expected. Those who know that they have permanently lost their jobs should be more willing to take a new job at lower pay than those who have some probability of recall.

TABLE 13.4

Months out of Work and Wage Ratios: Typists and Keypunch Operators Combined

Age at Hire	Changed Jobs Voluntarily			Changed Jobs Involuntarily[a]		
	Number	Mean Months out of Work	Mean Wage Ratio[b]	Number	Mean Months out of Work	Mean Wage Ratio[b]
Under 25	134	2.0	1.16	73	1.6	1.11
25–34	39	3.4	1.04	30	2.9	0.95
35–44	28	2.1	1.01	39	2.4	1.00
45 and over	21	3.6	1.01	17	3.4	0.96
Total	222			159		
Weighted mean		2.4	1.11		2.2	1.04

[a]Includes reason unknown.
[b]Starting wage on present job divided by last wage on previous job.

TABLE 13.5

Months out of Work and Wage Ratios for Janitors

Age at Hire	Changed Jobs Voluntarily			Changed Jobs Involuntarily[a]		
	Number	Mean Months out of Work	Mean Wage Ratio[b]	Number	Mean Months out of Work	Mean Wage Ratio[b]
Under 25	11	2.3	1.44	21	3.1	1.16
25–34	10	1.8	1.30	28	3.5	1.09
35–44	14	0.7	1.13	34	3.3	0.98
45 and over	20	1.7	1.01	40	3.2	0.95
Total	55			123		
Weighted mean		1.6	1.18		3.3	1.03

[a]Includes reason unknown.
[b]Starting wage on present job divided by last wage on previous job.

The number of workers who quit their last jobs because the journey to work was too long is substantial only for the female clerical occupations. This supports the inferences drawn earlier from other data about the greater importance of location to women than to men.

Tables 13.4 through 13.7 provide an alternative analysis of the same sample of job changers. The reasons for leaving the last job have been collapsed to two categories, voluntary and involuntary, with the unknown reasons included in the involuntary. Workers are classified by their age at the time of hire by their present employer, which was obtained by subtracting years of service from age in 1963.

In three of the four occupational groups the number of months out of work is higher for involuntary movers than for voluntary movers, which is the result to be expected. For many of the voluntary movers, a new job has been secured before the worker has stopped work on the old one, and the number of months out of work is zero. The occupational group that is the exception to this pattern is typists and keypunch operators, where the probability is highest that the voluntary moves include some temporary withdrawals from the labor force. The difference in months out of work between the two groups is largest for janitors, where involuntary movers were out of work for an average of 3.3 months, or twice as long as voluntary movers.

The relation between age and number of months out of work is not a close one. Some of the tables show a tendency for the number

TABLE 13.6
Months out of Work and Wage Ratios: Material Handlers and Fork
Lift Truckers Combined

Age at Hire	Changed Jobs Voluntarily			Changed Jobs Involuntarily[a]		
	Number	Mean Months out of Work	Mean Wage Ratio[b]	Number	Mean Months out of Work	Mean Wage Ratio[b]
Under 25	61	2.5	1.34	101	2.0	1.19
25–34	36	2.2	1.13	81	2.3	0.95
35–44	19	1.6	0.95	41	3.3	0.95
45 and over	9	1.1	0.91	12	1.8	0.92
Total	125			235		
Weighted mean		2.2	1.19		2.3	1.05

[a]Includes reason unknown.
[b]Starting wage on present job divided by last wage on previous job.

of months out of work to increase with age, but others show an opposite tendency, and in many the pattern is quite irregular.

As would be expected from the analysis of direction of wage change in table 13.3, the ratio of the starting wage on the new job

TABLE 13.7
Months out of Work and Wage Ratios: Maintenance Electricians
and Tool and Die Makers Combined

Age at Hire	Changed Jobs Voluntarily			Changed Jobs Involuntarily[a]		
	Number	Months out of Work	Wage Ratio[b]	Number	Months out of Work	Wage Ratio[b]
Under 25	9	2.1	1.03	11	0.6	0.90
25–34	18	0.8	1.01	27	1.6	0.95
35–44	19	0.5	0.94	27	1.1	0.95
45 and over	11	1.6	0.99	22	2.3	0.94
Total	57			87		
Weighted mean		1.1	0.99		1.5	0.94

[a]Includes reason unknown.
[b]Starting wage on present job divided by last wage on previous job.

to the last wage on the old job is consistently higher for voluntary than for involuntary movers. Nevertheless, in three of the four occupational groups the ratio exceeds unity even for those whose last job was terminated by the employer. There is also a very clear relation between the wage ratio and the age of the worker. In all but one of the eight cases, the ratio declines with age, and in several cases the decline is very pronounced.

In short, our conclusions about workers who changed jobs are of two kinds, neither very surprising. The first is that the experience of those who changed jobs voluntarily is generally more favorable than that of those who changed involuntarily. The second is that the experience is less favorable with respect to wage rates the higher the age of the worker at the time of the move. Since our sample was not designed as a sample of recent job changers, it is not surprising that our conclusions in this area are of limited scope.

The material on job search viewed as a whole leads to two principal conclusions. The first is that the varying circumstances of the different workers and different employers engaged in the process of search lead to a complicated pattern of search activities unlike those found in simpler markets. The second is that for both the employer and the employee, wages and search are related quite directly. The low wage employer finds that he must undertake costlier search activities. The worker who, because of age or inability to choose the time of his separation, is at a disadvantage in the search process, must frequently accept a wage reduction.

14

Conclusions

Our discussion has touched on many aspects of the labor market in the Chicago area, and no short summary could pull them all together. Yet we should attempt some assessment of how well we think we have done in relation to the goals we set for this study.

In general, we feel that our methods were successful. We used interviews with employers to help generate hypotheses, and collected individual personnel records on samples of employees to generate data against which hypotheses could be tested. The results have met or surpassed our expectations; we see this as a fruitful way of studying a labor market. If we were to do the study again we would do some things differently, but the basic sources of data would remain the same. We can recommend this approach as one that provides a variety of data in a richness of detail that is not available, to our knowledge, without employing the much more expensive method of interviewing large samples of workers.

We also feel that the use of random sampling to select the establishments for study was worth the difficulties it created in gaining access to data, because it permits some confidence in the usual measures of statistical significance. However, in retrospect we cannot defend the choice of establishment size as the variable on which the sample was stratified. Had we used industry instead, we might have improved some of our results.

Wage Differentials

In assessing the more specific achievements of the study, we turn back to the objectives set forth in chapter 1. It may be recalled that we listed there several theories of wage differentials that we hoped to test. The first of these is Adam Smith's theory of compensating differentials—differentials needed to offset nonpecuniary disadvantages of employment. Although Smith advanced the theory to explain interoccupational wage differences, we argued that it should also hold for some wage differences within occupations.

Not many of the wage differentials we were able to measure can be classified as compensating differentials. Those that can are the differentials associated with location. The clearest case, reported in

218

chapter 7, is the significant wage premium that seems to be needed to attract female clerical workers to work in nonresidential neighborhoods. More broadly, the strong positive association of wages with distance traveled to work, summarized in chapter 11, can be viewed in large part as a compensating differential needed to draw enough workers to the less accessible establishments. Alternative explanations of this association are possible, but seem less consistent with our evidence.

The second basic theory of wage differentials we wanted to investigate is that embodied in Alfred Marshall's concept of "efficiency wages." Stated in a weak form, this would hold only that there is a positive relation between wages and worker quality. On this level, a great deal of our evidence supports the theory. We find a clear positive relation between wages and schooling in seven of our twelve occupations; the schooling differentials range from 2 to 7 percent of mean earnings (see table 11.6). We also find a positive relation between wages and previous work experience in seven occupations with differentials ranging from 3 to 14 percent of mean wages (see table 11.7). In the two cases (typist and accountant) in which we were able to relate test scores with wages for subsamples of occupations, we also found positive associations (see tables 7.4 and 7.6).

The most important single determinant of individual earnings in our models—seniority—can be interpreted as an index of relevant experience, though other interpretations must also be considered. Firms that pay high wages and that advance wages substantially with length of service will have fewer quits and hence less need to train new workers. They will also tend to have high average seniority and few workers who are not thoroughly familiar with their work. This suggests that the higher pay associated with seniority may be, from the employer's perspective, a reward for familiarity with his operations—a familiarity that can increase productivity. The same differentials viewed from the standpoint of fellow employees or unions may be seen as due to senior employees on grounds of equity.

None of our evidence tests the strong form of Marshall's theory, which holds that competition will equalize efficiency wages, or that high wage employers get as much quality as they pay for. We doubt that the strong form would hold in much of the Chicago labor market, since we know of major noncompetitive elements in wage determination. An employer required by a union agreement to offer a higher wage than he cares to will adjust to this requirement by raising his hiring standards, but we would not expect this adjustment to prevent any rise in unit labor costs as a result of the union.

Not all employer preferences among workers are related to quality in the sense of objective performance on the job. To no one's surprise, we find clear evidence of wage differentials in favor of males over females, whites over nonwhites, and other whites over those with Spanish surnames (see tables 11.9 and 11.12). Employers may view these preferences as indexes of quality, but there is no reason for the objective observer to do so.

Our measures of wage differentials by sex and color are incomplete measures of discrimination in one very important sense. Since we observe them within occupations, they do not reflect discrimination in gaining entry to the better occupations. However, our measures are more precise than other available measures in another important way. They are measures of wage differences by color and sex after allowing for the effects of differences among workers in age, seniority, schooling, and experience. It therefore cannot be contended that differences between groups in these dimensions cause the intergroup wage differentials that we observe.

Regressions containing individual variables only are appropriate for testing the classical and neoclassical theories of wage differentials. Those containing establishment variables are more appropriate for testing institutional theories, such as those relating wages to unionization and establishment size. However, we have been somewhat less successful in measuring establishment variables associated with wage differentials than in measuring individual variables. This is a result, in general, of the small number of establishments in our sample and the wide variation in types of establishments.

Although we find important wage differentials by industry, they have proved difficult to summarize in any consistent pattern. Location of the establishment gave consistent results for blue-collar occupations. These results show a wage gradient with its highest point at the southeast of the Chicago area, where the concentration of heavy industry is greatest, and sloping downward toward the northwest (see table 12.1).

We expected to find a more consistent pattern by unionization than was in fact detected. We ascribe the absence of a clear union-nonunion differential largely to the potential threat that nonunion establishments will be organized if they fall too far behind union wage levels. We also expected to find that large establishments pay higher wages than small ones, but our results did not conform to these expectations (see table 12.4). The size-of-establishment differentials reported elsewhere in the literature thus seem to reflect a combination of other factors that have been controlled separately in this study.

The wage structure of a large metropolitan area, even within narrow occupations, is highly complex, and not all of its component forces can be identified and measured. However, most of our regression models do succeed in accounting for a substantial portion of observed variation with a reasonably small number of independent variables. The individual variables are of greatest importance in explaining wage variation in the white-collar occupations, whereas establishment variables play a greater role in the blue-collar occupations, especially the semiskilled ones. This is consistent with the view of Robert Raimon that firms have the greatest latitude in setting wages for semiskilled workers.

INFORMATION CHANNELS AND LABOR MOBILITY

Our approach to channels of job information is less novel than our approach to wage analysis. Our statistical findings on the ways in which workers found their jobs parallel those of several earlier studies. One new element in our analysis is the measurement of wage differentials by job source (table 13.2). So far as we know, this is the first statistical confirmation of George Stigler's hypothesis that low wage employers must engage in more costly search.

Our employer interviews also lead us to a somewhat different interpretation of the information channels in the labor market than that of some earlier studies. Like other investigators we find a heavy reliance, especially among blue-collar workers, on informal sources of information such as referrals from friends and relatives. However, we do not feel that this reliance is necessarily evidence of an imperfect market. Rather it suggests to us the importance of kinds of qualitative information about job seekers and about vacant jobs that could not be communicated well through formal channels, such as newspaper ads and employment agencies, at the time of our study.

We had hoped to get information about job changers as a by-product of a sample designed essentially for other purposes. This by-product material proved somewhat less rich than we had hoped. We nevertheless observed that those who left their last jobs involuntarily were less likely to improve their wages than those who left voluntarily. We also found that older job changers typically do not improve their wages as much as younger ones.

FINAL THOUGHTS

In closing, we return to a theme mentioned at the outset of our study—the tendency of some observers of labor markets to view them as heavily influenced by random and chaotic forces, and to judge them as poor or imperfect markets relative to markets for commodities or nonlabor services. We do not share this view, and although our position rests in part on views we held before we undertook this research, we feel that it is substantially supported by our findings.

We do find that large metropolitan labor markets are highly complex, and are made up of separate but interrelated occupational and geographical submarkets. Wage determination, job search, and the movement of workers among employers are all influenced by a great variety of forces—economic, institutional, locational, and personal. However, we cannot concur in the view that because economic forces are mingled with others they are inoperative, or that because a process is highly complex it is necessarily in large part irrational.

We think our statistical work shows that many important forces in wage determination, at both the individual and the establishment level, can be disentangled and measured. And we think most of our work also implies that the actors in the market—the workers, the employers, the unions, and the job market intermediaries—behave on the whole in rational ways. This is not to say that employers, for example, are wholly rational, any more than consumers or investors are. It seems highly irrational to us to refuse under any circumstances to employ Negro workers, as some of the employers in our sample admitted they did. But on the whole, employers and workers seem to pursue reasonable goals in appropriate ways. If at first their behavior does not appear to make sense, it may be simply because the employment of a worker is a much more complicated transaction, and one with many more dimensions, than the purchase of a contract in the wheat futures market. Perhaps, despite the large body of sound research in labor markets of the postwar period, economists and other social scientists have not yet tried hard enough to understand this behavior fully.

APPENDIX

Form Used to Record Information from Personnel Records

1. Firm name code
2. Occupation
   number

   01. Accountant I (highest level)
   02. Accountant II
   03. Accountant III
   04. Tab Machine Op. I (Supervisor)
   05. Tab Machine Op. II
   06. Tab Machine Op. III
   07. Key Punch Op. I (Supervisor)
   08. Key Punch Op. II
   09. Key Punch Op. III
   10. Clerk Typist I (Supervisor)
   11. Clerk Typist II
   12. Tool & Die I (Journeyman)
   13. Tool & Die II (Apprentice)
   14. Maintenance Electrician I
   15. Maintenance Electrician II
   16. Punch Press I (includes set-up)
   17. Punch Press II
   18. Truck Driver
   19. Fork Lift Trucker
   20. Material Handler
   21. Janitor
   22. Janitress

3. Individual
4. Address at hire _____
5. Address at date of recording _____
6. Residence

   1. Owns
   2. Rents
   3. Boards

7. Year of birth
8. Sex

   1. Male
   2. Female

9. Date of application (mo., day, yr.)
10. Race

    1. White
    2. Negro
    3. Latin
    4. Other

11. Place of birth

1. Zone of employment
2. Other Chicago or Calumet Region, Indiana
3. Other Illinois or Indiana
4. North, West or East; Urban
5. North, West or East; Rural
6. Southeast; Urban
7. Southeast; Rural
8. Puerto Rico
9. Mexico
0. Other Foreign

12. Height at hire

1. 5' and under
2. 5'1"–5'2"
3. 5'3"–5'4"
4. 5'5"–5'6"
5. 5'7"–5'8"
6. 5'9"–5'10"
7. 5'11"–6'
8. 6'1"–6'2"
9. 6'3"–6'4"
0. 6'5" and over

13. Weight at hire

1. 100 lbs and under
2. 101–20
3. 121–40
4. 141–60
5. 161–80
6. 181–200
7. 201–20
8. 221–40
9. 241 and over

14. Marital status at hire

1. Single
2. Married
3. Divorced or separated
4. Widowed

15. Position applied for (from supp. occupational list)

16. Education

1. 0–4
2. 5–8
3. 1–4 H.S.
4. H.S. graduate
5. 1–4 college
6. College graduate
7. Some graduate school
8. Master's degree
9. Ph.D.

17. Grade-school or high-school location (code same as item 11)

18. Other training or skills

1. None
2. Evidence of formal off-the-job training of direct and obvious reference to present occupation; e.g., Coyne Electrical School for a man now a maintenance electrician,

tool and die maker, Armed Forces tab operators' school for a tab operator.

3. Evidence of formal off-the-job training not of direct and obvious relevance to present occupation.
4. Has skills not reflected in work history of direct and obvious relevance to present occupation.
5. Has skills not reflected in work history not of direct and obvious relevance to present occupation.
6. CPA

19. Location of last prior employer _____
20. Dates of employment—last prior employer (qtr./yr. to mo., day, yr.)
21. Occupation—last prior employer
22. Wage—last prior employer
23. Reason for
    leaving—last
    prior employer
2. Laid off, plant shutdown or move
3. Laid off, reduction in force
4. Sickness
5. Quit, for better job
6. Quit, for family reasons
7. Quit, too far to travel
8. Quit, for other reasons
9. Discharged
0. Military

24. Location, next to last employer _____
25. Dates of employment (qtr., yr. to qtr., yr.)
26. Occupation—next to last employer
27. Wage—next to last employer
28. Reason for leaving next to last employer (see item 23)
29. Location—second from last employer _____
30. Dates of employment (qtr., yr. to qtr., yr.)
Blank
Repeat code columns 1–6 card 1
31. Occupation—second from last employer
32. Wage—second from last employer
33. Reason for leaving—second from last employer (see item 23)
34. How did
    applicant hear
    of this job?
01. Friend or relative employed at this firm
02. Friend or relative not employed at this firm
03. Union
04. Newspaper ad
05. Private employment agency
06. State employment service
07. Charitable or relief agency
08. Church

34. How did
    applicant hear
    of this job?
    (continued)
    09. Professional association
    10. School, public
    11. School, trade or vocational
    12. College
    13. Other employer
    14. Gate application
    15. Applicant is former employee
    16. Yellow pages
    17. Trade journals
    18. This employer contacted him
    (Add 20 for transfers)

35. Date hired
36. First job (code from supp. occupational list)
37. Date transferred to present occupation (qtr., yr.)
38. Job to which transferred (code from item 2)
39. Date job changed from one level to another within occupation (first such change)
40. Job to which changed (first such change) (code from item 2)
41. Date job changed from one level to another within occupation (second such change)
42. Job to which changed (second such change) (code from item 2)
43. Wage at hire
44. Wage at June 30, 1961
45. Wage at June 30, 1962
46. Wage at June 30, 1963
47. Wage increase at time transferred to present occupation (item 37) (use 9 in column 52 for wage decrease)
48. Wage increase at time transferred from one level to another within occupation (item 39)
49. Wage increase at time transferred from one level to another within occupation (second such change) (item 41)
50. Method of
    payment
    0. for time rate
    1. for incentive rate

51. Days of vacation and holidays
52. Wonderlic test score
53. Other test scores
54. Fringe benefits
55. Hours of work
    regularly
    scheduled
    0. for 30 hours
    1. for 35 hours
    2. for 36 hours
    3. for 37½ hours
    4. for 38¾ hours
    5. for 40 hours
    6. for 45 hours
    7. for 48 hours
    8. for 20 hours

56. Weight to be given this individual in sample. Code 1 if all persons in this occupation in this establishment were surveyed. If a subsample was surveyed code the reciprocal of the proportion taken, e.g., if took 1/2 code 2.
Blank

Index

Janitors, in study sample—cont'd
  individual characteristics, 58–67
  individual variables and wages,
    111–19, 190–91, 194, 198
  job changers, 212, 214, 215
  job source, 201
Janitress, defined, 57
Janitresses, Chicago area
  employer wage and manning strategy,
    46–49
  employment and earnings, 27–28
Janitresses, in study sample, 71–72,
    111–12
  analysis of wage dispersion, 111–21
  correlation of wages with other
    occupations, 46–47
  establishment variables and wages,
    114, 118–21, 196–97, 198
  fringe benefits, 78
  individual characteristics, 58–67
  individual variables and wages,
    112–19, 192–93, 196, 198
  job source, 201
Job changers, 4, 9, 210–17, 220
Job search, 199–207
  information channels, 9–10, 221
Journey to work, 10–11, 15–17, 169–75,
    218–19
  and hiring standards, 49–50
  of workers in this study, 66–67,
    169–74

Keypunch operator, definition, 55
Keypunch operators, Chicago area
  employer wage and manning strategy,
    46–49
  employment and earnings, 27–28
Keypunch operators, in study sample,
    71, 80
  analysis of wage dispersion, 80–90
  correlation of wages with other occu-
    pations, 46–47
  establishment variables and wages,
    81, 86–88, 195, 198
  fringe benefits, 78
  individual characteristics, 58–67
  individual variables and wages,
    80–88, 190–91, 194, 198
  job changers, 212, 214
  job source, 201, 206, 207–10
  test scores, 88–90

Labor force, Chicago area, 14–25
Labor market, Chicago area
  employers' view of, 36–54
  See also Local labor markets
Labor mobility
  and income differentials, 4

  and job information channels, 9–10,
    221
  legal restrictions, 6
  patterns, 9–10
Labor supply
  and employer wage policy, 36–49
  and wage differentials, 5–6
Laborers, material handling. See
    Material handler
Latin. See Spanish surnames
Lester, Richard A., 3, 6, 8, 185–87
Life insurance plans
  note on contribution to wages, 77–79
  not used in earnings data, 69
Linear variables, 70
Lisco, Thomas E., 174
Local labor markets
  Chicago pilot study, 29
  commuting costs, 10–11
  competitive model, 6, 8
  complexity, 222
  employers' view of, 36–54
  information channels, 9–10, 221
  mobility patterns, 3, 9–10
  previous research, 3–13, 221–22
  sources of research data, 13, 25–35,
    218
  spatial characteristics, 10–12
  wage differentials, 3–8, 218–21
Location of establishment, 10–12
  and hiring standards, 49–50
  regional scheme, 95–96
Location variable in wage regressions,
    by occupation
  summary of findings, 179–81, 195, 196
  accountant, 92, 95
  fork lift trucker, 122–23, 126
  janitor, 118–19
  janitress, 118–19
  keypunch operator, 81, 86–88
  maintenance electrician, 137, 139–40
  material handler, 104, 108–10
  punch press operator, 128, 131
  tabulating machine operator, 95–100
  tool and die maker, 143, 144
  truck driver, 134–35
  typist, 81, 86–88
Logarithmic variables, 70

Machinery industry, 30, 179–80
Maintenance electrician, definition, 57
Maintenance electricians, Chicago area
  employer wage and manning strategy,
    46–49
  employment and earnings, 27–28
  union wages, 44–45
Maintenance electricians, in study sample, 72, 136